# Deleuze and Education

## *Deleuze Connections*

'It is not the elements or the sets which define the multiplicity. What defines it is the AND, as something which has its place between the elements or between the sets. AND, AND, AND – stammering.'

Gilles Deleuze and Claire Parnet, *Dialogues*

**General Editor**
Ian Buchanan

**Editorial Advisory Board**

Keith Ansell-Pearson
Rosi Braidotti
Claire Colebrook
Tom Conley

Gregg Lambert
Adrian Parr
Paul Patton
Patricia Pisters

**Titles Available in the Series**
Ian Buchanan and Claire Colebrook (eds), *Deleuze and Feminist Theory*
Ian Buchanan and John Marks (eds), *Deleuze and Literature*
Mark Bonta and John Protevi (eds), *Deleuze and Geophilosophy*
Ian Buchanan and Marcel Swiboda (eds), *Deleuze and Music*
Ian Buchanan and Gregg Lambert (eds), *Deleuze and Space*
Martin Fuglsang and Bent Meier Sørensen (eds), *Deleuze and the Social*
Ian Buchanan and Adrian Parr (eds), *Deleuze and the Contemporary World*
Constantin V. Boundas (ed.), *Deleuze and Philosophy*
Ian Buchanan and Nicholas Thoburn (eds), *Deleuze and Politics*
Chrysanthi Nigianni and Merl Storr (eds), *Deleuze and Queer Theory*
Jeffrey A. Bell and Claire Colebrook (eds), *Deleuze and History*
Laura Cull (ed.), *Deleuze and Performance*
Mark Poster and David Savat (eds), *Deleuze and New Technology*
Simone Bignall and Paul Patton (eds), *Deleuze and the Postcolonial*
Stephen Zepke and Simon O'Sullivan (eds), *Deleuze and Contemporary Art*
Laura Guillaume and Joe Hughes (eds), *Deleuze and the Body*
Daniel W. Smith and Nathan Jun (eds), *Deleuze and Ethics*
Frida Beckman (ed.), *Deleuze and Sex*
David Martin-Jones and William Brown (eds), *Deleuze and Film*
Laurent de Sutter and Kyle McGee (eds), *Deleuze and Law*
Arun Saldanha and Jason Michael Adams (eds), *Deleuze and Race*
Rebecca Coleman and Jessica Ringrose (eds), *Deleuze and Research Methodologies*
Inna Semetsky and Diana Masny (eds), *Deleuze and Education*
Hélène Frichot and Stephen Loo (eds), *Deleuze and Architecture*

Visit the Deleuze Connections website at
www.euppublishing.com/series/delco

# Deleuze and Education

Edited by Inna Semetsky and Diana Masny

EDINBURGH
University Press

© editorial matter and organisation Inna Semetsky and Diana Masny, 2013
© the chapters their several authors

Edinburgh University Press Ltd
22 George Square, Edinburgh EH8 9LF

www.euppublishing.com

Typeset in 10.5/13 Adobe Sabon
by Servis Filmsetting Ltd, Stockport, Cheshire,
printed and bound in Great Britain by
CPI Group (UK) Ltd, Croydon CR0 4YY

A CIP record for this book is available from the British Library

ISBN 978 0 7486 4303 5 (hardback)
ISBN 978 0 7486 4302 8 (paperback)
ISBN 978 0 7486 6945 5 (webready PDF)
ISBN 978 0 7486 6946 2 (epub)
ISBN 978 0 7486 6947 9 (Amazon ebook)

# Contents

# Acknowledgements

We are grateful to the *Deleuze Studies* international conferences for providing a stimulating forum for discussions over the years and creating a valued opportunity for testing new thoughts and nonthoughts in a friendly intellectual environment. We specifically thank Ian Buchanan who enthusiastically supported the original idea for this book. Diana Masny expresses her gratitude to the Faculty of Education, University of Ottawa for a grant that provided the necessary technical support in the final phases of the book editing and specifically thanks Monica Waterhouse and Maria Bastien for their assistance. We also thank the anonymous reviewers for their invaluable suggestions and are especially grateful to the contributors to this volume for their scholarship, diligence, insight, and apprenticeship to Deleuze.

# Introduction: Unfolding Deleuze

## Inna Semetsky and Diana Masny

Unfolding Deleuze is at once a deterritorialisation and reterritorialisation of his philosophy. Perhaps this is what this book is about: constructing a Deleuzian transversal, which is particularly suited to diverse educational contexts. Unfolding Deleuze means to deterritorialise Deleuze while simultaneously reterritorialising him in a new context partaking of three interconnected problematic fields: educational theory, philosophy of education, and pedagogical practice. The chapters presented in this volume comprise a transversal line of flight along which, in Deleuze's spirit, a multiplicity of new concepts are created – concepts that will give us a new Sense of teaching and learning. Yet, these concepts may have always already been implicated in their virtual form in the field of education; this book unfolds or explicates them. Indeed Deleuze conceptualised the fold as the inside *of* the outside. Education is to be understood broadly as both formal – inside a classroom – and informal – outside the walls of a typical classroom but inside 'a' life, explicated in experience and culture.

The popularity of Deleuze's philosophy across disciplines is highly visible, especially in the areas of cultural studies, politics, gender studies and the like. While less visible in education, his body of work has been a subject of research and practical applications that have been continuously traced by the editors of this volume in their earlier works (e.g., Semetsky 2004, 2006, 2008; Masny 2010, 2012; Semetsky and Masny 2011). If we were to examine the programmes of the international conferences devoted to *Deleuze Studies*, there was one panel on the topic of education at the first conference in Cardiff in 2008; at the second conference held in 2009 in Cologne there were three panels, and there were several presentations at the conference in Amsterdam in 2010 and in Copenhagen in 2011. The fifth conference held in 2012 in New Orleans also had three education panels.

Positing philosophy as a method of inventing novel concepts, Deleuze and Guattari present this method in terms of the geography of reason expressing itself through the singularities of experiences and events. The creative – both constructive and expressive – element is a necessary condition for the very pedagogy of the concept. It is specifically the Deleuzian philosophy of life shared by the contributors to this volume that crosses the boundaries between the fragmented subject matters still prevalent in contracted forms of educational research, schooling and tertiary education. As Deleuze and Guattari wrote: 'If the three ages of the concept are the encyclopedia, pedagogy, and commercial professional training, only the second can safeguard us from falling from the heights of the first into the disaster of the third' (1994: 12). Deleuze and Guattari were interested in the concept as a vehicle for expressing an event as a singularity that would have secured 'linkages with ever increasing connections' (1994: 37). The unpredictable and unforeseen connections presuppose not the transmission of the same but the creation of the different; this is the process that has important implications for education as a developing practice of the generation of new knowledge, values and meanings.

This volume constitutes an experiment in educational philosophy as its instance of becoming-other. Such present-becoming comprises diverse assemblages that unfold the ideas represented by twelve essays written by Deleuze scholars across the globe. The chapters in the volume form assemblages along the four lines of creative becoming, namely: *The Art of Teaching/Teaching the Arts*; *Inside/Outside Classroom*; *Mathematics and Science*; and *Life, Sign, Time*. Tracing Deleuze's thought through the problematic of teaching and learning, the chapters in these assemblages explore pedagogy as actual and virtual; semiotics and apprenticeship in signs; affective and uncanny experiences; curriculum studies; the syntheses of time and educators as people to come; as well as multiple literacies, mathematics, arts, and science education, while traversing narrow disciplinary boundaries. Encompassing both the formal and informal modes, the book reterritorialises the field of education in terms of experimental and experiential nomadic processes of multiple encounters embedded in life, and represents the very becoming-other of Deleuze's original philosophical thought.

Assemblage I in this volume is titled *The Art of Teaching/Teaching the Arts*. Deleuze and Guattari expressed the importance of sensations, concepts and functions in, respectively, art, philosophy and science. Teaching as such might well be art, the art of genuine becoming when affects spill over beyond those who live through them, thus contributing to their becoming-other (Deleuze 1995). The interplay of philosophy with art – which 'thinks' no less than philosophy, yet does so pre-conceptually through affects and percepts – is traced through the chapters in this assemblage. The opening chapter by Ronald Bogue is called 'The Master Apprentice' and is in admirable counterpoint with the rest of the volume with its emphasis on learning as an apprenticeship in signs. Bogue draws from Deleuze's *Proust and Signs* and *Difference and Repetition*, both of which offer incisive remarks about learning yet, as he insightfully notes, may seem to downplay the importance of teaching itself. Referring to young Marcel in Proust's *À la recherche du temps perdu* as an apprentice, Bogue points out that he seeks guidance from others to understand signs; however his genuine teachers, if at all, are the signs themselves.

Bogue refers to Deleuze's example of learning to swim – a concept which is elaborated upon in a number of chapters in this volume as extremely significant for educational theory and pedagogical practice. There is a relation between the sea emitting the signs of experience and a swimmer's body forming a qualitative multiplicity responsive to an encounter with the sea as a heterogeneous other. Based on this example, Deleuze proposes an apprenticeship in teaching and learning so that students do *with* the teacher as opposed to doing as the teacher does. Bogue's chapter contends that the teacher as the emitter of signs plays an important role in education.

A unique feature of this chapter is Bogue's recourse to the figure of Deleuze himself as a teacher, a lifelong practitioner. With regard to pedagogical techniques, Deleuze, as Bogue argues, might appear to have been rather conservative: his chosen method of teaching was the *cours magistral*, a classical lecture. Yet, the goal of his lectures was not to directly communicate information but to model the process of thought as an experience, a singular event. Bogue says that Deleuze would commence by claiming a lack of preparation or a hesitation in how to start; then he would pose questions to himself and offer tentative responses. Only after that would he gradually reveal a line of thought leading to the construction of a full-fledged conceptual apparatus. Philosophical lectures, for Deleuze, bordered on musical concerts wherein he himself was a performer for an audience of students; and just as one would not interrupt a pianist in mid-concert, so one does not interrupt the lecturer-in-process with any questions and objections. And similar to concerts, when the full sense of performance cannot be comprehended immediately but would achieve its full effect well afterwards, Deleuze gave preference to an extended lecture course and not to short conference papers.

The time of comprehension (addressed, significantly, in the concluding chapter by James Williams as the 'later' time) in an extended course allows slow absorption, positing questions between lectures and then giving measured responses to questions in subsequent lectures. Still, Bogue claims, Deleuze's lectures exceeded mere performances because they were often instruments of a pedagogical discipline as training in the history of philosophy conceived in terms of the apprentice's workshop. Deleuze taught, in the final analysis, as a mentor who intervenes or participates in individuals' lives at decisive moments and can provide them with encouragement while outlining programmes of self-education and guiding individual research. Bogue asserts that in this regard Deleuze performed a role analogous to that of the master in Asian martial arts; for example, the Japanese art, *kyudo*, or the Zen art of archery. Through specific techniques, what is taught is not simply a history of ideas but a way of life as a mode of being in the world and an image of thought that amalgamates concepts with percepts and affects (addressed in detail in Semetsky's chapter). The practitioners of this art commit to a lifetime of apprenticeship that includes mastery of the techniques and principles of the art. Bogue concludes his chapter by reiterating that teaching is a continuous encounter with signs as an ongoing apprenticeship.

Chapter 2 by Julie Allan is called 'Staged Interventions: Deleuze, Arts and Education'. Deleuze testified to the arts' transformative capacities as offering multiple sensory, and even sensual, affects that by means of producing fragments, strivings and allusions would create affirmative conjunctions. For example, Deleuze and Guattari contend that music is an open system permeated by rhythms, which also permeates and is permeated by the world. Painting is thought of as blocs of sensations, affects and percepts which in their relationships become-other and create new concepts. Minor literature is proposed as a way to transform subjectivities. Allan argues that these examples of arts have a potential reach that enables teachers to engage all students and, furthermore, that Deleuze's concepts can assist teachers in thinking and practising both differently and equitably. Allan draws on Deleuze's analyses of various art forms so as to provoke altered forms of subjectivity and to promote an inclusive and affective kind of education. Her chapter considers creative interventions, which Deleuze's thought has the potential to generate, and illustrates these theoretical considerations implied by Deleuze's philosophy by setting out three practical educational performances.

The first performance opens up to a deterritorialised space of an art lab that provides a smooth space as different from formal schooling and where the students can experience arts activities, initiated by artists-practitioners that highlight an embodied engagement with education. Deleuze's concept of a rhizome allows us to reconceptualise learning with artists as opening up a multiplicity of different and unpredictable spaces (for example, physics-art) for all participants. The second example is an experiment with the United Nations Convention on the Rights of the Child when a group of students experience and experiment with rights by taking these rights – literally – on a walk in and out of school, and propose new actions and becomings for their teachers and fellow students. Allan points out that these students worked in groups focusing on integrating the rights of disabled people within a curriculum. The rhizomatic engagement with rights enabled one individual to recreate himself with a new subjectivity, educational trajectory and future. In the third and final performance, disability arts involve 'thinking with Deleuze', that is, bringing the participants, disabled artists and audience, into new territories of experience that provoke becomings. Allan's example of the performance conducted by disabled artists and seeking to educate audiences by inviting them to stutter and then to think differently is striking! The chapter concludes with an exercise in creative subtraction as an element of Deleuze's deterritorialisation with a specification of the negative orientations and practices which could open up possibilities for teachers to confound their students and pave the way for a different pedagogy.

Assemblage II posits a Deleuzian fold as *Inside/Outside Classroom* and comprises the chapters by Bonta, Masny, Cole and Drohan. In Chapter 3 '"We're Tired of Trees": Machinic University Geography Teaching After Deleuze', Mark Bonta investigates pedagogy in terms of becomings folded into machinic assemblages of bodies and collective assemblages of enunciation that populate the earth. Through a Deleuzian lens, education becomes nomadic, deploying rhizomatic movements as unpredictable and uncontrolled, and hence capable of destabilising a model of education with its built-in mechanisms of predictability and accountability. Bonta's chapter is a response to business models that have come to permeate universities and the whole knowledge economy. He takes a contra-stance with regard to the current implantation of business models of education. Nomadic pedagogy, by way of classrooms that are self-organising and rhizomatic (with rhizomes spontaneously sprouting during role-playing games as Bonta's example of his pedagogical model), inhabits the spaces of chaos and complexity that seek to deterritorialise a closed system heavily influenced by corporatisation and the imposition of a model akin to that of the profit-making business within global capitalism, yet unfitted to liberal arts education.

Through his analysis of the societies of control and instant communication, Deleuze foresaw in the French university system that which, as Bonta makes clear, also now applies to the US academic community. Bonta contends that the business model of education has attempted a takeover of US academe, thus normalising and reducing the concept of college to that of a 'job-training' site, where technical proficiency is reached via the pursuit of 'knowledge' understood (by Deleuze and Bonta) as a memorisation of objective facts and instructions imparted by authorities. Universities are thereby becoming trade schools, where testable and assessable demonstrations of proficiency in the actual realm replace unpredictable but creative explorations of the virtual realm and explicitly turn college students into docile and compliant workers as widgets. Still, asserts Bonta, resistance is possible through a liberal arts core curriculum, which itself is defended via the tenets of academic freedom, even if this freedom no longer appears present in all sites of 'higher learning'.

Bonta's chapter taps into the virtual while exploring the plane of consistency where abstract machines are 'instructions' for what happens in the actual. What would a Deleuzian classroom look like? Bonta's response is to practise nomadic education (see Semetsky 2008) as an experimentation with the Real that can take many forms. Nomadic pedagogy is pliable and non-repetitive; and experimenting in such a geography class transforms it into a self-organising classroom, in which hierarchical power structures are dissolved and communication becomes transversal. Bonta affirms that such exploration creates imaginary micro-worlds, submerging students in situations where they empathise with the Other – be it several families of Andean Quechua potato farmers displaced by a mining company or the diplomat faced with 'Third World War' over events occurring on the Korean Peninsula. Bonta creates a novel term: 'Deleuzifying' an institution. In an era of academe that relies on predictable learning trajectories, it is unpredictability, nonlinear transformations and rhizomatic movements that are important to counteract a tree-like structure of knowledge.

Chapter 4, 'Multiple Literacies Theory (MLT): Exploring Spaces' by Diana Masny, takes up an inside-outside connection by focusing on how literacies function and what they produce in spaces such as the classroom and at home. The chapter opens with a presentation of literacies through the lens of Multiple Literacies Theory. MLT takes on both theoretical and practical perspectives in reading, reading the world and self. Moreover, reading is disruptive and immanent. In other words, reading functions to destabilise. Destabilisation brings on a virtual unthought potential of what is yet to come, immanence. At the heart of MLT is becoming and the rhizomatic movement in which multiple literacies transform how one might live. Literacies involve reading, reading the world and self as text that creates potentialities for transforming life. Since an important aspect of literacies is to produce change, MLT is interested in how literacies change bodies, communities and societies: human, animal and vegetal.

How a life might be composed is linked to Deleuzian ontology, exposing a relationship to reality couched in transcendental empiricism. Transcendental empiricism, as conceived by Deleuze, was a response to his perspective on life as becoming and to the place of experience in life. Experience is not limited to the individual. The immanence of experience is the factor in the production and formation of subjectivity. From ontology the chapter moves onto concept creation, holding a lens to problems in literacy and literacies research that provides the context for concept creation of and within MLT. The chapter continues with an ontology of space(s), concept creation within MLT and conceptualising space. Ontology of space(s) exposes aspects of transcendental empiricism critical to concept creation (for example, reading, reading the world and self) and to understanding how literacies function. Moreover, Deleuzian ontology becomes interesting in conceptualising space(s). Smooth space is related to a-signifying machines, nomadic, intensive, non-metric and deterritorialising. Striated space is extensive, homogeneous, metric and territorialising. The interrelationship between smooth and striated space becomes important in establishing equilibrium in an open system.

The next section of this chapter brings together literacies, space(s) and becoming in an empirical study that examines how multilingual children conceptualise aspects of writing systems in home and school contexts. Experimenting with writing activities is an entry point in order to ask how literacies function and what they produce in smooth and striated spaces. The longitudinal study involves five girls between five and eight years old. Filmed observations occurred at home and school. Interviews took place with the children, their parents and teachers. Vignettes were selected on their power to affect and be affected within an assemblage that included 'data', researchers, research assistants and more. This study provides an entry into deterritorialising arborescent literacy, a hierarchical literacy valued in educational institutions, and into thinking differently about literacies. Accordingly, an intermezzo follows that proposes an ontology of reading that describes a reality of relationality and MLT as minoritarian.

Chapter 5, 'Affective Literacies: Deleuze, Discipline and Power' by David Cole, explores Deleuze's philosophy in view of understanding classroom management as moving power-structure(s) in the teaching and learning context. The classroom dynamic presents a form of affective literacy or literacies in the framework of Multiple Literacies Theory (see Masny 2006). The ways in which communication happens in the classroom demonstrates an affective map of the power flows in that context; and Cole deals with the power differential through *affectus* as the body's power to act. The affective interactivity of literacies in classroom management is complementary to and congruent with the conceptual framework of this writing. The chapter proposes a classroom management model based on contexts permeated by affective literacies when 'affect' is the act of changing in relation to an encounter with another. *Affectus* represents the material and immaterial elements of change and refers to the act of learning as a type, for Cole, of non-human pedagogy. The two conceptions of desire addressed by Deleuze and Guattari in *Anti-Oedipus* and *A Thousand Plateaus* are reconciled by Cole through applying affective literacies and in the power relationships as *affectus*. Cole explores Deleuze and Guattari's concepts of anti-production and order-words, unpacking them in the specific educational context of classroom management and as pertaining to teacher education. Anti-production locates the immovable and yet invisible points in the socius. Order-words 'flow' around places of learning like the routing of electricity in plasterboard walls, and present a means to explain how disciplinary triggers are shared communally and linguistically. Cole includes several scenarios illustrating the classroom management machine while also demonstrating how teacher education and classroom management could be modified from the Deleuzo-Guattarian philosophical perspective with the emphasis on the affective literacies that are at work in schools and on their potential impact on teaching and learning. This chapter contends that classroom management is made easier through understanding affective literacies as they apply to questions of power and by combining an analysis of anti-production with order-words to improve classroom management.

In Chapter 6, 'Deleuze and the Virtual Classroom', Christopher Drohan questions the current pedagogical usage of such terms as 'virtual' and 'computerised' as synonymous, and posits this use as being at the very least ambiguous, if not entirely problematic. Accordingly, his chapter explores the philosophical concept of the virtual through the work of Deleuze so as to gauge the various senses in which the contemporary classroom has become virtual. As educational institutions begin to increasingly demand that teachers incorporate computerised technology into the classroom, this chapter questions what it is exactly that they are inviting into the learning environment, and how this technology impacts on the acquisition of knowledge. The chapter begins by interrogating the ontological sense of the virtual as it is applied to education today. To this end, the author deconstructs the false dichotomy of virtual versus real classrooms, showing that for Deleuze the virtual is more than just a matter of retaining the 'essence or effect' of the classroom in a different form (for example, online methods of instruction or McLuhan's classroom without walls). Fundamentally, learning is always a matter of 'effectively' (derived from the middle-English '*virtuall*') producing virtual and immanent essences in the concrete. In this sense, education is more a matter of creating new forms rather than discovering them. We learn by exploring and apprenticing with the signs of new ideas, objects and worlds; this process in turn necessitating highly technical – and technological – classroom spaces that allow both teachers and students to extend their investigative powers. Finally, Drohan's chapter explores the ethical sense in which current pedagogy is virtual. Building on the virtual's Latin senses of excellence and goodness (*virtus*) and its French etymology as truth (*vertu*), the author considers the virtual as a means of living, learning and teaching ethically. A revised metaphysics as an ontology of the virtual demands a different kind of classroom, one that is more experimental than ideological, more pragmatic than disciplinary. Traditional hierarchical models of pedagogy are transformed into critical explorations, wherein teachers and students work through problematics together, symbiotically building their knowledge of the world. Drohan notices that, quite ironically, pedagogy is brought back to its classic, even if long-ignored, ideals: teachers as mentors; an academy of friends.

Assemblage III is devoted to *Mathematics and Science* as sites of education in the spirit of Deleuze's philosophy. Chapter 7 by David Holdsworth is titled 'Philosophical Problematisation and Mathematical Solution: Learning Science *with* Gilles Deleuze'. As Holdsworth notes, a number of educational theorists have taken up the thought of Deleuze as the inspiration for an approach to pedagogy that recognises the complexity of learning experiences and emphasises the importance of active creation by the learner. Referring to Semetsky's and Masny's innovative research in educational theory, Holdsworth starts from the observation that Deleuze's rather scattered remarks regarding the master-pupil relationship and those concerned with learning are almost always embedded in a context where he is discussing mathematics. In order to bring these reflections to bear on, specifically, science education, the author proceeds to discuss the mathematical proposition understood as a particular case of the proposition being a conscious expression of the virtual positivities of affirmation. He argues that, first, this shows in what way the multivocity of difference as differentiation/differenciation manifests itself as the multiplicity of scientific practices.

Second, he demonstrates that mathematical propositions, even in their conventional form (derived from Frege and Russell), ascend to the limit of formal language where we encounter mathematical simulacra, that is, axiomatic mathematical frameworks that reveal 'models' as folds of multiple structural interpretations into each other in a way that is already suggestive of the Deleuzian (and the Heideggerian) fold. Third, turning from the (ontological) proposition as found in Deleuze to the Deleuzian *problem*, Holdsworth considers the specific relationship of complexity theory, understood as a branch of axiomatic mathematics, to the complexity of scientific experience and the learning of science. Here, at the limits of theoretical knowledge, where we encounter that which cannot be thought, a Deleuzian conception of scientific practice and science education becomes compelling. The chapter concludes (somewhat speculatively, as the author makes clear) with a reflection on the pedagogical consequences for the teaching of mathematical science. Holdsworth proposes that, contrary to recent innovations in mathematical pedagogy (the so-called New Math of the 1960s), as well as more orthodox approaches that return to the rote learning of techniques, experimental methods are possible and desirable at all levels of education, including the teaching of higher algebra. He argues that to be consistent with a conception of the *mathesis universalis* (with a nod to *mathesis* as a universal science of life) science teaching must abandon its dominant (and contradictory) dispositions, on the one hand to valorise the concrete, while on the other hand treating abstraction as the ultimate expression of Truth. The resultant challenge for science education is to develop a pedagogy related to the science of life.

Chapter 8 by Rocco Gangle, 'From Brackets to Arrows: Sets, Categories and the Deleuzian Pedagogy of Mathematics', brings to the fore what the preceding chapter only touched upon, namely *mathesis*, problems and category theory. It focuses on how Deleuze's philosophy of mathematics and his more general emphasis on apprenticeship and semiotics might be understood to lay the groundwork for a specifically Deleuzian pedagogy of mathematics. In particular it addresses how the abstract and universal character of mathematical knowledge may be coordinated with a creative and experimental approach to teaching and learning. Gangle points out that it is necessary to recognise that *mathesis* in Deleuze's corpus names a concept ranging over a much broader field of phenomena and practices than the conventional understanding of mathematics would entail.

For Deleuze, *mathesis* is an integral component of all processes of life, growth, experience and experimentation. This insight already serves as an initial clue as to how a Deleuzian pedagogy of mathematics might proceed. A more definite direction for research then crystallises around the Deleuzian understanding of mathematics in *Difference and Repetition* in terms of a reversal of the usual privileging of solutions over problems. Gangle demonstrates that what is potentially new and creative in a Deleuzian mathematical pedagogy is posited in terms of the difference between two rival foundational branches of mathematics: set theory and category theory. He argues that category theory lends itself naturally to Deleuzian practices of teaching and learning due to its specific approach to mathematical objects in terms of structural relations on the one hand and its diagrammatic notational conventions on the other. On both these points, category theory is usefully contrasted with set theory, which proposes a static, object-based conception of mathematical structures. In category theory, mathematical objects are conceived as relational nodes, whereas in set theory, mathematical relations are reduced to objects (sets).

Gangle's chapter summarises the axioms of category theory and presents the key example of functions between sets as a concrete illustration of the difference between the respective approaches of set theory and category theory. In particular, the idea of the composition of arrows in categories is clarified by showing how it illuminates the composition of functions, in a diagrammatic example that also shows how the standard notational conventions of category theory lend themselves to demonstrative and intuitive modes of teaching and learning. In conclusion, the contrast between set-theoretical and category-theoretical approaches to mathematics is shown to resonate with issues in mathematical pedagogy in several ways. The relation-based and diagrammatic approach of category theory resonates strongly with Deleuze's pragmatic semiotics and his emphasis on learning as apprenticeship. But not only. The unique way that category theory translates across varying levels of abstraction lends itself to situating mathematical teaching and learning immediately within the problem of bridging the abstract and the concrete. Here, the application of mathematical knowledge no longer serves as a secondary and derived aspect of mathematical practice. Finally, category theory provides natural techniques and practices for investigating conceptual

– and not merely quantitative – relations, as well as offering a milieu for rigorous abstract experimentation.

The important themes that appeared in different guises through the previous chapters are put together in the conjunctive/disjunctive synthesis of the final Assemblage IV, called *Life, Sign, Time*. In Chapter 9, titled 'Learning the Uncanny', Joshua Ramey argues that Deleuze's approach to thought and unthought is uniquely placed to articulate the pedagogical possibilities implicit in uncanny experiences. Starting from Deleuze's disagreement with Plato over the status of difference, Ramey creates a background for his excursion into Deleuze's philosophy by critically examining Freud's 1919 essay and Hitchcock's *The Birds*. Freud advises modern folks to take a reductive approach to their experiences of the uncanny, because such feelings are nothing but a recursion to an immature 'animist' phase in development, one that is linked to narcissism and wish fulfilment. But Freud himself, as Ramey argues, cannot definitively demonstrate that an event felt as uncanny is not also indicating something about extra-psychic reality. Pupils of Freud are left haunted by the possibility that our sense of propriety in nature, derived from the image of nature given to us by modern science (pre-relativistic physics and Newtonian determinism) might be uncertain. Ever the astute observer of psychoanalysis, Alfred Hitchcock in *The Birds* puts Freud to the test, hinting that even when it is blatantly obvious that the uncanny aspect of the birds' attacks is linked to Mitch's regressive attachment to his mother, the attack is nevertheless *really* taking place and psychic disorder could *really* be manifest in anonymous forces of nature or the brute instincts of animals. Hitchcock's trailer to the film humorously suggests that we have yet to learn something 'scientific' from our feeling of the uncanny.

For Ramey, such is but one example of a specific pedagogical possibility implied by Deleuze's philosophy and semiotics. For Deleuze, the uncanny is an opportunity to learn something not merely about psychology but also about what he called 'naturing nature' as the impersonal, pre-individual field of intensities, with the uncanny often being a cipher for their proximity. For Deleuze, the uncanny is not a recursion to a primitive phase but advancement towards an experimental phase of human perception, which is – rather than being an aberration – the very essence of humanity. The language of uncanny signs is the language of a differentiating process that manifests as fundamentally creative in so far as such signs, by inviting the invention (rather than mere reception) of significance, provoke humanity to develop the world rather than passively inhabit it. A mind that experiences the presence of the unknown as an invitation, as commanding attention, is a mind that is willing to relinquish understanding for the sake of participation, seeking not to gain mastery in advance over as yet unknown potencies, but to risk identification with them. On the basis of Deleuze's account, it then becomes possible for our vision of what there is to learn from the uncanny to go beyond psychoanalytical reductionism towards a genetic account of the imagination in terms of a real experimental pedagogy that partakes of a politics of the uncanny and proceeds through a diagrammatic production of signs.

Addressing 'Morphologies for a Pedagogical Life' in Chapter 10, Jason Wallin reminds the reader of Nietzsche's influence on Deleuze's writings. The question of 'a' life emerges throughout the work of Deleuze, appearing most pointedly in his final published essay that addresses life as immanent and immanence as 'a' life (2001). For Deleuze, the three metamorphoses in *Thus Spoke Zarathustra* compose a diagram for Nietzsche's life, thorough the figures of a camel, a lion and a child. Wallin deploys metamorphoses as a response to a pedagogical question of how a life might be composed and lived. Through a Deleuze-Nietzsche fold, Wallin's chapter endeavours to rethink the notion of *currere* (the course of life) as a radical challenge to the presumptions of subjectivity, temporality and transcendence that continue to circulate in even the most progressive images of pedagogical thought. The question of how a life might go is intimate to the fundamental problematic of education. Indeed, the etymology of the word curriculum relates to *currere* and is implicitly concerned with the ways in which the course of 'a' life might be composed. As the chapter develops, it is in response to this implicate question that the educational project mobilises its intellectual and disciplinary resources in an attempt to capture students' desire in an *a priori* molar image (how life ought to go). Yet, the chapter contends that the molar image of life as proffered by the institution is inadequate.

In discussing becoming-camel, Wallin explores the curriculum-as-plan with prescribed objectives and outcomes, an arborescent molar image of a royal science. The transformation to becoming-lion brings forth a challenge in the manner of the lived curriculum (cf. Aoki 2005) that mobilises the question of how a life might be composed at an immanent contact point between the curriculum-as-plan and the virtual. Using films, Wallin illustrates that pedagogy takes on a different life when it escapes its previous image and reterritorialises in the smooth space. Addressing becoming-child, Wallin revisits antiquity and the role of a pedagogue. Becoming-child does not refer to an individual being but

rather to the art of pedagogy which is more-than-personal. Wallin
brings back the teacher Zarathustra to illustrate the return of difference
that requires new pedagogical practices and images. To infuse education
with Deleuzian concepts entails becoming-lion and affirming a people
yet-to-come. For Wallin, Deleuze's philosophy populates education with
the underexplored notions of pre-personal affective singularities, by
means of which a pedagogical life might be mapped. It is via the composition of such a life that educational and curriculum theorists might
more adequately rethink the task of education, emancipating it from
the dominion of instrumentalism and foundational presuppositions that
characterise the internal limit of the contemporary educational project
and opening what it means to compose a pedagogical life for people to
come.

The term *edusemiotics* in the title of Chapter 11, 'Deleuze, *edusemiotics*, and the Logic of Affects' by Inna Semetsky, translates as educational semiotics and designates a cutting-edge direction in educational
philosophy and theory taken by the author. Edusemiotics centres on
learning from signs which abound in experience, in life. An informal
milieu of signs cannot be confined to a formal classroom. For Charles
Sanders Peirce, the world is perfused with signs. Deleuzo-Guattarian
semiotics represents a mix of Peirce's relational logic and Hjelmslev's
linguistics. In contrast to substance metaphysics and the law of identity
based on the analytic tradition's logic of the *excluded* middle, Deleuze's
philosophy deploys process-ontology and the logic of multiplicities
or signs that function on the basis of the conjunction 'and' as the
*included* middle. The static logical copula 'is' gives way to the relational
dynamics of multiple becomings as a learning process oriented towards
inventing novel concepts for experiential events. The chapter addresses
Deleuze's pedagogy of the concept as a function of difference embedded in experience. All thinking proceeds in signs, and the continuous
process of what Peirce called semiosis as the evolution of signs provides
a stream of events for the practical experimentation on ourselves. Such
experimentation, argues Semetsky, is at the core of edusemiotics as a
theory-practice nexus for education by means of exploring the faculties
of perception irreducible to empirical sense-data. The chapter analyses
Deleuze's method of transcendental empiricism and his new image of
thought characterised by unconscious and yet-unthought-of affects.
The focus of the chapter is, specifically, the logic of affects that alone
allows for showing the imperceptible and thinking the unthinkable.
Semetsky presents Deleuze's metaphor of a rhizome as a model for
genuine learning that demonstrates an immanent power of creation. A

sign is structured as a triadic relation between affects, percepts and concepts; this irreducible triad, according to the author, represents a major Peircean inflection in Deleuze's philosophy with its emphasis on the production of sense. Deleuze understands semiotics as a-signifying, which defies a presupposed signifier-signified identity but demands a mediatory 'third' as a transversal connection along which becomings evolve and novel concepts emerge. The chapter blends Deleuze's ontology of the virtual with ethics as an apprenticeship in signs that embody values, and argues that the actualisation of the virtual in practical experience is equivalent to becoming conscious of the unconscious ideas that become intensified in experiential, singular, events. Importantly, education, when it becomes informed by Deleuze's pedagogy of concepts and the logic of affects, entails a shared process of deterritorialisation/reterritorialisation that involves both teachers and students, thereby challenging the dogmatic formula 'do as I do'. The concluding part of the chapter presents a Deleuzian-like (dis)solution to the learning paradox as the Socratic problem of new knowledge, and interrogates (together with James Williams) an apparent logical invalidity of paradoxes. Education as edusemiotics by its very logic embraces the pedagogy of novelty and creativity rather than a given curriculum. Teachers as edusemioticians, argues Semetsky, are genuine nomads and 'people to come' (the nuance also noticed by other authors) who would invent new modes of existence resistant to the oppressive present.

Such a future-oriented dimension is especially visible in Chapter 12, 'Time and Education in the Philosophy of Gilles Deleuze' by James Williams, as the crescendo to this volume. The chapter investigates the time-frames of education. It does so by following Deleuze's account of time as a nexus of interacting dimensions of time. According to this interpretation of Deleuze, time is a multiplicity of asymmetrical processes of reciprocal determination. There are many times; they determine one-another; they are process-like. When guided by this view, education becomes teaching and apprenticeship as active and passive practices in accordance with the processes of time. Williams' chapter then goes on to stress the importance of pure values and signs for Deleuze's account of apprenticeship, where practice is an experimental approach to values and to signs. The chapter closes around questions about novelty and dosage in teaching and apprenticeship.

A remarkable feature of this chapter is Williams' remembering his family lore and asking, 'what time-frame was that caring educator teaching for?' The answer provided by Deleuze (Deleuze-Proust, to be precise; as well as Deleuze-Williams) is transversal time, which simultaneously affirms disjoined pieces of different times and places. Referring to Deleuze's virtual reserve, Williams constructs a grid of the nexus of times juxtaposing all three syntheses. This grid is followed by another one as a set of practical guides comprising paradoxical maxims, questions and challenges for apprentice teachers and apprentice learners alike. A teaching process becomes a dedication to pass on pure and abstract values so lives have a greater potential to be lived well. Turning to 'ideas' associated with teaching and apprenticeship, Williams draws our attention to Deleuze's reversed Platonism and an ideal horizon embracing the realm of values.

The pedagogical task then is to intensify connections in actuality while seeking to release new potentiality. In this education, not only are actual lives enriched, but the condition for this gift as the reserve of pure, virtual, yet real values is affirmed. Williams notices that Deleuze admired teachers and apprentices (the likes of Sade, Masoch and Kafka) whose acts demonstrated the emptiness of eternal law exemplified in our present-time law of subservience to scientific method, liberal economics, centralised curricula and methodology. Affirming the 'otherness' of events and encounters, Williams emphasises a time-dimension of 'later' when learning is put into practice, thereby affecting the very definition of a sign for Deleuze as not just a symptom of the present but also a divination of/in the future beyond the boundaries that are currently known. A genuine education is thereby characterised by a transcendental movement as much as by being immanent to experiences and events.

This book is an experiment with the Deleuzian folds in education: becoming-educational. The chapters collected in this volume will inspire its readers not only to think differently about Deleuze's intellectual legacy in the specific context of educational theory and philosophy, as well as in plurivocal pedagogical contexts, but also to make a difference at the level of social practices and social institutions, among which the institution of education is the most important. It will contribute to a critical de-stratification of educational philosophy worldwide along the diverse lines of flight created by the volume's authors.

# References

Aoki, T. (2005), 'Legitimating Lived Curriculum: Toward a curricular landscape of multiplicity' in W. Pinar and R. Irwin (eds), *Curriculum in a New Key: The Collected Works of Ted T. Aoki*, Mahwah, NJ: Lawrence Erlbaum Associates, pp. 199–218. (Originally published in 1993.)

Deleuze, G. (1995), *Negotiations: 1972–1990*, trans. Martin Joughin, New York: Columbia University Press.

Deleuze, G. (2001), *Pure Immanence: Essays on A Life*, trans. A. Boyman, New York: Zone Books.

Deleuze, G. and F. Guattari (1994), *What is Philosophy?*, trans. H. Tomlinson and G. Burchell, New York: Columbia University Press.

Masny, D. (2006), 'Learning and Creative Processes: A poststructural perspective on language and multiple literacies', *International Journal of Learning*, 12(5): 147–55.

Masny, D. (2010), 'Multiple Literacies Theory: How it functions, what it produces', *Perspectiva*, 28(2): 337–52.

Masny, D. (2012), 'Multiple Literacies Theory: Discourse, sensation, resonance and becoming', *Discourse*, 33(1): 113–28.

Semetsky, I. (ed.) (2004), 'Deleuze and Education', special issue of *Educational Philosophy and Theory*, 36(3).

Semetsky, I. (2006), *Deleuze, Education and Becoming*, Rotterdam: Sense.

Semetsky, I. (ed.) (2008), *Nomadic Education: Variations on a Theme by Deleuze and Guattari*, Rotterdam: Sense.

Semetsky, I. and D. Masny (eds) (2011), 'Deleuze, Pedagogy, and *Bildung*', special issue of *Policy Futures in Education*, 9(4).

# ASSEMBLAGE I:
# THE ART OF TEACHING/
# TEACHING THE ARTS

# Chapter 1

# The Master Apprentice

## Ronald Bogue

Deleuze describes Proust's *À la recherche du temps perdu* as 'the narrative of an apprenticeship' (Deleuze 2000: 3). In Deleuze's reading, the narrator, Marcel, is engaged in an apprenticeship in signs, whereby he comes to understand first the signs of the world, then the signs of love and the signs of involuntary memory, and finally the signs of art. At times Marcel looks to others, like Swann or Charlus, to guide him in this apprenticeship, but they prove to be unreliable teachers. If Marcel has any teachers at all, they are the signs themselves.

In *Difference and Repetition*, Deleuze expands a bit further on the relation between signs and learning, saying that 'learning [l'apprentissage] takes place . . . in the relation between a sign and a response (encounter with the Other)' (Deleuze 1994: 22). To learn, says Deleuze, is 'to enter into the universal of the relations which constitute the Idea, and into their corresponding singularities' (1994: 165). As an example of this engagement with the Idea and its corresponding singularities, Deleuze considers the process of learning to swim in the sea. Following Leibniz, he states that the Idea of the sea 'is a system of liaisons or differential relations between particles and singularities corresponding to the degrees of variation among these relations – the totality of the system being incarnated in the real movement of the waves' (1994: 165; translation modified). To learn to swim is to create an interface between the 'distinctive [*remarquable*] points of our bodies' and the singular points of the sea. The physical sea is the object emitting signs, and it is a multiplicity of wave movements; the signs emitted constitute a system of connections or differential relations between particles (the Idea) and corresponding singular points, or degrees of variation among the differential relations; and the response to the signs involves the physical body of the swimmer, which engages the complex of the sea's system and its singular points via the body's own 'distinctive points' ('distinctive points', in my reading, being simply a synonym for 'singular points'). The body's movements do not resemble the sea's movements, but instead form a heterogeneous multiplicity responsive to an encounter with the sea as an 'other' heterogeneity.

It is within this complex relation between the multiplicities of the body and the sea that the teacher attempts to intervene. The 'swimming instructor [*maître-nageur*]' (Deleuze 1994: 23) perhaps initiates instruction by demonstrating strokes while standing on the shore, and then having the learner imitate the strokes. But such instruction is useless, since there is no relation between the mock-swimming on land and actual swimming in the sea. Only when the swimmer's body interacts with the waves of the sea can swimming begin, and it is the encounter between wave-signs and the responding body movements that does the teaching. Hence, 'we learn nothing from those who say: "Do as I do". Our only teachers [*maîtres*] are those who tell us to "do with me", and are able to emit signs to be developed in heterogeneity rather than propose gestures for us to reproduce' (1994: 23). Genuine teachers, it turns out, are simply emitters of heterogeneous signs that help students encounter other heterogeneous signs. In learning to swim, then, whether the signs are emitted by the sea or by the genuine *maître*, the signs themselves are the teachers.

At first glance, this characterisation of teaching seems to minimise the role of the teacher. Basically, the *maître-nageur* says, 'let's jump in the sea and start swimming', at which point the sea does the teaching. One might ask whether there is really any need for a *maître-nageur* at all, and whether the apprentice, like Marcel, might as well learn on her own. In part this portrait of the teacher as humble assistant is strategic, in that Deleuze is countering the orthodox image of the teacher as all-powerful master, the one who knows, the one who poses the questions and already possesses all the answers. 'According to this infantile prejudice, the master sets a problem, our task is to solve it, and the result is accredited true or false by a powerful authority.' Such is the 'grotesque image of culture that we find in examinations and government referenda as well as in newspaper competitions' (Deleuze 1994: 158). But in the final analysis, the true master as emitter of signs is indeed an important role in education, one that Deleuze does not specify in an explicit fashion, but which can be extrapolated from Deleuze's own practice as a teacher and his occasional remarks about the process of giving courses. The Deleuzian teacher, I hope to show, is both master and apprentice, a master apprentice engaged with the apprentice in their mutual apprenticeship in and through signs.

Deleuze spent most of his adult life teaching, with the exception of a four-year CNRS fellowship (1960–64) and one year of sick leave (1969–70). He began teaching at age twenty-three at the lycée d'Amiens (1948–52), followed by posts at the lycée d'Orléans (1953–55), the lycée Louis-le-Grand in Paris (1955–57), the Sorbonne (1957–60), the University of Lyon (1964–69), the University of Paris-VIII at Vincennes (1970–80), and Paris VIII at Saint Denis, following the government's destruction of the Vincennes site and relocation of the campus (1980–87). From the beginning, his students found in him an exceptional teacher, whose primary pedagogical tool was the venerable lecture (and remained so throughout his career). Michel Marié, one of Deleuze's Amiens students, recalls that

> With him, philosophy wasn't the severe discipline that I feared but an encounter, a fusion between a conceptual apparatus, a culture and its languages and learning techniques, its commentaries and links that you learn by reading generations of thinkers on one hand, and on the other hand, a sort of secret thrust, a mental attitude to perceive, to conceive of the simplest, most ordinary and yet most basic elements of existence. (cited in Dosse 2010: 101)

This notion of an encounter, and the dual focus on the history of philosophy and a prevailing mental attitude, are repeated time and again in accounts of Deleuze's teaching, whether conducted in the humblest lycée or the most exalted university.

In the video *Deleuze's ABC Primer* (*L'abécédaire de Gilles Deleuze*), Deleuze claims that his teaching never changed from the lycée to the university (Deleuze and Parnet 2004: 'P as in Professor'),[1] but it does seem that his sense of humour was more overtly displayed in the lycée context.[2] Alain Roger, a student at the lycée d'Orléans, says that although 'his courses were very arduous, based on a rigorous conception of philosophy and its history', at the same time 'he was hilarious, and this joking earned him the adoration of his students' (Roger 2000: 36). Generally, Deleuze would enter the classroom, impeccably dressed, briefcase in hand, take a sheet of paper from his coat pocket, and then launch into an amusing story. Misadventures constantly befell him in the commute from his Paris home to Orléans, and they often provided material for his anecdotes. Roger recalls one such account, in which Deleuze and a travelling salesman inadvertently picked up each other's briefcases. Deleuze described his own puzzlement at discovering a plethora 'of Colgates and Palmolives' (Roger 2000: 36) in his bag, and speculated on the panic the salesman would no doubt experience when presenting clients with the *Critique of Pure Reason*. At the close of the anecdote, Deleuze lamented that he had thus lost his lecture notes, but concluded that he would proceed anyway – and then did so in a flawless, magisterial performance.

This strategy of appearing to be unprepared was one Deleuze used often at Orléans, and in all his other positions. Roger recalls that Deleuze 'frequently gave the impression of having prepared nothing, expressing himself in a hesitant, uncertain fashion, as if unsure of himself'. He might begin '"Ah, there, you see . . . the transcendental . . . what is the transcendental? . . . Well, obviously, Kant tells us that it's the conditions of possibility of knowledge . . . Yes . . . Yes . . . But why call this transcendental, why? . . . I don't know . . . I don't know . . ."' And then, following this stuttering introduction, Deleuze would gradually put everything in place, such that 'at the end of an hour of what had seemed useless and blank gropings, Deleuze's thought would rise, luminous . . .' (Roger 2010: 37).

When Deleuze advanced to a university position, he soon gained a large following of enthusiastic students. His Sorbonne lectures were filled to overflowing, and his popularity was sufficient to arouse the jealousy of colleagues. Olivier Revault d'Allonnes reports that 'At three o'clock, when the course was over, everyone left, and the next professor, Raymond Polin, who taught in the same room, had six students. Utterly furious, he hated Deleuze' (cited in Dosse 2010: 116). Similar crowds jammed his Tuesday morning seminars at Vincennes, 'where the ritual was always the same. Deleuze arrived at a room already so packed with students that it was hard to get in the door. The place where Deleuze was supposed to sit was already filled with a forest of tape recorders' (Dosse 2010: 356–7).

The Vincennes seminars seem to have been especially memorable, and several former students have attempted to capture the atmosphere of those courses. Pierre Blanchaud speaks of the 'party atmosphere' (Dosse 2010: 358) of the courses, which Philippe Mengue confirms, noting that at Vincennes in general there was 'a climate of mad effervescence, a breath of total contestation, a wind of intellectual creation, of a liberation of mores and the imagination' (Mengue 2000: 49). Pascal Criton remembers vividly the 'encounter' presented by the 'peculiar climate of the seminars':

> the presence of the regulars, a mixture of all generations, the curious, those with a passion for philosophy, art, or those with a vaguer disposition – all this coalesced as a disparate, improbable composition. Were certain

audience members students, philosophers, writers, actors, musicians? Yes, no doubt, but their presence was circumspect, because they came to be fused with that thought of the imperceptible, which embodies the vital impulses of thought rather than brandishing it, which proceeds by hesitations, interrogations . . . A shared experience, almost a *sotto voce* island, adjacent to the intimacy of the work of thinking, the elaboration of thought in 'real time', distant from stupidity and sad passions; and then, beyond the silence created by this island, sinuously would become manifest Deleuze's special craving to make things operational, to bestow on them the grace and necessity requisite for possible explorations of thought. (Criton 2007: 57)

Here again, the themes articulated by Deleuze's first students – hesitations, interrogations, encounters with the thrust of thought, the action of thinking 'in real time'.

For Philippe Mengue, the essence of Deleuze's teaching was distilled in his voice, a voice that Mengue continues to discern faintly in Deleuze's writings. The *ABC Primer*, says Mengue, conveys only weak hints of the charm and intensity of Deleuze's voice, which were made fully present in the seminars alone.

A voice full of softness, but devoid of any flaccidity or pity, as is so often the case, free as well of that false amenity that poses as modesty the more easily to seize the opportunity of biting or stinging . . . One sensed, in that softness, a great firmness of thought, without a trace of rigidity, as if, in the tone of this flexible voice, were expressed the agility and subtlety of his mind, characteristics that allowed him to reject ready-made problems and to slip past static, obstructive contradictions. (Mengue 2000: 52)

In his work on Nietzsche, Deleuze stressed that affirmation does not mean blanket acceptance of everything, but must also include critique of the negative Will to Power; but that critical dimension, says Mengue, was scarcely evident in the seminars. Rather, Deleuze gave voice to the Nietzschean Yes 'that precedes all negation, the affirmative yes', leaving to others the critique of the philosophical priests of *ressentiment*. Deleuze's 'Yes' took a particular form, one that for Mengue made incarnate the spirit of Deleuze's thought.

When he began a seminar, or in the first moments of an encounter, when dealing with a question, Gilles Deleuze would respond with a Yes whose sound was an exaggerated suspension, prolonged, and then slowly, indefinitely diminished . . . And, in that moment of suspension, you suddenly saw all the possibilities of thought surge forth, light and free like birds, liberated from ponderous habits and mediocre objections. How welcomed you felt!

> How intelligent you felt! The marvellous sensation of a sudden expansion
> of the space of thought, an opening to everything [*une ouverture à tout*], an
> open whole [*un tout ouvert*]. (Mengue 2000: 54)

In this suspended time, 'everything could be said, and even non-sense
became a weapon for thinking' (Mengue 2000: 54).

Clearly, Deleuze put the standard lecture format to new use, imbuing
it with a purpose beyond that of conveying information. The lecture
functioned as an enactment of thought – fluid, halting, soft, yet thoroughly firm, intense and passionate. That intensity was not without
humour, but its spirit resembled the playfulness of Lewis Carroll, rather
than the biting satire and savage irony of Juvenal or Swift. And both
the spontaneity and humour of the seminars were evident in the ludic
pretence that Deleuze often offered of being thoroughly unprepared.

In fact, Deleuze put considerable effort in preparing his courses.
François Dosse tells us that Deleuze

> attached enormous importance to his Tuesday seminar and spent most of
> the week preparing his class. Pierre Chevalier, a family friend who lived
> with the Deleuzes on rue Bizerte between 1973 and 1983, remembers the
> care Deleuze took in preparing the seminar for Vincennes. 'I saw Gilles set
> to work on Sunday morning, sometimes on Saturday, polishing the seminar
> for three days and before he left to teach, there was a physical preparation,
> as if he were going to take part in a race. He would turn up on Tuesday
> mornings, no longer needing the little page of notes in his hand because
> he knew by heart what he was going to say. Yet he gave the impression
> of thinking on his feet, that his class was a pure improvisation of mental
> development in harmony with his public.' (Dosse 2010: 354)

Given the thoroughness of Deleuze's preparation, one might ask
whether the seminars were genuine enactments of thought 'in real
time', or mere performances, re-presentations of the act of thinking. A
preliminary, hopelessly Platonic defence would be that, even if simple
re-enactments, the seminars must have had as their models previous,
original actions. But Deleuze himself indicates that the seminars were
so carefully rehearsed in order to exceed the limits of preparation. In
a 1988 interview, shortly after his retirement, Deleuze offered a rare
glimpse into his conception of the seminars to which he devoted much
of his life. 'Giving courses has been a major part of my life, in which
I've been passionately involved ... It takes a lot of preparatory work
to get a few minutes of inspiration. I was ready to stop when I saw it
was taking more and more preparation to get a more taxing inspiration'
(Deleuze 1995: 139). Deleuze's goal, then, was to make present, within

the prepared performance of thought, unpredictable and spontaneous moments of inspiration. In this regard, Deleuze's object was that of such performing arts as theatre, dance and music. In these arts, performers succeed only to the extent that they attain a zone of indiscernibility, in which performer, audience and performance become indistinguishable elements of an a-personal event. This essential dimension of the seminars is what Deleuze signals in the same interview when he says that 'a course is a kind of *Sprechgesang*, closer to music than to theatre' (1995: 139). The positions of performer and audience in music are not those of emitter and receiver of messages, but co-participants in a sonic event. In another interview, while paying tribute to Foucault, Deleuze says that 'good lectures, after all, are more like a concert than a sermon, like a soloist "accompanied" by everyone else. And Foucault gave wonderful lectures.' Audiences 'accompany' Foucault 'because they're doing something with him, in their own work, in their own independent lives. It's not just a question of intellectual understanding or agreement, but of intensity, resonance, musical harmony' (1995: 86). As Deleuze argues in *Difference and Repetition*, the genuine teacher says, 'do with me', not 'do as I do'.

The seminar is also like a musical performance in another important sense. After describing the seminar as a kind of *Sprechgesang*, Deleuze reflects on the diverse audience he addressed at Vincennes. 'It was there that I realized how much philosophy needs not only philosophical understanding, through concepts, but a nonphilosophical understanding, rooted in percepts and affects' (Deleuze 1995: 139). In *What Is Philosophy?*, Deleuze and Guattari associate percepts and affects most closely with the arts, arguing that just as philosophers invent concepts, so artists invent percepts and affects. Such percepts and affects are not personal perceptions and emotions, but anonymous, autonomous manifestations of the 'being of sensation' (Deleuze and Guattari 1994: 164), elements that permeate and pass through the individuals who serve as their vehicles. As *Sprechgesang*, the Deleuzian seminar aims to infuse concepts with percepts and affects, giving them a necessary intensity, resonance and harmony. It is this musical and philosophical essence that Mengue felt in the voice of Deleuze, a sonic materialisation of concepts, percepts and affects belonging no longer to Deleuze the individual, but to thought itself. In the language of *Difference and Repetition*, the voice had become an emission of signs, a trajectory passing through the singular points of the cadences and rhythms of performance.

Deleuze's conception of the seminar as *Sprechgesang* has further implications concerning time and audience response, which he sketches in his 1988 interview. Here Deleuze contrasts seminars and professional conferences, finding in the latter a time and atmosphere that inhibit genuine thought. Conferences consist of discrete, short lectures, followed by 'discussion', by which Deleuze means fractious debate. 'Philosophy has nothing to do with discussing things, it's difficult enough just understanding the problem someone's framing and how they're framing it' (Deleuze 1995: 139). The short duration of the conference paper is insufficient for understanding the specific problem under consideration, for which reason conferences give rise to battles over pre-established territories, forensic skirmishes that in no way foster co-participation in thought. By contrast, seminars 'have to be carried on over a long period with a relatively fixed audience, sometimes for a number of years. It's like a research laboratory [*un laboratoire de recherche*]: you give courses on what you're investigating [*sur ce qu'on cherche*], not on what you know' (1995: 139). Understanding problems proceeds in a slow rhythm, stretching well beyond the limits of a given seminar. At Vincennes, says Deleuze, there were 'long sessions [two and a half hours], nobody took in everything, but everyone took what they needed or wanted, what they could use, even if it was far removed from their discipline' (1995: 139). Only in this time of 'a long period of time' [*une longue durée*] could comprehension take the form of a musical accompaniment, in which intellectual understanding would become a matter of 'intensity, resonance, musical harmony' (1995: 86).

In the *ABC Primer* ('P as in Professor'), Deleuze distinguishes two basic conceptions of the seminar: one which aims at provoking an immediate audience response, soliciting questions, establishing a dialogue among the students and the teacher; and the model Deleuze followed, the traditional lecture, known in French as the *cours magistral*, the magisterial course, the course of the *magister*, the master (a name, Deleuze tells Parnet, with which he is not particularly happy). Deleuze claims that he used the *cours magistral* because that was what he had always done, but it was obviously a method well-suited to his talents. Essential to the *cours magistral*, as Deleuze conceived it, was an uninterrupted delivery, and in this sense, very much like a musical performance, during which the audience is expected to remain silent. Since the courses were so long and comprehension only occurred slowly, there necessarily would be stretches of time when students would be baffled, or lose their concentration, but questions at every juncture of confusion would only impede understanding. The point of the lecture was to allow students to drop out of the flow of words, to give them opportunities to rejoin the flow, and to encourage them to wait for illumination. As in a musical performance, says Deleuze, a phrase or motif may only become coherent later in the piece, so the elements of the seminar often coalesce only towards the end of the presentation, or perhaps days later. Deleuze notes that his best students asked their questions the week following the lecture, when they had allowed the temporality of the seminar experience to exercise to the full the power of its *longue durée*.

Clearly, one of Deleuze's goals in his seminars, and one that he met with considerable success, was that of performing the action of thinking and creating moments of inspiration during which the rehearsal of thought became thought 'in real time'. The pursuit of that goal suited a particular format, with its own temporality and mode of audience participation. But what of the content of his courses? What did he talk about? Deleuze gave lectures on the material in *Anti-Oedipus*, *A Thousand Plateaus*, *Cinema 1*, *Cinema 2* and *Francis Bacon*, but he also devoted several seminars to other philosophers, notably Kant (1978), Spinoza (1978, 1980, 1981) and Leibniz (1980 and 1986–87). These courses in the history of philosophy are especially important in considering the Deleuzian teacher as master apprentice.

In *Dialogues*, Deleuze speaks disparagingly of the traditional function of the history of philosophy:

> The history of philosophy has always been the agent of power in philosophy, and even in thought. It has played the repressor's role: how can you think without having read Plato, Descartes, Kant and Heidegger, and so-and-so's book about them? A formidable school of intimidation which manufactures specialists in thought – but which also makes those who stay outside conform all the more to this specialism which they despise. An image of thought called philosophy has been formed historically and it effectively stops people from thinking. (Deleuze and Parnet 2002: 13)

One might assume from this critique that Deleuze had no use for the history of philosophy, but a few pages later Deleuze explains that he found his way out of this repressive regime via philosophers who had escaped from philosophy's orthodox history 'in one respect, or altogether: Lucretius, Spinoza, Hume, Nietzsche, Bergson' (Deleuze and Parnet 2002: 14–15). In fact, as Deleuze explains in the *ABC Primer* ('H as in History of Philosophy'), the history of philosophy played an essential role in his own education.

For Deleuze, the history of philosophy is a form of portraiture in thought. The object of a historical study is to paint a philosopher's portrait by delineating the concepts he or she invented and to uncover the problem that gave rise to those concepts and to which they responded.

Throughout his life, Deleuze defined philosophy as the invention of concepts, an activity parallel to that of the painter, who creates with colour,
the musician, who creates with sound, and the writer, who creates with
words. But he insists in the *ABC Primer* that the invention of concepts is
extremely difficult and requires considerable training if one is to succeed
in that endeavour. Deleuze speaks of the great respect, awe, hesitation, and even fear and panic that Van Gogh and Gauguin felt when
approaching colour. They were great colourists, but it took them years
to feel capable of exploiting colour to the full, of being 'worthy' (*digne*)
of creating with colour. Deleuze expresses a similar respect towards concepts, and in his books on Hume, Nietzsche, Bergson and Spinoza, he
was gradually learning to master the art of concept creation by working
with and through these master concept-creators. This 'research into the
concepts of others', he says, constituted an 'indispensable apprenticeship' that allowed him eventually, in *Difference and Repetition* and
*The Logic of Sense*, to attempt the invention of concepts himself, to feel
worthy of such an enterprise. He regards as absurd the idea that one
can simply start 'doing philosophy' without training in the history of
philosophy, an absurdity equal to that of a writer who claims to have no
time to read other writers and hence simply creates *ex nihilo*.

Thus Deleuze's own development involved an extended apprenticeship, well beyond his years as a student, and in his seminars on Kant,
Spinoza and Leibniz, he re-enacted that apprenticeship, and in the
process led his students in their own training. Before creating concepts,
one must know what concepts are, and one can only understand them
by studying the concepts of the great masters. One must also comprehend the relationship between concepts and problems, a task even
more difficult since problems are only hinted at, partially articulated,
or at times completely tacit and hidden. Without an understanding of
the problem, the concepts remain abstract; once situated in relation to
the problem, however, everything becomes concrete. Plato's 'Idea' is a
genuine concept, Deleuze explains, which one may define as 'something
that is only what it is'. An actual mother, for example, is a wife, a sister,
a friend and so on, but the Idea of 'mother' is nothing more than mother,
a pure mother. But this concept remains vague and seems unmotivated
until one understands the problem that led Plato to invent the concept
of the Idea. The problem arose in the democratic city-state of Athens,
and concerned the determination of the rights of claimants (*prétendants*)
before various tribunals, legislative bodies or other venues for public
decisions. Who is the genuine claimant? Who possesses the right to a
given role, a given title, a given property? This problem, claims Deleuze,

forces Plato to invent the Idea of pure things – the Idea of Justice, Truth, the Good and so on, as pure things that are nothing more than what they are – in order to address the very concrete situation of adjudicating claimants and their petitions, of ranking the claimants according to the extent to which their claims approach the purity of a given standard.

Hence, when Deleuze says in *Difference and Repetition* that teachers only teach by saying 'do with me', he is not downplaying the role of the teacher, but simply clarifying it. The teacher as emitter of signs does not provide apprentices with answers, but guides them in the art of discovering problems, an art that can only be mastered by practising it. Such practice is mysterious in its inner workings, and unpredictable in its effects. As Deleuze remarks in *Difference and Repetition*, 'We never know in advance how someone will learn: by means of what loves someone becomes good at Latin, what encounters make them a philosopher, or in what dictionaries they learn to think.' As a result, 'There is no more a method for learning that there is for finding treasures.' Nevertheless, learning involves 'a violent training, a culture or *paideïa* which affects the entire individual' (Deleuze 1994: 165). The violent training, culture and *paideïa* of philosophy take place in the workshop of the history of philosophy. There, the master apprentice offers apprentices encounters with the concepts and problems of great philosophers, as well as the processes of thought involved in their disclosure. Not a method, but an art, not a programme of study, but a rigorous discipline.

The seminar played a central role in Deleuze's life as a teacher, but he also paid attention to individual students, fostering their development in accordance with the traditional master-apprentice relationship. In the *ABC Primer* ('E is for *Enfance*' [Childhood]), Deleuze himself singles out a certain Pierre Halwachs, a young teacher whom Deleuze met at age fourteen during an extended beach vacation at Deauville, as his first '*maître*'. Before meeting Halwachs, Deleuze was an indifferent student, but Halwachs introduced him to Gide, Anatole France, Baudelaire and other writers, and these encounters with Halwachs and great writers 'completely transformed' him. He grew passionate about learning, and during the ensuing fall term, when he studied philosophy, he discovered something important that he knew he would do the rest of his life.

Deleuze himself assumed the role of *maître* early in his career. At Amiens, when still in his twenties, he discovered that a student, Michel Morié, intended to become a worker-priest, but Deleuze insisted that he study philosophy. Morié persisted and did become a priest, but later followed Deleuze's advice and studied at the Sorbonne (Dosse 2010: 107). Another Amiens student, Claude Lemoine, developed a love of philosophy while in Deleuze's course, but Lemoine's parents planned that he follow in his father's footsteps and become a lawyer. Deleuze told Lemoine that he would not allow that to happen, and then asked to meet Lemoine's father, 'who agreed, unenthusiastically, and was finally persuaded that his son would study philosophy' (Dosse 2010: 102). At Orléans, Deleuze assumed an especially important role in the life of Alain Roger. Transformed by Deleuze's courses, Roger planned to pursue advanced study in philosophy, but disastrous year-end examinations in other subjects led him to question the viability of that career, and he contemplated instead pursuing his other passion and becoming a professional cyclist. He spoke with Deleuze about his decision, and Deleuze responded by taking Roger to the lycée library and removing three books: Epictetus' *Discussions*, Spinoza's *Ethics* and Nietzsche's *Genealogy of Morals*. He then instructed Roger to prepare a class presentation according to these instructions: '"You are going to look for the centre of gravity in this triangle, the intersection of the three medians, it's easy"' (Dosse 2010: 104). Roger did not dare say no, and he spent the next few days feverishly reading and formulating his preparation. The exercise helped dislodge Roger from his cyclist plan. Later he wondered '"how Deleuze was able to foresee that those three names were going to become my preferred authors for half a century"' (Dosse 2010: 104). During the ensuing four academic years, Deleuze drew up a rigorous programme of study for Roger and tutored him through regular discussions of his various assigned expositions of philosophical texts. Later, when Roger moved to Paris to study, he became friends with Deleuze, who, aware of Roger's lack of money, frequently took him out to eat. The winter of 1956, Roger was stricken with pleurisy 'and stuck in the lycée infirmary for several weeks, where, despite everything, I continued to work. Gilles came to see me and I don't know whether, without him, I would not have surrendered to that adversity' (Roger 2000: 40).

Such stories are touching, and one might view Deleuze's action simply as the caring attention of a decent human being, but there is more one may draw from this intense commitment to the master-apprentice relationship. These anecdotes provide evidence of Deleuze's conception of philosophy as more than mere thought, as a way of living that extends beyond the classroom. It is important, however, to recognise that in serving as a master to apprentices Deleuze was not recruiting disciples. Even when he had become a prominent philosopher, he always scorned the cultivation of acolytes and the project of building a Deleuzian 'school of thought'. In the *ABC Primer* ('P as in Professor'), Deleuze tells Parnet with a smile that he never had disciples because no one wanted to follow him, and then speaks of the 'awful', 'terrible' notion of a 'school'. A school, he says, should be contrasted with a 'movement'. Surrealism, for example, was a school, with a leader, tribunals, grudges, expulsions and so on, whereas Dada was a 'movement', with no orthodoxy, no structure, no collective purpose other than the pursuit of art in hetero-geneous directions. If anything, he would have liked to have engendered a movement through his teaching. The ideal of such a movement would disperse its participants, not bring them together, since for Deleuze, the ultimate aims of his teaching, he says, are (1) to help students 'be happy with their solitude' and (2) to provide students with pliable concepts, applicable in diverse spheres, such that each student, in his or her solitude, may encounter something that stimulates genuine thought.

The master-apprentice relationship in philosophy is part of a mode of existence, and, I would argue, understandable in terms of Deleuze's ethics. In *The Logic of Sense*, Deleuze expounds on the Stoic notion of being worthy of the event, a concept that he himself embraces. He offers as an example of such worthiness Joe Bousquet, who had been paralysed by a bullet and yet refused to lament his misfortune. This Stoic ethics has a single goal: 'to become worthy of what happens to us, and thus to will and release the event' (Deleuze 1990a: 149). Deleuze identifies this worthiness with Nietzsche's *amor fati* and the rejection of all forms of *ressentiment*, and given the example of Bousquet, one might conceive of this ethics primarily in terms of a reaction to what befalls us. But being worthy of the event is more than this. An event is an encounter, and the essence of learning, as well as thinking, resides in encounters. True, Deleuze says that thought only begins with a violence external to thought, but it is also important to do something with such violence, actively to become worthy of the encounters that occur. And one may also work to create encounters, to seek others with whom we may build ongoing encounters, to find what Deleuze calls '*intercesseurs*' (translated as 'mediators' in Deleuze 1995: 121), such as he found in Guattari. In his courses, Deleuze provides encounters for his students, events of which they then must become worthy. And as a master to individual appren-tices, Deleuze again is being worthy of the event, not seeking affection, loyalty or adulation, but endeavouring to create individual encounters and thereby help his apprentices themselves become intercessors who actively fashion their own encounters.

In some ways, Deleuze's practice as a teacher resembles that of the master of a Japanese martial art. For example, in *kyudo*, the Zen art of archery, when the *sensei*, or master, accepts students, the apprentices enter into a bond that should last for a lifetime. The *sensei*'s concerns for the students extend to all aspects of their lives. The *sensei* has reached a state of mastery by passing through all the stages of a rigorous apprenticeship, a disciplinary practice through which the *sensei* then guides the students. Students learn the eight basic postures of *kyudo* and practise them for years, gradually perfecting them and integrating them with breathing techniques and the regulation of mental activity that allows full concentration. The postures, breathing techniques and mental exercises, however, are only means to an end. *Kyudo* distinguishes between *ri*, or skill, and *ji*, or inspiration. *Ri* involves discipline, repetition and specific configurations of mind and body, but *ji* is allied to genuine mastery of the principles of the art of *kyudo*.

> Understanding the principles underlying a Zen art is not based on cognitive or intellectual understanding. Rather it is based on an intuitive awareness of the underlying principles of the Universe as they apply to that particular art . . . The philosophy of teaching in the Zen arts is to teach underlying principles through the repetitive practice of techniques. The techniques of the arts represent formalizations of the masters' understandings of the principles. They can be seen as approximations of the underlying principles . . . Each student ultimately must see into those underlying principles by himself. This can only be done by endless repetition of the eight stages of kyudo. (Kushner 2000: 17)

*Kyudo* means literally 'the way of the bow', *do* being the suffix that means 'way' (the Japanese equivalent of the Chinese 'tao'). Hence, the designation of karate as *karatedo*, the way of the empty hand, or the Zen art of sword fighting as *kendo*, the way of the sword. The various ways of the martial arts, as well as the art of writing (*shodo*), the art of tea (*chado*), and so on, are 'fractional expressions of Zen in limited fields . . . These actions become Ways when practice is not done merely for the immediate result but also with a view to purifying, calming and focusing the psycho-physical apparatus, to attain to some degree of Zen realization and express it' (Leggett 1978: 117). The final goal, then is to go 'beyond technique, and indeed beyond thought' (Leggett 1978: 118) and reach a point at which the *ri* of technique gives way to the *ji* of inspiration.

The *ri* of philosophy, its ensemble of skills and techniques, is the history of philosophy. The *ji* of philosophy is the inspiration that arises in the process of creating concepts. The discipline of philosophy, 'a violent training, a culture or *paideïa* which affects the entire individual' (Deleuze 1994: 165), gradually takes shape through the collective practices of former masters of the art, such as Plato, Spinoza, Nietzsche and Bergson, each master adding something to the *ri* of the 'way' of philosophy. The master trains apprentices in the workshop of the history of philosophy, sometimes conducting group lessons, sometimes offering individual instruction. The master discloses the concepts and problems of past philosophers, and in the process models the activity of philosophical thought. Apprentices must undergo this rigorous *paideïa*, but only as a means of commencing a true apprenticeship in signs, one that they will pursue on their own until, perhaps, they master the 'way' of philosophy and manage to find the *ji* of philosophical creation. How this will happen, when, or by what means is mysterious, beyond any method or programme. But if such mastery is attained, its effects will be all-pervasive. The 'way' of philosophy is a way of living, a mode of existence, and like the way of Zen, one that applies to all aspects of life.[3] Philosophy's way is that of the event, the encounter, the forceful interference, intercession, reverberation and resonance of signs meeting signs. The master, as producer of signs, is filled with a lightness, a gentle humour, but also with a passionate intensity. When producing signs, the master is no longer a human being, but a selfless, a-personal concentration of thought itself, an amalgam of concepts, percepts and affects. In the philosophy seminar, the material vehicle of thought is the voice, and conducting a *cours magistral* is nothing other than giving voice to philosophy. The master's enunciation of the way is the affirmative Yes, hesitant, prolonged, suspended in time, in an intermezzo, a meanwhile (*entretemps*), a between-time, a floating time that opens towards the possibility of something new. It is in this Yes, a single sign of all signs, inseparable from the asignifying matter of the master's *Sprechgesang*, that the *ji* of philosophy, its inspiration, appears. At that moment, the master apprentice discloses the essence of teaching, the way towards a perpetual encounter with signs, an ongoing apprenticeship in which masters and apprentices alike continue to learn from the world.

## Notes

1. There is no transcription of Deleuze's remarks in the *ABC Primer* available in print. Charles Stivale informs me that Deleuze's estate declined to grant permission for such a transcription (personal communication). Stivale has, however written an invaluable detailed synopsis of the seven-hour video and has made it accessible on the internet (Stivale 2000).
2. In the *ABC Primer*, Deleuze tells Parnet that he once taught a lycée lesson by playing a musical saw, a pedagogical technique, one must assume, that he abandoned at the university level.
3. In the *ABC Primer*, Parnet asks Deleuze if he goes to art exhibits or films in the pursuit of culture, and he says no, that he is simply seeking encounters. She then asks if he ever goes to films for entertainment rather than 'work', and he

replies that it's not a matter of work, but of being alert, looking for something disturbing, amusing, stirring, anything that has the energy of something 'passing', something in the process of becoming-other. This vigilance is not restricted to the realm of the arts, he suggests, but informs all of his experience. And indeed, given the wide range of subjects Deleuze addresses in his books, it is evident that the 'way' of philosophical encounters is one that he pursued in all aspects of his life.

# References

Criton, P. (2007), 'L'esthétique intensive ou le théâtre des dynamismes' in Bruno Gelas and Hervé Micolet (eds), *Deleuze et les écrivains*, Lyon: Cécile Defaut, pp. 57–69.

Deleuze, G. (1990a), *The Logic of Sense*, trans. M. Lester, with C. Stivale, ed. C. V. Boundas, New York: Columbia University Press.

Deleuze, G. (1990b), *Proust and Signs: The Complete Text*, trans. R. Howard, London: Athlone.

Deleuze, G. (1994), *Difference and Repetition*, trans. P. Patton, New York: Columbia University Press.

Deleuze, G. (1995), *Negotiations: 1972–1990*, trans. M. Joughin, New York: Columbia University Press.

Deleuze, G. (2000), *Proust and Signs*, trans. R. Howard, Minneapolis: University of Minnesota Press.

Deleuze, G. and C. Parnet (2002), *Dialogues II*, trans. H. Tomlinson and B. Habberjam, London: Continuum.

Deleuze, G. and C. Parnet (2004), *L'abécédaire de Gilles Deleuze*, dir. Pierre-André Boutang, Paris: Montparnasse.

Dosse, F. (2010), *Gilles Deleuze and Félix Guattari: Intersecting Lives*, trans. D. Glassman, New York: Columbia University Press.

Kushner, K. (2000), *One Arrow, One Life: Zen, Archery, Enlightenment*, Boston: Tuttle.

Leggett, T. (1978), *Zen and the Ways*, London: Routledge and Kegan Paul.

Mengue, P. (2000), 'En hommage à Gilles Deleuze: Vincennes, une voix, un personnage proustien . . .' in Yannick Beaubatie (ed.), *Tombeau de Gilles Deleuze*, Tulle: Mille Sources, pp. 49–56.

Roger, A. (2000), 'Gilles Deleuze et l'amitié' in Yannick Beaubatie (ed.), *Tombeau de Gilles Deleuze*, Tulle: Mille Sources, pp. 35–48.

Stivale, C. (2000), *Synopsis of Deleuze's ABC's* <http://www.langlab.wayne.edu/CStivale/D-G/ABCs.html> (accessed 17 September 2012).

# Chapter 2

## Staged Interventions:
## Deleuze, Arts and Education

*Julie Allan*

As a young boy, film director Anthony Minghella listened to the Leonard Cohen song 'Suzanne', played to him in class by his English teacher. This experience 'confounded' him and established within him a love of poetry which lasted a lifetime. Just before his death, in 2008, he implored teachers to confound the young people in their charge in the way that his English teacher had done with him. Teachers, he argued, had to be able to engage students with the extra-ordinary, and he suggested that film, music and other art forms could help them to achieve this. Deleuze also testifies to the arts' transformative capacities, offering individuals sensory, and even sensual, affects and producing 'fragments, allusions, strivings, investigations' which create 'affirmative injunctions' (1998: 111). I would argue further that the arts have a potential reach that enables teachers to engage *all* students and, furthermore, that Deleuze's concepts can assist teachers to think and to practise both differently and equitably (Allan 2008). This chapter examines the potential of the arts, drawing on Deleuze's analyses of various art forms, to provoke altered forms of subjectivity and to promote a more affecting kind of education. It also considers the creative interventions which Deleuze's thought have the potential to generate. The chapter then sets out three educational performances. The first of these shows students experiencing arts activities within a deterritorialised space, initiated by practising artists, and highlights the embodied engagement these provoked. In the second performance, a group of students experience and experiment with rights, take these rights – literally – on a walk in and out of school, and propose new actions and becomings for their teachers and fellow students. The rhizomatic engagement with rights also enabled one individual in the group to recreate himself with a whole new subjectivity, educational trajectory and future. The final performance is work by disabled artists which seeks to educate audiences by altering the space in which they encountered difference and to provoke new becomings. The chapter concludes with an exercise in creative subtraction, an element of Deleuze's deterritorialisation, with a specification of the negative orientations and practices which could open up possibilities for teachers to confound their students.

## Affecting Arts

The arts have long been proclaimed as having life-enhancing properties, being depicted as the food of life itself by Shakespeare, and as capable, as Robert Browning contended, of speaking the truth. Deleuze is convinced of the capacity of the arts to create 'new percepts and new affects' (Deleuze 1995: 164). Percepts differ from perceptions in that they are independent of the person experiencing them (Deleuze 2004); affects, following Spinoza (1985), extend beyond the affections and feelings experienced to denote transformations in bodily capacities. Affects 'transpierce the body like arrows, they are weapons of war' (Deleuze and Guattari 1987: 356). Percepts and affects are separate '*beings* whose validity lies in themselves and exceeds any lived' (Deleuze 2004: 164). The arts achieve their affects through expression, as opposed to emotion, and this is 'capable of taking the ground away' (Uhlmann 2009: 64). It is the 'critical enmeshment of the newness' (Hickey-Moody 2009: 172) which provides the content of expression and which removes the possibility of self-consciousness and the need for interpretation and understanding.

The essences of particular art forms are such that they escape conventional structures and forms. Music, for example, is seen as prophetic (Attali 1985), able to explore possibilities much faster than other forms of enquiry. For Deleuze, music 'Deeply traverses our bodies and puts an ear in our belly, in our lungs etc. . . . it rids bodies of their inertia, of the materiality of their presence. It *disincarnates* bodies . . . it gives the most mental entities a disincarnated, dematerialized body' (1981: 38). This provides greater scope for connectivity with individuals and for more embodied experiences. Yet, while music can embrace and envelop us, it also excludes us from articulating our experience of it, if, as McClary (1985) observes, we cannot access the self-contained structure and language of music. Deleuze and Guattari (1987) dispute this inaccessibility, contending that music is an open structure that permeates and is in turn permeated by the world (Bogue 2003), and is machinic and rhythmical rather than mechanical and mathematical. Deleuze and Guattari draw attention to composers such as Messiaen who draw everything in and make music a complete engagement with cosmic forces.

Visual art also requires connectivity and embodied engagement from individuals in order to produce. The artist Paul Klee describes the period just before art is made as a 'nowhere existent something' or 'a somewhere existent nothing' (1961: 4), which, once established by the artist, leaps into a new order. Cézanne's account of making art conveys an assemblage of himself and the world to be painted and from which there needs to be some emergence: 'At this moment I am one with my canvas. We are an iridescent chaos. I come before my motif, I lose myself there . . . We germinate' (1978: 150). For Deleuze and Guattari (1994) painting is a block of sensations that produces percepts and affects and creates a 'becoming-other' and they exalt Cézanne's landscapes of 'iridescent chaos' as examples of percepts and Bacon's heads-becoming-animal as exemplars of affects (Bogue 2003: 164). The artist, by provoking percepts and affects, both of which are separate from the person who experiences them, can claim to be producing something new and unimagined.

The moving image, says Anthony Minghella, helps to interrupt and punctuate the drone of the voice. This capacity is profound, according to Mazzei who bemoans how the 'barrage of speech-acts blurs identity to the point that subjects themselves disappear' (2010: 518), and Barad argues that film can enable us to see speech as image such that 'conceptions of materiality, social practice, nature and discourse must change to accommodate their mutual involvement' (Barad 2007: 25). Deleuze, through his engagement with film (1986, 1989), successfully reframes the speech-act as an image, allowing us to view voice and engage with it differently. What this means is that we no longer depend on voice to tell us the authoritative story – the truth – and that we have no absolute need to comprehend or even apprehend what is held within. It leaves us open to experience voice – and indeed language – both for what it is and what it might become, in other words, in its own 'state of perpetual disequilibrium' (Deleuze 1994a: 27).

Minor literatures that have been created in major languages by minorities (Deleuze and Guattari 1986) offer great possibilities for the articulation of new political subjectivities. The literatures could be used to help name minorities, marginalised groups, including disabled people, those whose voices are normally subjugated, and to mobilise politically around these names, while at the same time working to undermine the sovereign subject. A minor literature has three features: the language used is affected by deterritorialisation, that is, a smoothing out of space or a stripping out of syntax so that it loses all symbolism and signification; everything is political (and individuals are connected to a political immediacy); and everything has a collective value (Deleuze and Guattari 1986). Two great writers, James Joyce and Samuel Beckett, are lauded by Deleuze and Guattari for their production of very different, but equally potent, minor literatures: Joyce achieves 'exhilaration and overdetermination' while Beckett produces 'dryness and sobriety, a willed poverty' (Deleuze and Guattari 1986: 19). Beckett also produces affects by interfering with space, time and sound and interpellating speech into gesture, movement, place, physical position and posture (Chabert 1980). In contrast with the interruption of sound by the image achieved in film, Beckett inserts voice over the seen, as for example in *Catastrophe*:

> DIRECTOR: How's the skull?
> ASSISTANT: You've seen it.
> DIRECTOR: I forget. Say it.
> (Beckett 1984: 298)

Both Joyce and Beckett succeed in creating deterritorialisation that takes language to its limits, makes it stand still and forces a reterritorialisation. Kafka, observe Deleuze and Guattari, uses syntax against itself to render language inert:

> Kafka will turn syntax into a cry that will embrace the rigid syntax of this dried-up German. He will push it toward a deterritorialization that will no longer be saved by culture or myth, that will be an absolute deterritorialization, even if it is slow, sticky, coagulated. To bring language slowly and progressively to the desert. To use syntax in order to cry, to give a syntax to the cry. (1986: 26)

The act of creating a minor literature is 'to find points of nonculture or under-development, linguistic Third World zones by which a language can escape, an animal enters things, an assemblage comes into play' (Deleuze and Guattari 1986: 27). The accomplishment – and use – of a minor literature goes against the dream of major styles, genres and movements of assuming major functions and aspiring to be authoritative: 'Create the opposite dream: know how to create a becoming-minor. (Is there hope for philosophy, which for a long time has been an official, referential genre? Let us profit from this moment in which antiphilosophy is trying to be a language of power)' (Deleuze and Guattari 1986: 27). The use of minor literatures to name and privilege particular voices and identities is described usefully by Rancière as a process of making a discourse of that which has formally been a noise and as a process of rupture which renders certain identities visible:

For me a political subject is a subject who employs the competence of the so-called incompetents or the part of those who have no part, and not an additional group to be recognised as part of society. 'Visible minorities' means exceeding the system of represented groups, of constituted identities . . . It's a rupture that opens out into the recognition of the competence of anyone, not the addition of a unit. (2008: 3)

Critchley argues that the scope for political action has been reduced by the disarticulation of names which are inherently political, such as the 'proletariat' or the 'peasant', and cites the examples of 'indigenous' peoples achieving the status of a force for change in Mexico and Australia. Critchley usefully advocates a kind of demonstration as demos-tration, 'manifesting the presence of those who do not count' (2007: 130). Minor literatures, because they take language beyond being merely representative, moving 'head over heels and away' (Deleuze and Guattari 1986: 26), offer great potential for addressing inequalities. They do so productively and creatively, by 'setting fire to the unjust state of things instead of burning the things themselves, and restoring life to primary life' (Deleuze and Guattari 1986: 108).

## Becoming Creative: With Deleuze

We are in a tenor of relaxation – I am speaking of the tenor of the times. Everywhere we are being urged to give up experimentation, in the arts and elsewhere. (Lyotard 1993: 1)

Deleuze's thought is capable of producing profound creative experiences and requires 'a whole new pedagogy . . . because we have to read the visual as well as hear the speech-act in a new way' (Deleuze 1989: 237). His philosophy opens us up to 'intensity, resonance, musical harmony' (Deleuze 1995: 86), producing us as creative artists 'capable of thinking the unthinkable' (Semetsky 2004: 318). It takes us outside of the confines of language, while enabling us to subject language to its own becoming in which it is in-between: 'like silence, or like stammering . . . something letting language slip through and making itself heard' (Deleuze 1995: 41). Thus he offers us concepts which are more than simply concepts, but which cross senses, requiring that we experience these as more than utterances. These concepts have a multiplicity, a history and a 'becoming', the 'plane of immanence' (Deleuze and Guattari 1994: 18, 35) on which the concept can emerge along with the conceptual personae who can activate the concept, such as the nomadic teacher or the rhizomatic learner.

Deleuze's work offers an opportunity to respond ontologically, with a series of questions: 'Does it work? What new thoughts does it make possible to think? What new emotions does it make possible to feel? What new sensations and perceptions does it open in the body?' (Massumi 1992: 8). The body can respond in terms of its functions and capacities, for example for movement and expression, producing 'transvaluation of negation into affirmation, reactive into active' (Smith 1998: 263). Such a response is necessary, since, according to Deleuze, problems 'do not exist only in our heads but occur here and there in the production of the actual historical world' (Deleuze 1994b: 190), and the significance of this is that they can be worked upon through thought. The act of thought, for Deleuze, is a throw of the dice, a form of experimentation. This is vital in today's educational contexts in which the simple, the reducible or the replicable has primacy and where, as Deleuze and Guattari warn, 'we constantly lose our ideas [and] that is why we want to hang on to fixed opinions so much' (1994: 201).

## Educational Performances

Deleuze and Guattari's model of rhizomatic thought challenges both conventional knowledge and the means of acquiring this knowledge, but Deleuze contends that children are already *in* the rhizome, in their processes of learning: 'Children never stop talking about what they are doing or trying to do: exploring milieus, by means of dynamic trajectories, and drawing up maps of them' (Deleuze 1998: 61). Several writers have argued that artwork undertaken by children and young people can be highly educative as work of experimentation (Greene 2004; Deleuze 1998; Gardner 1982; Matarraso 1997), providing dynamic play and allowing them to create what Braidotti calls 'fabulations', or a 'fiction that offers us a world clearly and radically discontinuous from the one we know, yet returns to confront that known world in some cognitive way' (Braidotti, cited in Gough 2004: 256).

The three educational performances that follow are being read as enactments of key 'conceptual bits' (Rajchman 2001: 21). The first example was an explicit and knowing attempt to provide a deterritorialised space for a group of students. The second and third examples are interpreted and made sense of through thinking with Deleuze (Mazzei 2010). Each of these take the participants out of the reach of the familiar and into new territories of experience. They also command a complete and unequivocal engagement from all and hence are equitable. The affects that are produced, for the participants and for others, are confounding and afford them no possibility of returning to the original territory.

## Art Lab

Students aged eleven to twelve were invited to *Art Lab,* promising a variety of activities led by practising artists from music, theatre, dance, film animation, visual art and circus (Lynch and Allan 2006). The experiences provided in *Art Lab* were distinctive, as a deliberate act of deterritorialisation, an attempt to provide a smooth space that was explicitly different from school. They involved the students in embodied learning, requiring movement rather than passivity from them, and expression rather than understanding. The learning was also rhizomatic, in that it took the students off in new and unanticipated directions, and was 'entirely oriented toward an experimentation in contact with the real' (Deleuze and Guattari 1987: 12). The *Art Lab* encouraged and enabled students of all levels of ability to participate, and the actor who led the theatre activity was himself disabled and engaged the youngsters in activities involving his own wheelchair in a way which was inventive and, in their words, 'cool'.

The students' experiences were embodied in the most obvious sense – as one individual commented, 'you get to do stuff' – and appeared in the focus group discussions held after the event to contrast starkly with the passivity of their usual school routine. According to one group of students, 'doing stuff' was more effective because 'you think more'. The activities had been deliberately presented to the students as embodied. For example, a musician, working with the students on percussion, told them: 'You don't need a drum to make good rhythm – you've got lots of bodily surfaces' – and encouraged them to explore these. He also distinguished what they were doing at *Art Lab* from their school lessons: 'This is a drumming class. And, let's face it, it's not maths. It's not chemistry. It's certainly not physics. Enjoy yourself.' He called to the students with rhythm that initially involved their own bodies and then instruments; gradually, but overwhelmingly, he had the entire group rocking, pulsating and seeming extremely pleased with themselves. The other workshops involved the students almost immediately in action, doing some things they had never done before, such as spinning a plate, or making a piece of animation, and other things that were familiar, such as drawing. The focus of the dance workshop was science, but not as the students normally experienced it. Here, they were required to create patterns and connections with others which simulated attraction and repulsion. So, this was physics, but on the move.

The theatre workshop appeared to be the most provocative and intensive and to have the greatest impact on the students. The session involved a series of activities in which the students were called upon to be inventive, using their own bodily resources – voice, expression, gesture, posture and movement. In one episode, they were asked to insert punctuation, of their own choice, into a continuous passage read by one of the leaders. They came up with a short sigh for a comma, a long one for a full stop, 'ping' for a question mark and a slap on the floor with both hands for an exclamation mark. In another piece, they had to find different ways to say 'I don't want to be a skydiver', and in yet another, they each had to come up with a different – and loud – exclamation, and many riotous variations were produced. In one particularly inventive activity, the group leader, Robert Softley, an actor with the company *Birds of Paradise*, came out of his wheelchair and turned it upside down on the floor. The students were then asked to compile words or phrases and accompanying actions around the wheelchair. They chose a range of actions either directly involving the wheelchair, for example spinning wheels, or gestures towards or away from it. The sounds they produced were both musical and machinic and came together in an impressive cacophony: 'Cool, wow, wah, check it out, just weird, that's dreadful'. Robert asked them to turn up both the speed and the volume, then to bring it down again. The youngsters' 'performance' seemed to represent a productive kind of repetition through which rhythmic difference is produced. This kind of repetition 'has nothing to do with a reproductive measure' (Deleuze and Guattari 1987: 314), of the kind which produces exclusion. Rather, it was inventive, creative and affecting.

The extent to which the students had engaged in the arts activities was revealed in the discussions, during which they expressed delight in their active participation and in their achievements. One youngster proudly boasted: 'I learned how to juggle, spin plates, drum' while another described his experience of animation as 'awesome'. The participants in the drama expressed great satisfaction with what they had produced and pleasure at 'watching other people'. There was also an interestingly matter-of-fact engagement with the disabled actor and his wheelchair in their reflections. One of the participants, for example, referred to the actor as someone who 'could be quite funny' and who had 'that machine thing'. The students appeared to have engaged with difference as interesting rather than problematic. There was some dispute over whether what they had experienced was 'work' or not: 'You didn't have to do work; You just got to do the fun stuff. It is work, but it is fun work.'

The students highlighted the contrast between the teaching they had received from the artists within this smooth space and that which they normally experienced in school. The artists made their activities more interesting and appealing than their teachers managed, albeit, they admitted, with more intrinsically interesting subjects than those in school. The artists also accorded the youngsters a level of respect which they did not enjoy in school; they thought most teachers lacked a sense of humour and often shouted or, as one person commented, 'speak down to us'. For many of the students, the musician was the living embodiment of their ideal teacher. Clearly his hat and 'cool' demeanour was part of his attraction, but his main strength, as far as the youngsters were concerned, was his ability to relate to them in a respectful way and to allow them to make such great noise.

## Performing Rights

The second performance involves a group of students in one school in which the school principal was experimenting with how far she could go with the UN Convention of the Rights of the Child (Allan and I'Anson 2004; Allan et al. 2005). This is being read as a performance of rights through which the students experienced rhizomatic learning and new affects for themselves, for disabled people and for the wider school community. As researchers tracking the principal's activities and progress within the school, we were not clear that she was having much success with her early efforts. The principal also realised that her attempts to bring students' rights into what we termed the 'bureaucratic spaces' (Allan and I'Anson 2004: 126), pupil councils and school assemblies, had little effect, largely because the power relations in the school were unchallenged. Incorporating rights within the curriculum was somewhat more successful as it enabled students to explore their own conceptions of power and their place within the school and to make connections with the subject content. However, the principal's greatest success was achieved when she gave a small of group of students the chance to experience and experiment with rights within ethical spaces. The group that was formed to look at inclusion in the school and the group, which called itself the Special Needs Observation Group (SNOG), was initially established by a parent of two disabled students in the school, but the students gradually assumed responsibility for their own activities. The group experienced a form of rhizomatic learning in which they experimented with, and experienced, inclusion. They took rights – literally – on a walk through the school in order to discover the points at which exclusion arose. Simulation exercises of this kind, in which non-disabled individuals pretend to be disabled, can be superficial and essentialist, but these young people directed their gaze to the disabling barriers and found themselves able to imagine the exclusion experienced by their disabled peers. This kind of learning about rights seemed to be particularly effective because it took them off in new and unanticipated directions. Having *dealt with* disability, the group decided to move on to ethnicity, and identified some concerns about the level of participation of some individuals. They then decided to tackle weight issues when they became aware of some of their peers' discomfort when changing for gym. Their experience and experimentation with rights had alerted them to new forms of exclusion that they wished to do something about.

For one young person, Alistair, the experience of being part of the SNOG group, and of rhizomatic learning, was particularly significant in enabling him to rescue himself from a downward spiral of misbehaviour and exclusion and to remake his identity. He described himself as having been out of control, often getting into trouble in the playground for fighting and being regularly excluded. Prior to joining SNOG, he had become a buddy to a disabled child and being responsible for someone else had made him alter his own behaviour. His membership of SNOG had, by his own account, transformed him into someone else, someone who had to have regard for others, and had allowed him to escape the deviant identity that was being ascribed to him. It was a dramatic line of flight:

> Well, when I started to know [disabled students] I was, like, I need to show them I want to be good, 'cos I used to get into fights and stupid things like that but when I started to get to know them and got into the SNOG group I started my behaviour; I wanted to start again and be good . . . I didn't want everybody to know me as Alistair the bad boy. I want to be good now. So that's what I was trying to do when I went into the SNOG group . . . sometimes I'm amazing. (Allan and I'Anson 2004: 133)

Alistair had transformed himself, but recognised that he had to police his own newly formed identity and occasionally he lapsed:

> I get into a fight or I get angry because it didn't happen. If I didn't get to sit beside my friends I start to get angry. I just want to be a good boy now. As everybody says 'good boy'. That's what I want to be – I want to prove them all wrong. They all think I [can't] behave but I want to prove them all wrong that I can behave . . . some people just know me as 'there's Alistair – stay away from him'. But I'm to prove them all wrong – that I'm good. I'm going to be good. I just want to be good now. (Allan and I'Anson 2004: 134)

Alistair reflected on his former self and recognised his initial motivations for becoming involved with disabled people as being misplaced:

I just wanted to have them 'cos I thought they looked amazing. I just wanted to be with them . . . I thought they looked so cute and things like that. But everybody feels sorry for them but they're just the same as us so they should just be treated the same. 'Cos they don't like being felt sorry for – just because they have disabilities doesn't mean they should be treated differently. That's what the group's all about – to make sure people don't treat each other differently because they look different. So that's what we've been doing. (Allan and I'Anson 2004: 133)

He had come to understand how damaging pity and differential treatment could be to individuals and he became intent on ensuring this was understood by others. He saw his future as a bright one in which he would continue to work against the destructiveness of pity and to shape himself as someone who cared: 'I think everyone that's got a disability feels better when you treat them the same . . . I think that's how they feel – they just like to get on with their life. I care about a lot of people with disabilities . . . It makes me feel like I'm more important. And keeps me out of trouble.' Alistair's remaking of himself delighted all those with whom he was connected – the principal, the teachers, the janitor, Alistair's mother, and the researchers. Most impressed of all was Alistair himself, who came to know himself as 'amazing'.

## Disability Arts

Disability arts offers a very particular kind of becoming for the spectator which is also educative and transformative. While not all the artists have read their work as Deleuzian, it can be interpreted as producing a minor literature which profoundly alters the audience and forces upon them a series of becomings. It provides an embodied display of difference, but also works upon able-bodied people's perceptions of normality and unravels these, creating dissonance and doubt and forcing them to rethink. Disabled artists provide a unique take on the body that is not available to able-bodied people. It also engages the spectator in ways of looking that are powerful and transformative:

> While the able body is often defined by the need to enhance an otherwise dulled network of sensations, the disabled body finds itself drawing an undue amount of attention to itself. For disabled artists, the socially abhorrent body is forced to engage in an exchange. First the disabled body offers itself for consumption by audiences alienated from their own bodies. And then the artist turns that spectacle into a rearticulation of disability as a source of insight and power. (Nussbaum 2004)

Deleuze and Parnet remind us that the capability of the body, whether disabled or not, is limitless when we step away from seeking to apprehend its substance:

> 'What can a body do?', of what affects is it capable? . . . Spinoza never ceases to be amazed by the body. He is not amazed at having a body, but by what the body can do. Bodies are not defined by their genus or species, by their organs and functions, but by what they can do, by the affects of which they are capable. (1987: 60)

Much of disability arts is playful and cheeky, seeking to disrupt the commonplace and the taken-for-granted in both the art form and in everyday life. The kind of art practised here can be likened to a form of kynicism (Allan 2005; Sloterdijk 1987), a Greek term denoting a form of solemn mockery which is also outrageous, 'pissing against the idealist wind' (Sloterdijk 1987: 103) to achieve its disruptive goals:

> Ancient kynicism begins the process of *naked arguments* from the opposition, carried by the power that comes from below. The kynic farts, shits, pisses, masturbates on the street, before the eyes of the Athenian market. He shows contempt for fame, ridicules the architecture, refuses respect, parodies the stories of gods and heroes. (Sloterdijk 1987: 103)

Kynicism attacks the piety of seriousness through the 'physiologically irresistible energy of laughter' (Sloterdijk 1987: 110). The disabled artists confront non-disabled people with their own banality and force them to look at themselves and the way they disable and exclude through their attitudes and behaviour and through the structures and practices they participate in. They are made to experience the comedy and irony of these and are taken to the 'horror of the comic', where they are inside the 'guts of a joke' (Kundera 1986: 104) and are forced to think again about how they relate to disabled people. Disabled artists, involved in a range of activities including music, visual art, photography, dance, film and stand-up comedy, have used their own bodies as material, or, as some see it, as weapons to subvert and undermine disabling barriers. Some of the artwork portrays disabled people themselves as emboldened or empowered, while other work depicts the disabling environment in which disabled people have to live.

There is a great deal of work within disability arts, but the following examples from poetry and dance illustrate the powerful interventions that they constitute. Cheryl Marie Wade, in her poem 'I Am Not One Of The' (2007), teases her audience with a set of oppositions. She solicits a becoming from her audience by forcing them to encounter her disabled self as at once beautiful and grotesque, portraying herself as both a sexual object – with lace panties – and as deformed – with a stub. She also playfully denies the benevolent labels put on disabled people such as 'physically challenged', preferring to reclaim language, such as 'gimp' and 'cripple' which has been left behind, while also declaring herself an 'epitaph for a million imperfect babies left untreated' and an 'ikon carved from bones in a mass grave at Tiergarten'. In offering herself as a 'French kiss with a cleft tongue' she is demanding a sexual presence which has hitherto been denied (Davis 1997), but recognises the distaste this provokes: 'I'm orthopedic shoes sewn on a last of your fears'. Her becoming, therefore, has an impact on her own identity and on how she portrays these, but more importantly on those who read the poems and who are forced to examine their own normalising and disabling knowledge and actions.

Movement offers a space to open up the possibilities for knowing difference in new ways that are not yet fixed by notions of otherness. Deleuze refers to this space as the Open: 'If the whole is not giveable it is because it is the Open, and because its nature is to change constantly, or to give rise to something new, in short, to endure' (1986: 9). The educative function of the Open – or of the act of opening – has been aptly illustrated by Masny (2009) in relation to literacies, enabling the self and the world to be read as texts and provoking new becomings. The Open is, however, a fragile space for disabled people because, as Kuppers points out, spectators inevitably impose a diagnostic gaze upon them, marking them as other and judging their performance accordingly. Kuppers seeks to find a way through this by creating performances which are acts of 'witnessing', in which:

> Change is present but not clearly categorizable into the 'other' . . . the unclearly, imperceptibly moving and breathing bodies withholding their inner experience would be *alive*, that is not fixed into difference. Something would be moving and the fact that it would not be clear *what* is moving and *how* would draw attention to the not-quite-stillness of the performers and the spectators' desire to see and to witness. (Kuppers 2003: 131, original emphasis)

Disabled dancers have the opportunity, according to Hickey-Moody (2009), to catalyse the construction of affect or sensation by virtue of their own disabilities. This interaction within the performance space has the potential to enact a 'turning away' from a history of intellectual disability which imposes limitations upon disabled people, especially in the eyes of a mainstream public. Through the act of turning away, disabled dancers can participate in an act of becoming other, an act which 'wrest[s] the percept from perceptions of objects and the states of a perceiving subject [and wrests] the affect from affections as the transition from one state to another' (Deleuze and Guattari 1994: 167). At the same time, non-disabled participants, and indeed audiences, can experience a 'turning away' from their own presumptions and misapprehensions about disabled people and other minorities in a process that is for them also a becoming: 'Creativity is always a becoming, a reterritorialisation and an establishment of new affective systems of relation. One cannot become-other unless there is something from which one turns away' (Hickey-Moody 2009: 178). As Kuppers warns, artwork which cuts into the known is a 'risky business', but 'new rhythms, new ways of knowing social space can emerge in it' (2003: 84).

## Creative Subtraction

There is an urgent need to address the inequalities produced by an education system that insists that 'everyone do better than everyone else' (McDermott 1993: 274). The arts potentially allow a response to this challenge and Deleuze's thought helps to ensure such a response is appropriate. The 'creative subtraction', an element of deterritorialisation proposed by Deleuze and Guattari (1987: 109), is particularly helpful in achieving a recalibration towards the negative that is also creative. This involves three lines of obligation for the educator which are outlined below.

*Refraining from that which the student does not desire*: As well as underlining the actions and attitudes that should be removed, Kunc and Van der Klift (1995) offer an alternative to helping in their *Credo for support*.

> *Do Not help me*, even if it does make you feel good.
> *Ask me* if I need your help.
> Let me show you how you can assist me.
> *Do Not* admire me.
> A desire to live a full life does not warrant adoration.
> *Respect me*, for respect presumes equality.
> Do not tell, correct, and lead.
> *Listen, support, and follow.*
> Do not work on me.
> *Work with me!*

*Failing better*: Beckett enjoins us to 'Try again. Fail again. Fail better' (1992: 101), and if educators are to experiment and experience, and also to expose the students in their charge to this, it is vital to be able to mark failure as a positive event. Developing criteria for failure keeps us within the language of educational performance while also making it stutter.

*Knowing worse*: The urge to know the student and what he or she is capable of appears to be irresistible and uncertainty seems to further provoke a return to knowing (Mazzei and McCoy 2010); but it is here that closure occurs and where learning is stifled. Resisting the urge to know opens up new possibilities for students but also for the teachers themselves.

These staged interventions offered by the arts, and given provocation through Deleuze's thought, invite us to see education itself as an act, but one which commands a performance from all and which refuses bland perceptions and affections. It produces a teacher-becoming-artist, one who can stand before his or her students with the excitement of what is to come, and experience, together with them, sensation and confoundment.

# References

Allan, J. (2008), *Rethinking Inclusive Education: The Philosophers of Difference in Practice*, Dordrecht: Springer.

Allan, J. (2005), 'The Aesthetics of Ideology as a Productive Ideology' in L. Ware (ed.), *Ideology and the Politics of (In)exclusion*, New York: Peter Lang, pp. 37–51.

Allan, J. and J. l'Anson (2004), 'Children's Rights in School: Power, assemblies and assemblages', *International Journal of Children's Rights*, 12(2): 123–38.

Allan, J., J. l'Anson, A. Priestley and S. Fisher (2005), *Promising Rights: Children's Rights in School*, Edinburgh: Save the Children.

Attali, J. (1985), *Noise*, trans. B. Boone, New York: Paragon.

Barad, K. (2007), *Meeting the Universe Halfway: Quantum Physics and the Entanglement of Matter and Meaning*, Durham, NC: Duke University Press.

Beckett, S. (1984), 'Catastrophe' in *Collected Shorter Plays of Samuel Beckett*, London: Faber and Faber.

Beckett, S. (1992), *Nohow On*, London: Calder.

Bogue, R. (2003), *Deleuze on Music, Painting and the Arts*, New York and London: Routledge.

Cézanne, P. (1978), *Conversations avec Paul Cézanne*, Paris: Macula.

Chabert, P. (1980), 'Samuel Beckett as Director', trans. M. A. Bonney and J. Knowlson, in J. Knowlson (ed.), *Theatre Workbook 1, Samuel Beckett: Krapp's Last Tape. A Theatre Workbook*, London: Brutus Books, pp. 85–107.

Critchley, J. (2007), *Infinitely Demanding: Ethics of Commitment, Politics of Resistance*, London and New York: Verso.

Davis, L. (1997), *The Disability Studies Reader*, London: Routledge.

Deleuze, G. (1981), *Francis Bacon: Logique de la sensation*, Vol. 1, Paris: Editions de la différance.

Deleuze, G. (1986), *Cinema 1: The Movement-Image*, trans. H. Tomlinson and B. Habberjam, London and New York: Continuum.

Deleuze, G. (1989), *Cinema 2: The Time-Image*, trans. H. Tomlinson and R. Galeta, Minneapolis: University of Minnesota Press.

Deleuze, G. (1994a), 'He Stuttered', in C. Boundas and D. Olkowski (eds), *Gilles Deleuze and the Theater of Philosophy*, London: Routledge.

Deleuze, G. (1994b), *Difference and Repetition*, trans. P. Patton, London: Athlone.

Deleuze, G. (1995), *Negotiations 1972–1990*, trans. M. Joughin, New York: Columbia University Press.

Deleuze, G. (1998), *Essays Critical and Clinical*, trans. D. W. Smith and M. A. Greco, London and New York: Verso.

Deleuze, G. and C. Parnet (1987), *Dialogues*, trans H. Tomlinson and B. Habberjam, London: Columbia University Press.

Deleuze, G. and F. Guattari (1986), *Kafka: Toward a Minor Literature*, trans D. Polan, Minneapolis: University of Minnesota Press.

Deleuze, G. and F. Guattari (1987), *A Thousand Plateaus: Capitalism and Schizophrenia*, trans. B. Massumi, London: Athlone.

Deleuze, G. and F. Guattari (1994), *What is Philosophy?* trans. H. Tomlinson and G. Burchell, New York: Columbia University Press.

Gardner, H. (1982), *Art, Mind, and Brain: A Cognitive Approach to Creativity*, New York: Basic Books.

Gough, N. (2004), 'RhizomANTically Becoming-cyborg: Performing posthuman pedagogies', *Educational Philosophy and Theory*, 36(3): 253–65.

Greene, M. (2004), *Releasing the Imagination: Essays on Education, the Arts, and Social Change*, Washington, DC: National Association of Independent Schools.

Hickey-Moody, A. (2009), 'Becoming-dinosaur: Collective process and movement aesthetics' in L. Cull (ed.), *Deleuze and Performance*, Edinburgh: Edinburgh University Press, pp. 161–80.

Klee, P. (1961), *Notebooks*, trans. P. Findlay, London: Faber and Faber.

Kunc, N. and E. Van der Klift (1995), *Credo for Support* <www.mtcdd.org/transition/Web%20trainings/Disability%20History/Credo_text_with_uTubeLinks.pdf> (accessed 1 August 2011).

Kundera, M. (1986), *The Art of the Novel*, London: Faber and Faber.

Kuppers, P. (2003), *Disability and Contemporary Performance: Bodies on the Edge*, New York: Routledge.

Lynch, H. and J. Allan (2006), *Social Inclusion and the Arts*, Report to the Scottish Arts Council, Stirling: University of Stirling.

Lyotard, J. (1993), *The Postmodern Explained*, Minneapolis: University of Minnesota Press.

McClary, S. (1985), 'The Politics of Silence and Sound', Afterword to J. Attali, *Noise: The Political Economy of Music*, trans. B. Massumi, Minneapolis: University of Minnesota Press, pp. 150–1.

McDermott, R. P. (1993), 'The Acquisition of a Child by a Learning Disability' in C. Chaiklin and J. Lave (eds), *Understanding Practice: Perspectives on Activity and Context*, Cambridge: Cambridge University Press, pp. 269–305.

Masny, D. (2009), 'Literacies as Becoming', in D. Masny and D. Cole (eds), *Multiple Literacies Theory: A Deleuzian Perspective*, Rotterdam/Boston/Taipei: Sense.

Massumi, B. (1992), *A User's Guide to Capitalism and Schizophrenia: Deviations from Deleuze and Guattari*, Cambridge, MA: MIT Press.

Matarasso, F. (1997), *Use or Ornament? The Social Impact of Participation in the Arts*, Stroud: Comedia.

Mazzei, L. (2010), 'Thinking Data with Deleuze', *International Journal of Qualitative Studies in Education*, 23(5): 511–23.

Mazzei, L. and K. McCoy (2010), 'Thinking with Deleuze in Qualitative Research', *International Journal of Qualitative Studies in Education*, 23(5): 503–9.

Nussbaum, M. (2004), Commentary, *Self Preservation: The Art of Riva Lehrer*, dir. S. Snyder, Brace Yourselves Productions.

Rajchman, J. (2001), *The Deleuze Connections*, Cambridge, MA: MIT Press.

Rancière, J. (2008), 'Jacques Rancière and Indisciplinarity: An interview', *Art and Research*, 2(1): 1–10.

Semetsky, I. (2004), 'Becoming-Language/Becoming-Other: Whence ethics?', *Educational Philosophy and Theory*, 36(3): 313–25.

Sloterdijk, P. (1987), *Critique of Cynical Reason*, Minneapolis: University of Minnesota Press.

Smith, D. (1998), 'The Place of Ethics in Deleuze's Philosophy: Three questions of immanence' in E. Kaufman and K. J. Heller (eds), *Deleuze and Guattari: New Mappings in Politics, Philosophy and Culture*, Minneapolis: University of Minnesota Press, pp. 251–69.

Spinoza, B. (1985), *The Collected Works of Spinoza, Vol. 1*, trans. E. Curley, Princeton: Princeton University Press.

Uhlmann, A. (2009), 'Expression and Affect in Kleist, Beckett and Deleuze' in L. Cull (ed.), *Deleuze and Performance*, Edinburgh: Edinburgh University Press.

Wade, C. M. (2007), 'I Am Not One Of The', *The Gimp Parade* www.thegimpparade.blogspot.com/2007/04/poetry-cheryl-marie-wade.html> (accessed 12 October 2011).

# ASSEMBLAGE II: INSIDE/OUTSIDE CLASSROOM

# Chapter 3

# 'We're Tired of Trees': Machinic University Geography Teaching After Deleuze

*Excellt* [handwritten]

*Mark Bonta*

*this is dio/ free-spirit expertise / development / learning.* [handwritten]

## Resisting the Business Model of University Education

> We've got to hijack speech. Creating has always been something different from communicating. The key thing may be to create vacuoles of noncommunication, circuit breakers, so we can elude control. (Deleuze 1995a: 175)

Gilles Deleuze understood well the plight of post-secondary public education in France, and decried the undermining of traditional philosophy professor and teacher roles by the implantation of a business model that attempted to align curricula to the workplace, in essence transforming universities into training schools (Deleuze 1994, 1995a; St. Pierre 2008; Stivale 2011). In US academe, the ever-weakening bulwark protecting the core undergraduate liberal arts curriculum from a wholesale takeover by the business model is the American Association of University Professors' *1940 Statement of Principles on Academic Freedom and Tenure* (2011). The liberal arts curriculum includes liberal doses of courses in the humanities, social sciences and natural sciences that students would not otherwise necessarily take to fulfil the requirements of their specialisations. These so-called 'general education' classes, even in non-liberal arts colleges, may comprise a third to a half of all courses taken. Removing them from a student's requirements would quicken their move into the job market and eliminate what could be regarded as unnecessary burdens. Needless to say (given the presumed audience of this volume), the skills gained in liberal arts classes are crucial to the very continuity of creative thought, language and action in our societies.

Deleuze warns us against the evolution of education into a continuum of control and instantaneous communication (1995a). Sheltered by the academic freedom model are his 'vacuoles of noncommunication' where academics may yet elude control and resist instantaneity. By 'communication', Deleuze does not mean all significant interaction between people, but rather that type of discourse acceptable to the job-training mentality, to corporate-think: discourse that is simply the relaying of purported actual knowledge and attendant opinions. In the communication of knowledge, there can be no real exploration.

Paolo Freire (1984) called this situation the 'banking method of education' and resisted it with an activist, revolutionary approach that has directly or indirectly infused education praxis in the liberal arts to a substantial degree. Nevertheless, the liberal arts themselves are certainly not immune to the banking method or knowledge transfer. Indeed, it often seems that the business model makes headway as we remove creativity and exploratory, collaborative approaches and replace them with surveillable and accountable pedagogical methods. Do we memorise Shakespeare or act him out? In turning from the Canon to subaltern writers, do we steer our 'inclusive' conversations this way and that to guarantee that students do not stray from accepted thinking (no matter how radical and transformative) – or do we simply serve as guides? Do we test them, or let them test themselves; is testing even necessary? Crucially, do we who are teachers at the postsecondary level deterritorialise the course, the classroom and the lecture, or do we only suggest that someone out there do so?

There is room, still, in the academic freedom model for a Deleuzian university course. If we plan to infuse Deleuzian thinking, as 'nomadic education' (Semetsky 2008a), into university pedagogy, we most likely must tinker in our own laboratories. The bulk of literature on creativity and complexity ignores the university classroom and focuses on primary and secondary school as well as adult education and professional training (we have adapted the most important authors in what follows). An advanced degree in the 'subject matter' is the only prerequisite for being allowed to teach in the university classroom, and rarely do graduate degree programmes focus on pedagogy. Though post-graduate students, I am told, are paying increasing attention to pedagogical methodologies, the tenets of academic freedom also dictate against the imposition of requirements for professors to have lesson plans on file or otherwise adhere to a specific methodology or curriculum (obviously, this varies extremely widely by discipline, department and university, and is to a certain extent monitored via student review, peer review, the tenure process and requirements to have syllabi on file, for example). Not having a methodological orthodoxy usually allows considerable latitude for pedagogical creativity and experimentation by the professor (or any postsecondary instructor), but we need more models – alternative, open-ended

dionysos // free-spirit education.

models – that are recognised and defendable as 'nomadic education'. This chapter attempts to do just this: it is argued herein that nomadic education can end up turning a group of students into a (Deleuzian) machine, a rhizome, part of an open system with emergent properties that by its very definition cannot be predicted or easily controlled.

A course with elusive goals and unpredictable outcomes goes counter to the accountability system demanded by the university hierarchy, accrediting bodies and, ultimately, the non-creative job market. If we infuse a course-vacuole with learning rather than knowledge, if we can't control what we end up with and simply seek to liberate students' minds and bodies, and then to some extent the spaces in which they exist, we pose an implicit threat to the 'knowledge economy'. Clearly this is the idea, but such radicalism is nevertheless small consolation for the legions of university instructors without tenure or even the chance to receive tenure, or whose programmes are defunded and removed in part because of these very tendencies to sow creative chaos and to unleash nomads and their war machines on respectable society. Nonetheless, the alternative is to give in to the business model, at least by accommodating oneself to such a 'safe' degree that any real creativity is hopelessly hobbled and quashed.

## Whither Nomadic Education?

University education should be rhizomatic and challenge arborescent models of thought (Gough 2006). Hopefully we are not techno-fetishists, but few of us miss observing that the horizontal linkages made possible by social media and the internet, albeit in a surveilled and commercialised milieu, do free education to a considerable extent. Inasmuch as 'technology' seems to be universally favoured by the business model, there can be some superficial compatibility of methods, but there will probably be precious little overlap with what we actually wish to achieve. Nevertheless, the potential to deterritorialise university education and smooth the striations imposed by the business model is being explored through various non-hierarchical approaches in the generic milieu of higher education that has begun to accept, perhaps without even understanding it, the advances in our understanding of nonlinear systems.

Inna Semetsky (May and Semetsky 2008, Semetsky 2005, 2008a, 2008b, Semetsky and Lovat 2008) has championed the cause of Deleuze-inspired 'nomadic education' without attempting to box in Deleuze's concepts or the concepts he created collaboratively with

Guattari (Deleuze and Guattari 1985, 1987). She has called for 'transcoding' involving creativity and invention, following the Deleuzian dictum that matter is inherently creative and that becoming, not being, is the normal condition of existence. Semetsky (2008b) follows authors such as Elizabeth St. Pierre, who pioneered qualitative research based on Deleuzian 'nomadic inquiry' in the 1990s.

Under the umbrella of 'nomadic education' we can place several other authors and pedagogical concepts inspired by Deleuze. Gregoriou (2008) puts forth a 'minor philosophy of education', following Deleuze and Guattari's (1987) call for the becoming-minoritarian of disciplines and realms of inquiry. Gregoriou advocates an experimental encounter with Deleuze so as to foster multiplicity through the linkage of disparate elements – this suggests that nomadic education involves the creation of machinic assemblages (Bonta and Protevi 2004). Experimentation and deterritorialisation are evoked by both May and Semetsky (2008) and Allan (2004). The latter author considers these movements critical for teacher education. Finally, Zembylas (2007), drawing from the language of *Anti-Oedipus* (Deleuze and Guattari 1985), calls for a 'pedagogy of desire' and envisions education as a 'landscape of becoming' that interconnects forces, surfaces and flows of teachers/students in what Deleuze and Guattari would term 'desiring-production'.

Bonta and Protevi (2004) have provided definitions of Deleuzian terminology hinging on the assertion that Deleuze's project involved developing an ontology and epistemology adequate to exploring and explaining the *Nouvelle Terre* as revealed in the researches of complexity theory and the dynamics of nonlinear systems. Nearly every text by Deleuze and by Deleuze and Guattari introduces neologisms that can obscure the underlying project, but the key components of opposition (though not rigid, and often mutualistic) between hierarchy and rhizome, striated and smooth spaces, beings and becomings, and their numerous iterations across diverse realms of inquiry are what have penetrated effectively into theories and methodologies we can group as 'nomadic education'. But Deleuze also allows us to go beyond advocating the 'flattening' of education to support the very shift from knowledge back to learning, nothing less than the movement from the actual to the virtual.

## From Knowledge to Learning: Tapping Into the Virtual

> For Deleuze genuine teaching and learning are simply names for genuine thought. The goal of teaching and learning is to think otherwise, to engage the force of that which is other, different and new. (Bogue 2008: 15)

In 'On Philosophy' (Deleuze 1995b), Deleuze comments that courses should be like laboratories and investigations rather than bland settings-forth of what one already knows. This is an oblique reference to abstract machines on the plane of consistency, to use terminology from *A Thousand Plateaus* (Deleuze and Guattari 1987), a tension between the actual and the virtual. Bogue (2008) utilises concepts from Deleuze's basic ontological treatise, *Difference and Repetition* (Deleuze 1994), to get at this distinction in terms of 'learning' – exploration of the Idea on the virtual plane – versus 'knowledge', which involves rules and solutions applicable in the actual realm. Learning is an explorative and collaborative activity undertaken as a partnership between equals, whereas knowledge signifies the memorisation of facts and technical abilities relayed from an authoritative source and that must be standardised between operators. Universities, Deleuze argues, are for learning.

Following *Difference and Repetition* (1994), we can observe that the move from the virtual to the actual is via a series of intensive 'steps' both backward and forward. The realm in which several of these occur – the transformations that take place in the embryo, for example – is called the 'intensive' (Bonta and Protevi 1994). We mustn't see education, university or otherwise, as either learning or knowledge alone; they infuse each other. We need creative mechanics and creative doctors, but we also need them to be competent. In the social sciences, where I concentrate, we need creative geographers, but it never hurts to also have technical prowess in the art of cartography. In the language of *A Thousand Plateaus*, machinic assemblages of bodies and collective assemblages of enunciation draw from but also redraw the plane of consistency. Abstract machines are the sets of instructions in the virtual realm for what occurs in the actual realm, but the evolution, or involution, of the actual realm changes the virtual configurations – 'becoming' is best understood as an incessant intensive process capturing the unending movement of desiring-production. As a good geographer, I would favour the expansion of the term 'mapping' for the activity of exploring becomings.

## Creating Alternative Realities

> We never know in advance how someone will learn . . . (Deleuze 1994: 165)

In Deleuze's *ABC* discussions with Claire Parnet (Stivale 2011), he explains that the university course occupies a particular space-time. His lectures, we are informed, were not infrequently interrupted by 'wild interventions' from the audience. Given his philosophy, one can hardly imagine Deleuze as the classroom dictator, and indeed 'it's not a question of following everything or of listening to everything, but to keep a watch so that one grasps what suits him or her at the right moment'. He mentions that students seem to wake up when they hear something important to them.

What would the space-time of a course inspired by Deleuzian thought look like? What would happen in such a course? What if suppressed forces were unleashed by a loosening of authority on the part of the instructor? Would creative chaos result, desiring-production commence, or simply chaos and fear in response to a vacuum of order and suspension of hierarchy: confused and dismayed students? If nomadic education is about uprooting the tree of knowledge – because 'we're tired of trees' (Deleuze and Guattari 1987) – and fostering a rhizome connecting students, professor and space, then it is necessary to explore what learning can become. This 'experimentation in contact with the real' (Deleuze and Guattari 1987: 13) is risky in that it removes professorial authority and tests the boundaries of what is allowable in the institution with which the professor has a contractual obligation. There are boundaries, no doubt – a framework within which nomadic education can operate given that a course delivers a product that is paid for, and focuses on some range of topics of interest to an academic discipline. These and other parameters of the system can perhaps with time be modified, but let us focus on what can be achieved on the understanding that there are numerous constraints: initial conditions in a system that we can insist on prying open. Thence, the observations that follow build from eleven years of boundary-testing backed by plenty of Deleuzian concepts on the part of the author, though no explicit engagement with theories of nomadic education. The author as *bricoleur* tinkered in the laboratory, mixing and matching disparate elements. Rule-breaking did take place: I would define it as the 'pedagogical parenthesis' suggested by Daignault (2008), in which the norms of teaching are suspended to allow the unpredictable to occur.

Each course is as distinct as each configuration of students (number, ages, personalities, backgrounds) and whatever investigations and experiments seem exciting and important at the time (terrorism did, for a while, and natural disasters exacerbated by global warming are a perpetual favourite). The subject matter is geography, which broadly speaking involves open-ended exploration of the earth. Exploring without conquest, if you will. The courses wander about with threads of arguments that hold the disparate sections together loosely over the course of fifteen weeks. Course goals are on the syllabus and can theo-retically be assessed, but, as commented above, this is extremely hard to do in an open system. The goals involve instilling empathy in students for the 'Other', towards building a real 'community of those who have nothing in common' (Lingis 1994) but are increasingly better connected via social media (the 'friend' function on Facebook seems to have run far ahead of any constituents' desires to limit how connected they are to humanity-unlike-them, for example). The general idea is to explore societies and situations to such an intensity as to become-other – a mindset that doesn't necessarily fade entirely at the end of the course. By bringing students into other worlds, they are afforded the possibility of becoming-multiple, which enhances their potential connectivity in the future. (Role-playing exercises allowing students to have multiple identities at the same time help ease this process along.) That is to say, the course itself becomes some sort of rhizome connected to other rhizomes. The vacuole shields us from the business model but not from the new earth.

To a certain extent, regardless of course 'content', modifications can be made that favour a rhizome. Typically, the college classroom, particularly the 'lecture hall', contains rows of fixed seats all facing the same direction. At the front is the instructor, podium, screen and board (white, black or 'smart'), where appropriate Knowledge appears for consumption. This can be disordered: the room's mobile elements – desks, students and instructor – can be moved to shape diverse spatial conditions adequate to what is being learned. Desks can be placed in any location whatsoever, favouring non-hierarchical communication (as one might see in a kindergarten). They can retain their functionality as places-to-sit-and-work, or in other cases their functions can be deter-ritorialised and they can be deployed as distinct objects. Thus, desks might serve to define or delimit islands or to create blockages of flows between one space and the other ('chokepoints' in the lingo of political geography). In impromptu theatre, participants can throw desks and otherwise disrupt the 'normal' seating pattern (normal flow of events). In demonstrations of geography lessons that could be used in schools, students may pile and stack desks or move them into various constella-tions, once they understand that such behaviour is permissible (this helps if they have made the rules to allow it). Naturally, walls, ceiling, floor, columns and so forth can also be used creatively, if needed. Boundaries between zones are easily defined with tape. The door can serve as an obvious threshold, for example a border post. It can simulate a barrier to communications and concepts, for example when different discursive communities are role-played by groups of students. Naturally, space and noise level-restrictions permitting, activities can spill into hallways and occupy other classrooms and sites across campus.

Another challenge is unsealing the 'learning-time' envelope – deterritorialising time – to disabuse students in the age of social media of the assumption that what they call 'taking a class' can only occur in discrete locations at defined times (in the classroom during class time, and outside it during times allotted to study and homework). The implementation of continuous role-plays, where strategic advantage is gained by engagement in activities around the clock, in any physical location as well as online, forges a continuum where, in the best cases, class time becomes only the most concentrated part of an experience that in some cases can stretch in one form or another over weeks or even months. (In the worst cases, I am only feeding a culture of distraction and multitasking and not helping students concentrate and manage their time effectively.)

Disorganising and re-experiencing space and time helps set the stage for radical modifications of the tree of knowledge. Indeed, without some alteration of the traditional course space-time, it is difficult or at least not necessary for students to do more than wonder, mildly, about the 'other world' that the lecturing professor purports is possible. The introduction of kinaesthetic and ludic elements, so central to learning in primary school, is childish, perhaps, but adults, like children, learn through active play (see Rieber 1996).

## Role-playing Games

Fantasy role-playing games ('rpgs') both live, online and as a hybrid of the two, have been the subject of extensive study. Fine's (1983) classic participant-observer ethnography of gamer culture helped make the study of these microworlds acceptable in the social sciences. Rieber (1996) argued strenuously for the value of play in interactive learning environments, but it was with the emergence of complexity theory that the full potential of rpgs and related simulation activities for learning came to be appreciated. I have not encountered another author specifically linking Deleuze to rpgs in university education, but nomadic education and gaming have brushed against each other on several occasions, as illustrated below.

Colella's (2000) work on participatory simulations has suggested strongly that personal experience garnered in rpgs helps students learn how to learn, which involves learning how to ask and how to investigate problems. Guyot and Honiden (2006) provide a very useful synopsis of the three 'non-ludic' applications of rpgs, following Olivier Barreteau's work in Senegal. These are training, observation and negotiation support; they coincide, the authors assert, with the triad of education, sociological research and action as advocated by Participatory Action Research (PAR) proponents. Training, in particular, helps rpg participants link individual and collective behaviours, which leads to problem-solving.

Guyot and Honiden (2006) advocate employing 'breaching methodology' (from ethnomethodology) to intentionally yield bad results, from which students learn, and suggest tactics for avoiding students' shouldering excess guilt after an rpg goes awry. Debriefing after the exercise is thus crucial. My approach has been to neither favour nor disfavour a bad outcome in the building of rhizomatic communities within the microworld of the rpg. It usually turns out that some groups opt for 'bad' solutions that are offered (such as the exploitation of others for personal gain) while others do not. The key is, indeed, in the debriefing, though I invariably explain that given the lack of an overall system to monitor what has transpired in a role-play, it is impossible to know or understand exactly what went on; by design, I leave large parts of the post-rpg reflection to the individual students (as the basis of essays for grades, for example).

The explorations of the earth favoured by geography easily lend themselves to role-playing. The complexities of land use as explored by rpgs and participatory modelling are discussed by Barreteau et al. (2001), D'Aquino et al. (2003), Etienne (2003) and Voinov and Bousquet (2010), for example. These tend to be technology-heavy, if not altogether online, and far more elaborate approaches than those that are possible in a typical university classroom (I have dabbled in fully online role-plays with mixed results, which I exclude from this discussion). An important distinction should be made at this juncture – most research on rpgs and related activities, no matter how well-intentioned, goes towards solving 'problems' defined by governments, aid agencies and military/intelligence strategists. The levels of tolerance of subaltern standpoints and distrust of the state may not be anywhere near what is possible or desirable in academe (or engagement with subaltern stances may be for wholly distinct reasons). This should be borne in mind equally in the discussion below of self-organising systems and emergence in role-plays.

Geography as I practise it must have social relevance and some relation to social and usually environmental justice. In role-playing the struggles of communities living in poverty, the *Pedagogy of the*

*Oppressed* is an obvious starting point (Freire 1984). Goodley's 'socially just pedagogies' (Goodley 2007) provide another point of departure. Goodley opposes the arborescent model of education to 'weeds', equating socially-just pedagogies to rhizomes that spawn spaces for becoming rather than being. Goodley's focus is on the disabled, but in relationship to the market and to global capitalism, for example, we are all disabled. Empathy involves the realisation of the dysfunctionality behind the 'American dream', which allows students to reinterpret their own taken-for-granted realities in light of struggles occurring elsewhere. Adapting the concept of 'curriculum otherness' in schools (Cole 2008) to the university course, geography is well-positioned to address multiculturalism, critiques of the surveillance of space, and further modes of otherness that Cole envisions. Perhaps the best-documented study on role-playing games yet, in their potential for creativity in the investigation of socio-environmental problems as experienced by subaltern groups, is the doctoral thesis of Colucci-Gray (2007), which examines a university course in Turin that explored water and soil management issues in central Africa. Though Colucci-Gray does not invoke Deleuze or nomadic education per se, there is a close sympathy with the projects of other authors cited in this chapter – and a common relationship to Freire.

## Pandemonium and Self-organisation

Semetsky (2005) provides nomadic education with the connection to role-playing in her call for the construction of a self-organising classroom wherein the hierarchical power structure is dissolved, deterritorialisation becomes a shared endeavour, and communication becomes transversal. Pandemonium results. Cole discusses this Manuel DeLanda concept wherein 'messages [are] broadcast to concurrent independent objects' (Cole 2008: 24), a chaotic situation which is commonly encountered in decentered learning apparatuses employing some form of online mode. Pandemonium, as it turns out, does not need to be enabled by computers – it is also the hallmark of success in the flesh-and-blood rpgs that I most commonly utilise in my introductory geography classes. In an rpg wherein distinct groups of people confront an impending natural disaster, pandemonium marks the complete immersion of the players in their microworld, no longer for them a simulation of reality but rather an alternative reality. The hub-bub of the 'international community' attempting to stop an imminent conflict between North Korea and the United States is also indicative of an advanced degree of transversal communication without any reference to an external signifier. The noise of a Peruvian neighbourhood marks the taking-place of myriad interactions in a third rpg dedicated to the internalisation of Latin American social struggles.

Complexity theory has begun to be examined in its relevance to education through studies such as Davis and Sumara (2006) and Mason's edited volume (2008). Resnick and Wilensky (1998) provide a solid framework for incorporating rpgs in classroom demonstrations of self-organising systems such as termite and ant societies; they blame the lack of emphasis on rpgs on 'centralised' and 'deterministic' mindsets. In their discussion of an rpg simulating the Veracruz coffee market, Guyot et al. (2005) documented the emergence of new social roles that were not in the original design (which was extremely elaborate, like that of most rpgs). This provides us with solid evidence that the rpg as part of a self-organising classroom does indeed enable emergence – that the rhizome, if we let it, is inherently creative. This is where, in the age of complexity, we must depart from deterministic models to allow for open-ended results. In my rpgs (all of which I have authored, and tinkered with incessantly), initial conditions are quite detailed, but no rpg ever ends the same way. Results have depended on characteristics of the players (more than anything else) but also on the structure of the classroom; in 2011, for example, I was enormously frustrated by being assigned for the first time to a classroom with immobile seats. The rpgs that semester were not nearly as successful as on other occasions.

## Inhabiting Poverty

To reiterate, role-playing games are not representations of reality but rather offshoots from reality that diverge at the precise moment students finish reading the description of initial conditions and begin to interact with one another under assumed identities. The scenario that evolves, depending on its length and complexity, becomes an internally coherent rhizome that retains considerable resemblance to the 'real world' but is nevertheless something else entirely. Accuracy and realism become increasingly warped as the divergent narrative progresses, perhaps because the instructor has only limited means to steer and control the course of events. It is this loss of control over what is being learned that would appear to pose the greatest threat to the instructor's ego, as well as sparking the fear that the role-play might not result in the correct knowledge being internalised in time for the test. (This is not to say that the instructor is uninvolved: my role is generally scripted as some authority that is capable of manipulating events in an 'unfair' way, and/ or some embodiment of 'fate' or another seemingly transcendent agent.) At worst, a role-play gone awry could interfere with the successful implementation and measurement of the 'Learning Objectives' listed on the syllabus (a requirement for university and programme accreditation). But competency is always at risk in experimentation that involves unpredictable creativity and imaginations run rampant.

The culminating rpg in my introductory geography class involves the building of community solidarity among 'nameless' 'non-people'. Because the overall intent of the course is to leave students feeling hopeful about the world, rather than overwhelmed by it, it is crucial to expose them to the struggles of those 'at the bottom' and in this way attempt to reverse the objectification of the 'Third World' so blithely commonplace in the US. The scenario involves several families of Andean Quechua potato farmers who were expelled from their village by a mining concession and have migrated to a patch of desert on the outskirts of Lima, Peru. There, they use whatever means at their disposal to survive (first) and then, if successful in that endeavour, to thrive, starting essentially from scratch with the bare resources to procure the reed mats that characterise the living quarters of this austere environment, as millions have done. (As a teenager, I was first exposed to 'Third World poverty' through the 'pueblos jovenes' of Lima, and had always thought that a 'Prince and the Pauper' exercise in such an environment might successfully jar complacent Americans out of their biases and misconceptions.)

The initial conditions for this role-play include many pages of rules, and the initial challenge is simply for each family to structure a set of living conditions whereby they can work enough hours to earn enough money to survive. The scenario is structured in such a way that the full extent of absolute poverty can be experienced – to the point that some students have even suffered emotionally from coming to realise the challenges faced by the 'less fortunate'. Each student takes on the identity of an adult or child, and after extensive study, it generally becomes possible for some sort of basic survival plan to take shape. In the beginning stage, math skills are paramount, and thus some insight is gained to the complex calculations that the poor must make, their extremely narrow margins of error, and the consequences of failure.

The essential rule for the exercise is that each student must follow the same code of ethics that s/he follows in real life. Moral dilemmas are thus not solved easily by dismissive decision but tend to build a greater sense of empathy. Not shying away from the 'dark side' of human marginalisation, numerous choices are available for families, ranging from narcotics trafficking and prostitution to guerrilla activity and incorporation into organised crime networks. The instructor plays any and all 'transcendent' forces, ranging from government and security forces to patrons always available to dole out money for the purpose of ensnaring players in unpayable debts.

Students are told outright at the beginning of the exercise that they are 'nobody' and that they will be exploited to the greatest extent possible. The intent is to encourage families to interact with each other to create a web and safety net of connections that can become the basis for a coherent and politically viable settlement similar to the hundreds of so-called 'shantytowns' that ring Greater Lima (and conurbations across the planet), where the material poverty observed by the casual viewer masks the tenacity and strength of community organisation. As families settle into rhythms of survival, they are encouraged to think about schooling and additional means of employment such as small businesses that may become possible through microloan programs. The exercise is structured in such a way that just the solvency to purchase a rooster and a couple of chickens becomes a major achievement, and (for example) the way to earn enough extra income to reduce or even eliminate the assignment of a family's seven-year-old to daily scrounging at the garbage dump.

'Fate' intervenes several times to sow chaos: the jailing of street vendors and the seizure of their goods; accidents; diseases; and so on. The families are encouraged to 'walk the straight and narrow' but the relationship between their 'moral performance' and their fates is anything but fair – often, the one or two families who turn to dangerous activities fare better than those who believed they would be richly rewarded by not doing so. One way or the other, after a couple of weeks, which equal two years, the classroom has become a functioning neighbourhood and the family association is beginning to discuss formal legal recognition from the government of Greater Lima. At this point, some sort of economic development activity such as the 'Mall of Peru' is introduced, wherein the illegal squatters and their chickens are threatened with removal. All means at the disposal of the transcendent force, which has become a consortium of government and powerful investors, with private as well as public security forces, are used to evict the community, which must, conversely, demonstrate to the politically sensitive elected city officials that its usufruct land-rights claim merits consideration. The existence of powerful popular organisations and heavy media coverage is assumed, thus not making it an easy case of eminent domain and bulldozers for the 'Company'. Bribery of the 'clean' families, often via a family that has come under the sway of the Company (via debt entrapment), is employed to lure the other families out with promises of future employment, and all efforts are made to split the community apart.

In the final stage, any students or entire families who are persuaded to evacuate to be resettled in a promised better area are asked to leave the classroom. In the rare case that the evacuation is successful, and the community is entirely removed, the game is ended by a brief slideshow presentation of a garbage dump or ravine where the students have been relocated, as well as the denial of promises and even signed agreements where the residents would have become employees at the mall. This has happened only a handful of times; usually, the community maintains solidarity and refuses to move, so the Company is eventually forced to back down and the neighbourhood becomes politically recognised by the government. This completes the transition from 'informal' (technically, illegal – a huge percentage of human endeavour and existence) to 'formal' and also almost always effects a transformation in attitudes among the majority of students.

Overall, the game interferes with students' casual understanding of poverty as the result of laziness and dependence. Towards the latter stages, conflict is created between students' real innate attraction to malls and other 'good' things of US consumer society, and their embarrassment and revulsion at being mired in poverty. However, by inhabiting poverty, it is typically possible to gain a much deeper sense of empathy than would be possible via any detached, analytic approach.

## Deleuzifying the Institution?

Inasmuch as transformations are effected in nonlinear ways, open-ended role-plays are rhizomatic implants within the layered and tree-like 'pursuit of knowledge' schema that characterises US academe. However, the overall perceptible effect is never any radical change in attitudes or behaviours in the class as a whole – no sweeping transformation occurs in any measurable way. What does occur is the deployment of students into the 'System' with certain altered internal measures of the world that create dissonances between what is taken for granted in US society (and perhaps taught in other classes, if it is addressed at all) and what has been experienced. The cumulative effects of this are unknown and unknowable, and in any case the intent has never been to indoctrinate but rather to deterritorialise, to deprogram, to reset – to remove the striations long enough that the 'new earth' can at least be glimpsed. The imaginary realms created during the duration of the role-play implant a war machine in students' minds – 'We've struggled with absolute poverty'; 'We've been Iran'; 'We've been refugees from the flood' – comprised of a bundle of intense memories, images and passions, constituting a strategic geographic knowledge that can be tapped into repeatedly and deployed as necessary. This could be useful.

But what effect does or can this example of nomadic education have within the institution? It is fair to say that if the extensive assessment structure required for programme accreditation and accountability procedures that exists now had been in place when I began employment in 2001, there would have been no question of developing a Deleuzian approach at my university. Today's increasingly restrictive rules demand that professors track, measure and report on exactly how their students are learning. Such demands, emanating from an increasingly corporatist regime in American academe, favour a closed, predictable learning trajectory that goes almost entirely counter to the creative, imagination-heavy, nonlinear and thus ultimately unpredictable pedagogy that I have practised. The only feasible alternative is 'gaming' the assessment apparatus itself, which can be a risky proposition now that funding of degree programmes and ultimately salaries is tied increasingly to perceived 'relevancy' in the face of what we not-so-fondly call the 'job-training mentality'. The increasingly restrictive structures of accountability in the liberal arts seem to dictate more and more each year against innovative approaches. Deleuze's fear of the business model was well-founded, and we have seen it advance by leaps and bounds in the past few years.

Thankfully, academic freedom is still an umbrella of sorts for us marginal types, and at least for the time being, administrations and accreditors must remain mindful of its implications. Furthermore, at least in my institution, the constant struggle to recruit and retain students tends to favour any pedagogical approach that is popular; thus, for example, my transition to role-playing in online classes that resulted in a substantial drop in the failure rate due to enhanced student engagement has been sufficient, so far, to protect my variety of nomadic education from full accountability to the strictures of the job market. Beyond this, I cannot say.

# References

Allan, J. (2004), 'Deterritorializations: Putting postmodernism to work on teacher education and inclusion', *Educational Philosophy and Theory*, 36(4): 417–32.

American Association of University Professors (2011), *1940 Statement of Principles on Academic Freedom and Tenure* <http://www.aaup.org/AAUP/pubsres/policydocs/contents/1940statement.htm> (accessed 19 September 2012).

Barreteau, O., F. Bousquet and J. M. Attonaty (2001), 'Role-playing Games for Opening the Black Box of Multi-agent Systems: Method and lessons of its application to Senegal River Valley irrigated systems', *Journal of Artificial Societies and Social Simulation*, 4(3) <http://jasss.soc.surrey.ac.uk/4/2/5.html> (accessed 19 September 2012).

Bogue, R. (2008), 'Search, Swim and See: Deleuze's apprenticeship in signs and pedagogy of images' in I. Semetsky (ed.), *Nomadic Education: Variations on a Theme by Deleuze and Guattari*, Rotterdam: Sense, pp. 1–16.

Bonta, M. and J. Protevi (2004), *Deleuze and Geophilosophy: A Guide and Glossary*, Edinburgh: Edinburgh University Press.

Cole, D. R. (2008), 'Deleuze and the Narrative Forms of Education Otherness' in I. Semetsky (ed.), *Nomadic Education: Variations on a Theme by Deleuze and Guattari*, Rotterdam: Sense, pp. 17–34.

Colella, V. (2000), 'Participatory Simulations: Building collaborative understanding through immersive dynamic modeling', *Journal of the Learning Sciences*, 9(4): 471–500.

Colten, C. (2005), *An Unnatural Metropolis: Wresting New Orleans from Nature*, Baton Rouge: LSU Press.

Colucci-Gray, L. (2007), 'An Inquiry Into Role-play as a Tool to Deal with Complex Socio-environmental Issues and Conflict', PhD thesis, Open University.

Daignault, J. (2008), 'Pedagogy and Deleuze's Concept of the Virtual' in I. Semetsky (ed.), *Nomadic Education: Variations on a Theme by Deleuze and Guattari*, Rotterdam: Sense, pp. 43–60.

D'Aquino, P., C. LePage, F. Bousquet and A. Bah (2003), 'Using Self-designed Role-playing Games and a Multi-agent System to Empower a Local Decision-making Process for Land Use Management: The SelfCormas Experiment in Senegal', *Journal of Artificial Societies and Social Simulation*, 6(3) <http://jasss.soc.surrey.ac.uk/6/3/5.html> (accessed 19 September 2012).

Davis, B. and D. J. Sumara (2006), *Complexity and Education: Inquiries into Learning, Teaching, and Research*, Mahwah, NJ: Lawrence Erlbaum.

Deleuze, G. (1994), *Difference and Repetition*, trans. P. Patton, New York: Columbia University Press.

Deleuze, G. (1995a), 'Control and Becoming', *Negotiations 1972–1990*, trans. M. Joughin, New York: Columbia University Press, pp. 169–76.

Deleuze, G. (1995b), 'On Philosophy', *Negotiations 1972–1990*, trans. M. Joughin, New York: Columbia University Press, pp. 135–55.

Deleuze, G. (1995c), 'Postscript on Control Societies', *Negotiations 1972–1990*, trans. M. Joughin, New York: Columbia University Press, pp. 177–82.

Deleuze, G. and F. Guattari (1985), *Anti-Oedipus: Capitalism and Schizophrenia*, trans. M. Seem, R. Hurley and H. R. Lane, Minneapolis: University of Minnesota Press.

Deleuze, G. and F. Guattari (1987), *A Thousand Plateaus: Capitalism and Schizophrenia*, trans. B. Massumi, Minneapolis: University of Minnesota Press.

Etienne, M. (2003), 'SYLVOPAST: A multiple target role-playing game to assess negotiation processes in sylvopastoral management planning', *Journal of Artificial Societies and Social Simulation*, 6(2) <http://jasss.soc.surrey.ac.uk/6/2/5.html> (accessed 19 September 2012).

Fine, G. A. (1983), *Shared Fantasy: Role-playing Games as Social Worlds*, Chicago: University of Chicago Press.

Freire, P. (1984), *Pedagogy of the Oppressed*, New York: Continuum.

Goodley, D. (2007), 'Towards Socially Just Pedagogies: Deleuzoguattarian critical disability studies', *International Journal of Inclusive Education*, 11(3): 317–34.

Gough, N. (2006), 'Shaking the Tree, Making a Rhizome: Towards a nomadic philosophy of science education', *Educational Philosophy and Theory*, 38(5): 625–45.

Gregoriou, Z. (2008), 'Commencing the Rhizome: Towards a Minor Philosophy of Education' in I. Semetsky (ed.), *Nomadic Education: Variations on a Theme by Deleuze and Guattari*, Rotterdam: Sense, pp. 91–110.

Guyot, P., A. Drogoul and C. Lemaître (2005), 'Using Emergence in Participatory Simulations to Design Multi-agent Systems', in F. Dignum et al. (eds), *International Joint Conference on Autonomous Agents and Multiagent Systems (AAMAS-05)*, pp. 199–203.

Guyot, P. and S. Honiden (2006), 'Agent-based Participatory Simulations: Merging multi-agent systems and role-playing games', *Journal of Artificial Societies and Social Simulation*, 9(4) <http://jasss.soc.surrey.ac.uk/9/4/8.html> (accessed 19 September 2012).

Lingis, A. (1994), *The Community of Those Who Have Nothing in Common*, Bloomington: Indiana University Press.

Mason, M. (ed.) (2008), *Complexity Theory and the Philosophy of Education*, Oxford: Wiley Blackwell.

May, T. and I. Semetsky (2008), 'Deleuze, Ethical Education, and the Unconscious' in I. Semetsky (ed.), *Nomadic Education: Variations on a Theme by Deleuze and Guattari*, Rotterdam: Sense, pp. 143–58.

Resnick, M. and U. Wilensky (1998), 'Diving into Complexity: Developing probabilistic decentralized thinking through role-playing activities', *Journal of Learning Sciences*, 7(2): 153–72.

Rieber, L. P. (1996), 'Seriously Considering Play: Designing interactive learning environments based on the blending of microworlds, simulations, and games', *Educational Technology Leadership and Development*, 44(2): 43–58.

Semetsky, I. (2005), 'Not by Breadth Alone: Imagining a self-organised classroom', *Complicity: An International Journal of Complexity and Education*, 2(1): 19–36.

Semetsky, I. (ed.) (2008a), *Nomadic Education: Variations on a Theme by Deleuze and Guattari*, Rotterdam: Sense.

Semetsky, I. (2008b), '(Pre)Facing Deleuze', I. Semetsky (ed.), *Nomadic Education: Variations on a Theme by Deleuze and Guattari*, Rotterdam: Sense, pp. vii–xxi.

Semetsky, I. and T. Lovat (2008), 'Knowledge in Action: Towards a Deleuze-Habermasian critique in/for education' in I. Semetsky (ed.), *Nomadic Education: Variations on a Theme by Deleuze and Guattari*, Rotterdam: Sense, pp. 171–82.

St. Pierre, E. (2008), 'Deleuzian Concepts for Education: The subject undone' in I. Semetsky (ed.), *Nomadic Education: Variations on a Theme by Deleuze and Guattari*, Rotterdam: Sense, pp. 183–96.

Stivale, C. (ed.) (2011), 'P as in Professor' in Part III of Overview of *L'Abecedaire de Gilles Deleuze, avec Claire Parnet*, dir. Pierre Andre Boutang (1996) <http://www.langlab.wayne.edu/cstivale/d-g/ABC3.html> (accessed 19 September 2012)

Voinov, A. and F. Bousquet (2010), 'Modelling with Stakeholders', *Environmental Modelling and Software*, 25(11): 1268–81.

Zembylas, M. (2007), 'Risks and Pleasures: A Deleuzo-Guattarian pedagogy of desire in education', *British Educational Research Journal*, 33(3): 331–47.

## Chapter 4

# Multiple Literacies Theory: Exploring Spaces

*Diana Masny*

Deleuze and Guattari individually or together were continuously involved in concept creation. Affect, deterritorialisation, becoming, smooth and striated spaces are just some of the concepts created in relation to their own work. Concept creation, in their view, was a response to real problems whether it be through literature, cinema or painting. The concepts that emerged had their own specificity because of the problems to which the concepts were a response. If we turn to Deleuze and education and particularly literacies education, what, in the current context, are some problems in literacies education that require plugging-in[1] to Deleuze and Guattari's notion of concept creation so that concepts created within literacies education emerge as responses to those problems? A rhizomatic entry at this time would be to ask what literacies do, how they function and what they produce when they plug-in to Multiple Literacies Theory (MLT), and the concepts that emerge, in particular that of space. The concept of space becomes a response to a problem of literacy/literacies viewed through education and the role of institutions.

The chapter opens with a presentation of MLT and the reciprocal relationship between becoming and reading, reading the world and self. The concepts created with MLT bring us to the question of ontology, that is, of the nature of reality or the real which provides the genesis for concept creation. Deleuze, contrary to some thinkers of his time, was very interested in ontology (May 2005). Deleuze's perspective on ontology unfolded as a response to certain ontology prevailing at that time, that of reality as fixed or represented. Deleuze's response was to posit a reality that is anti-representational and mind-independent. Deleuzian ontology becomes important because it is with a particular sense of reality that concepts are created. Accordingly, ontology becomes the second entry point and a link for MLT to plug into transcendental empiricism. The key concepts that characterise transcendental empiricism are: anti-representation, decentered subjectivity, interpretosis and relationality. The third entry point focuses on concept creation. Concept creation happens in response to a problem. What problems arise (*être aux aguets*) that deterritorialise literacy and reterritorialise as MLT? The problem is linked to the role of school-based literacy and the place of ontology and epistemology in literacy research. A potential response might lie in the relation between becoming-MLT and smooth and striated space. Therefore, what follows is the fourth entry which explores the concept of space. As Deleuze has pointed out, concept creation happens in relation to other concepts. These other concepts are affect, difference, immanence and virtual-actual. In the fifth entry, MLT plugs in to the different concepts created that are enfolded with Deleuzian ontology in order to map the sense that emerges in relation to a research study on conceptualisations of writing systems vignettes with multilingual children. The exit is an intermezzo that proposes first, an ontology of reading that connects with an ontology of difference and how one might live, and second, MLT becoming minor/minoritarian.

## Multiple Literacies Theory

MLT, developed by Masny (2006, 2009b, 2011), refers to literacies as a construct both virtual and actual. In the virtual, they are an assemblage of asignifying desiring machines, an assemblage of events from which sense emerges. Literacies actualise as words, gestures, sounds, listening, writing: ways of becoming with the world. Human, animal and vegetal encounters with social, intellectual and environmental processes such as affect, gender, race, culture, power, genes and digital remixes produce paintings, music, mathematical equations, speakers, writers, artists, genetic mutations, digital avatars. Literacies can emerge as visual, oral, tactile, olfactory and in multimodal digital forms, 'between mutations from plant to animal, from animal to humankind . . .' (Deleuze and Guattari 1987: 313). Given the nomadic tendencies of literacies, they are not wed to *a* context, but emerge in unpredictable ways in a particular time and space. Literacies involve reading, reading the world and self as texts that create potentialities for transforming life (how one might live). An important aspect of literacies is to produce change. Accordingly, MLT is interested in how literacies function and how they change bodies, communities and societies: human, animal and vegetal.

In terms of concept creation, reading is intensive and immanent. To read intensively is to read disruptively, to deterritorialise. The question is no longer what a text means but rather how it works and what it produces. To read immanently refers to the unthought potential of reading and it is from investment in reading that a reader is formed. Consider the following example. You are walking along a corridor at work when reading the smell of coffee disrupts. What could happen next? The clock on the wall says it is four o'clock: a visual and printed reading. The disruption might invite walking in an unpredictable direction. There is a rhizomatic rupture; whatever has been going on has been deterritorialised. The rupture brings on perhaps an unthought (pre-personal) coffee break, a going home, a vacation: reading as immanent. Where the smell of coffee could lead is unpredictable.

## Reading, Reading the World and Self (RRWS)

Reading the world and self are intricately intertwined but distinct, and draw on both the virtual and actual. In the virtual, reading the world is the point at which language and the world meet and sense actualises *in situ*. Reading self in the virtual consists of asignifying machinic encounters in an assemblage that resonates and produces sensations (affects and percepts) within an assemblage. This process is one of becoming, deterritorialisation. Reading self is actualised and sense emerges as an effect of signifying machines that come together in an assemblage charged with affection and perception. It is the power to affect and be affected. Take the example of coffee once more. A territorialisation: a particular assemblage of reading of self (different social and material desiring machines) and reading the world (a certain assemblage of the smell of coffee, the clock, the time of day, place, etc.). This assemblage deterritorialises and creates a different reading, a becoming on a plane of immanence. Transformations happen in the process of becoming. Then there is a reterritorialisation of reading self and the world. It is not a return to what was. The assemblage is different. What constitutes an assemblage are events of life, 'creations that need to be selected and assessed according to their power to act and intervene in life' (Colebrook 2002b: xliv) while reading intensively and immanently.

## Literacies as Processes

The focus is on how literacies intersect in complex and nonlinear ways in becoming. This is what MLT produces: from continuous investments in literacies (reading, reading the world and self), human, animal and vegetal are formed as literate. There is the example of the wasp and the orchid, a transcoding across species. There is a reading of the wasp and the orchid happening in relation to the world (the environment) that creates a deterritorialisation in which the wasp becomes 'a piece of the orchid's reproductive apparatus' and reterritorialises the orchid by transporting the pollen. In this process, there is a becoming: 'a becoming-wasp of the orchid and a becoming-orchid of the wasp' (Deleuze and Guattari 1987: 10).

## Sense

MLT is not interested in what a text means. Rather, it is interested in how a text functions and what it produces: sense. 'The event is sense itself' (Deleuze 1990: 20). An event transforms sense. An event transforms 'multiple interactions running through bodies ... and virtual structures (such as emotional investment)' (Williams 2008: 1). Sense has virtual/actual components. Language for instance is the virtual dimension of sense because language is more than its actual element (Colebrook 2002a). Perhaps sense as virtual becomes actualised, just as the event is actualised as an 'instantaneous production intrinsic to interactions between various kinds of forces' (i.e., as an assemblage) (Stagoll 2005: 87). This product (i.e., sense-event) is not a state of affairs, but a transformation, a becoming.

## MLT Theory and Practice

For a theory to be effective, it has to be used and seen to be able to work (Deleuze 2004). Therefore, MLT creates concepts that can be used and are able to work. Concept creation in MLT is not separate or opposed to practice. MLT, in theory and practice, generates a toolbox for the purpose of creating concepts not predetermined nor pre-given; rather, they are asignifying machines. They are tools that work once actualised *in situ*, in relation to a particular problem that presents itself in the world. In this way, MLT is available to experimentation, forming assemblages each of which is different each time. In sum, MLT is a concept that connects with other concepts rhizomatically. These concepts emerge in relation to an ontology that espouses a reality which is anti-representational and immanent, in which the subject is decentered, relationality is vital, and concern/vigilance for interpretosis critical. MLT evolves in a social world, one in which MLT navigates in and out of institutions, formal and informal learning. It is in this context that MLT, theory and practice, experiments with the toolbox to create concepts and becomes a response to what might be deterritorialising moments on a plane of immanence.

## Ontology of Space and Transcendental Empiricism

Ontology refers to reality and how reality is constructed. It provides the backdrop to epistemology (knowledge that exceeds the human knower). Deleuze's ontology or relationship to reality is couched in terms of transcendental empiricism. Transcendental empiricism as conceived by Deleuze was a response to his perspective on life as becoming and to the place of experience in life. Deleuzian transcendental empiricism is characterised by: anti-representation, decentered subjectivity, immanence,[2] interpretosis and relationality. In transcendental empiricism, representations limit experience to the world as we know it rather than as a world that could be. Representation also considers that there is an object present but that it also has another meaning (e.g., Romeo and Juliette representing forbidden love). Moreover, experience is not an event ascribed to the autonomous thinking subject, which means that experience is not grounded in the individual. She is not at the centre controlling thoughts; rather, the mind is a site where experience is conceived as an unthought experience. Recall the example of coffee presented earlier. The smell/reading of coffee produced an intensive disruption. This rhizomatic rupture opens up unpredictably to a pre-personal experience of a break, a going home, a reading as immanent and not pre-given.

Moreover, transcendental empiricism is not interested in the autonomous thinking subject that grounds experience through explanation or interpretation. Representation and interpretation are closely linked. For example, when looking for meaning in a relationship between two characters in a short story (What does this relationship represent? Fear? Harmony?) instead of looking at the sense that emerges through the power of affect. Looking for meaning in a short story is also seeking an interpretation. Deleuze and Guattari (1987) refer to interpretation as an illness, interpretosis. They would argue that 'interpretosis is typical of Western representational schema, whereby every experienced affect is read as the signifier of some original scene' (Colebrook 2002a: 134). Instead Deleuze and Guattari favour pragmatic experimentation (Bonta and Protevi 2004). Concerning relationality, we will return to the example of the coffee smell. The decentered subject becomes part of an assemblage (clock, time of day, the furniture, the colour scheme, etc.) and the reading that goes on is the result of encounters in an assemblage. In other words, the different bodies in the assemblage and their encounters or relation to each other in the assemblage contribute to reading. However, relationality is unpredictable:

> We know nothing about a body until we know what it can do, what its affects are, how they can or cannot enter into composition with other affects, with the affects of another body, either to destroy that body or to be destroyed by it, either to exchange actions and passions with it or to join with it in composing a more powerful body. (Deleuze and Guattari 1987: 257)

## Concept Creation

Concepts are created in response to a problem. Accordingly, this section is devoted to describing what problems in literacy research/education gave rise to concept creation and MLT. Literacy has had a very functional definition, perhaps more so in the field of education than in applied psychology and applied linguistics where the term reading was most often used, perhaps because it referred to a specific skill while literacy in many ways implied more than reading (Masny 2009a). Reading throughout the centuries was always important (Cook-Gumperz 1986). Reading was assigned to specific members of a community to perform certain tasks within the community (oral story telling, note-taking, letter writing, religious readings, communicating with government institutions) (Street 1984), what we might consider today as community literacy. By the turn of the twentieth century, reading had become a more democratic skill as school became compulsory. Reading and writing in schools and in the workplace became increasingly important for the economy of a society. School-based literacy is still today in a hierarchical fashion how literacy is defined, that is, as the ability to read, write and process information from printed text (UNESCO 2008). Other forms of literacy have become disenfranchised and with the power of institutions, other literacies have become invisible. If individuals do not demonstrate a certain functional level of school-based literacy, they are considered illiterate or non-functionally literate.

Moreover, ontological and epistemological considerations were problematic. In educational quantitative research, methodology was primary to the extent that both ontology and epistemology collapsed into methodology with the assumption that research was objective and the researcher stance neutral (Denzin and Lincoln 2005). This perspective is steeped in the binaries of postpositivism with its traditions stemming from the natural sciences that aim for replication, laboratory-like controls, generaliseable results and universal appeal (Gort 2006). It is not uncommon for meta-analyses on literacy research (Juzwik et al. 2006) to be conducted in order to develop a meta-narrative on literacy research.[3]

But there is also another perspective, that of qualitative research which allows for extraneous variables to free flow or to be factored in, on the premise that learning to be literate does not happen in laboratory conditions. Social and psychological constructs described as constructivism play a role in becoming literate. In addition, literacy has come to be regarded in terms of multiplicities: literacies plural (Barton and Hamilton 2005). While constructivism as it is known today is conceptualised in many ways, in most constructivist perspectives, ontology and epistemology are implicit. It is against this backdrop that MLT and concept creation emerge. MLT offers an alternative to other literacy frameworks as a response to thinking differently about literacies through concept creation. MLT adopts a rhizomatic outlook that maps literacies equally, regardless of the context (for instance, school, community, home, technology).[4] MLT consists in reading, reading the world and self, and releases school-based literacy from its privileged position by not allowing it to govern all other literacies but to have its place among other literacies.

## Conceptualising Space

Deleuze and Guattari, in line with transcendental empiricism and its espousal of a decentered subject, considered that human dependent space was a problem which required a different conceptualisation of space, immanent space. In positing immanence, space is conceived as virtual and actual, intensive and extensive, and exceeding any lived form of space. The potentiality of space opens up an affirmation of difference and how one might live. Smooth space is conceptualised to be virtual and intensive while striated space is considered to be actual and extensive. The characteristics of smooth space are: amorphous, nomadic, haptic, vectorial and deterritorialising. It is occupied by events, intensities and asignifying machines. Intensities are implicated in spontaneous and abrupt changes in structure, deterritorialisation. Smooth space is haptic. Examples are art and architecture. Smooth space is linked to close vision when the painter is nearest to the painting, 'to lose oneself without landmarks in smooth space' (Deleuze and Guattari 1987: 493). As in the example of Cézanne, there is no need to see the wheat fields. Haptic, since it is virtual, refers to a nonoptical function. Deleuze and Guattari contend that 'smooth space is both the object of close vision and the element of haptic space' (1987: 493). In addition, smooth space is vectorial. The former refers to points subordinated to the space/ trajectory between the points. It is a nomadic space that 'distributes people (and animals) in an open space, one that is indefinite and non-communicating' (1987: 380).

Striated space is homogeneous and territorialising. It is extensive, emerging from intensive singularities, such that intensity is 'turned inside out and distributed in such a way as to be dispelled, compensated, equalized and suppressed in the extensity which it [intensity] creates' (Deleuze 1994: 233). It is optical striated space that requires 'long distance vision: constancy of orientation, invariance of distance' (Deleuze and Guattari 1987: 494). 'Two spaces in fact exist only in mixture: smooth space is constantly being translated, transversed into a striated space; striated space is constantly being reversed, returned to a smooth space' (1987: 474); 'passages between the striated and the smooth are at once necessary and uncertain, and all the more disruptive' (1987: 493). In sum, the interrelationship between smooth and striated space is important in establishing an equilibrium in an open system. Creating smooth spaces along lines of flight cannot be continuously sustained. A system could not maintain itself in a constant disequilibrium. Meanwhile, striated spaces are considered sedentary and underline the importance of segmentary lines, lines that are rigid and provide no space for becoming. Therefore, a system such as an educational institution would want to accommodate both spaces with lines of flight that nomadically happen over striated space and the converse. Both are vital to achieve an equilibrium that incorporates becoming (smooth space) and progress (striated space) (Masny and Waterhouse 2011).

## Literacies and Space

This section connects literacies, space and education. There are a limited number of studies exploring literacy in Deleuzian spaces (Alvermann 2001; Eakle 2007; Hagood 2009; Leander and Rowe 2006). In most instances, space is taken up in terms of the rhizome as a spatial methodology. Eakle (2007), for instance, draws on the work of Foucault and Deleuze and Guattari to explore relationships between power and literacies in 'spaces'. In addition to mapping the lines of power amidst literacy spaces, Eakle deploys spatial/rhizomatic methods to show distances or ruptures made possible by the texts, the pedagogies, and the spaces present in the study. Thus, this 'space study' looks at expansions, limitations or reductions, and network systems to better understand how 'transactions of power' unfold in spaces such as the classroom.

MLT takes up the concept of space in this chapter in terms of forces flowing through striated and smooth space. 'What interests us in operations of striation and smoothing are precisely the passages or combinations: how the forces at work within space continually striate it, and how in the course of its striation it develops other forces and emits new smooth spaces' (Deleuze and Guattari 1987: 500). Accordingly, we are interested in a combination that connects MLT's relation to space (virtual and actual) and becoming (deterritorialisation), immanence, difference, and power of affect. All of these concepts are interrelated. Reading within MLT is virtual (intensive and deterritorialising) and actual (signifying material machines, (re)territorialising). Space is virtual (asignifying and smooth) and actual (signifying, striated). In the present context, addressing how multiple literacies may affect multilingual children at home and school, the flow of forces through striated spaces can emit smoothness that destabilises and creates lines of flight, or becomings. And in the interest of stabilisation, the flow of forces in a space can also striate a space.

The vignettes that follow involve two of five children who participated in a two-year longitudinal research study exploring conceptualisations of different writing systems with multilingual children. The five girl participants, aged five to seven years old, were filmed in class (language arts, mathematics, science and social sciences), at home (meals, homework, reading, recreational time), and where applicable, in the day-care centre (library, computer, games). Each filmed session was followed by an interview. In addition, each child was filmed participating in a mini lesson in which she gave a lesson on how to write in her home language (Spanish, Mandarin, Afar and English). Finally each child received a disposable camera and took pictures of people, places and things that were linked to literacies (music, road signs, animals, flags, etc.). Filmed sessions and the photo sessions were followed by an interview. These activities happened twice during the school year. The vignettes presented below are from Estrella and Dora, self-selected pseudonyms.

Seven-year-old Estrella is an only child born in Canada. Her mother speaks Spanish. Both parents have graduate degrees. Estrella's mother settled in Ottawa because in addition to Spanish she wanted the bilingualism (French and English) that characterises Canada. She wanted a similar experience for her daughter. She chose to send Estrella to a school where French is the sole language of instruction because French was the closest in terms of language structure to Spanish. She claimed it would help Estrella to make connections between French and Spanish. Estrella has made a personal decision to speak French at all times. The exceptions are Spanish to her mother and English to her neighbourhood friends.

## Vignette: Estrella

This exchange between the researcher and Estrella happened after taping a combination French Language Arts and Social Studies period in class. The children were asked to write a story on the theme of winter. They were to create a character and give it a name that each child would invent by combining two syllables that they had never put together before. Estrella created the penguin, Silgo. The following exchange took place about the story.

> Researcher: What did you write here?
> Estrella: Gift [pronounced *kado*/conventional spelling: *cadeau*; Estrella wrote '*cadoue*'].
> R: Gift is a difficult word to write. How did you come to write this word?
> E: Because I thought and I said I know that there is a 'c' and an 'a' and a 'd'. I decided to do 'o' with 'a' and then 'u' and then I put 'e'. [*cadoaue*]
> R: How did you know that that was the way to write it?
> E: But it is a word that I was not sure if I had to put an 'e' and I chose the shortest to make an 'o' [*cado*]
> R: And the longest . . . (interruption from Estrella)
> E: It is 'eau' [*cadeau*] and I did not want that because it was too long.
> R: And you did not want to write it [the other word, *cadeau*].
> E: Only if it is necessary.
> R: How do you know it is necessary?
> E: I know when it is necessary like a date and someone obliges me. If it is something that is not important, I do not do it.

In the actual, *cadeau* is the conventional spelling accepted in standard French. In the virtual, a word is part of asignifying machines in an assemblage. Let us explore the deterritorialising trajectory, the in-between vectorial space travelled between points that is immanent becoming. Based on instructions from the teacher, the problem is set in Estrella's mind and thinking happens. The story-writing might set off an immanent reading, an intensive event. What kind of space would gift occupy? Is it an asignifying thought of gift with an 'ou'? with 'e'? 'ea'? Each response might be considered the product of an assemblage reconfiguring differently each time. Moreover, have these responses been travelling in nomadic space, and with a haptic vision with no landmarks? MLT-becoming connects with processes of deterritorialisation happening as different orthographies emerge in the actual and reterritorialisation taking place

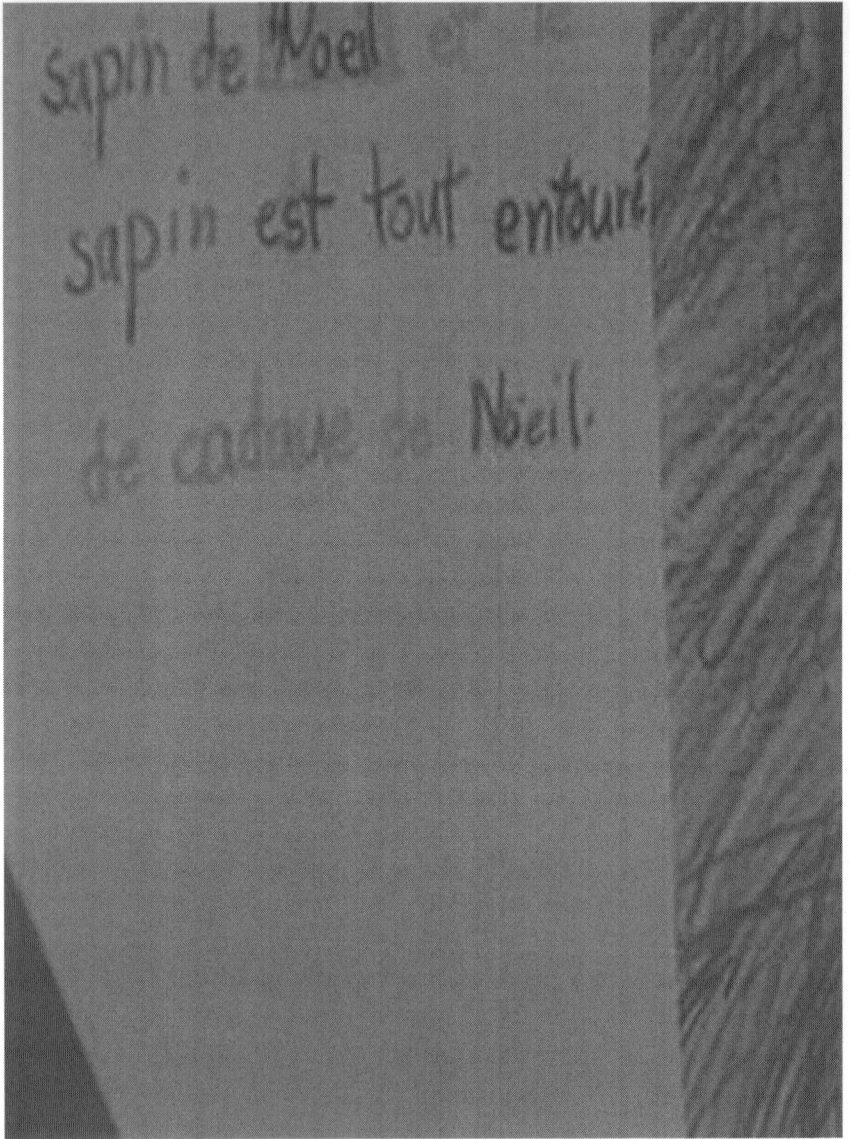

Figure 1 Estrella and *cadoue*

as a new orthography for *cadeau: cadoue, cado*. Whatever sense-word emerges in the actual is dependent on the space a word occupies. In this case, the reference point is the standard norm, *cadeau* in striated space. It is resisted because it is too long. A shorter form (that we never saw, *cado*) that ends with 'o' is possibly created. The resistance to the norm is qualified by stating that it is not necessary in this situation. Resistance is the opportunity to create and experiment. The space occupied by norms is striated, and in this vignette, both smooth and striated spaces intertwine.

## Vignette: Dora

Six-year-old Dora, the second participant, is the youngest of four children. All the children attend French language school. The oldest siblings (fifteen and thirteen years old) were born in Djibouti. Dora was born in Canada. The parents speak Arabic, Afar, Somali, French and English. The children speak French, English and Afar in the home. Mother is a day-care educator and father teaches French as a second language to immigrant adults.

In this vignette the researcher and Dora are discussing video footage of Dora writing on the chalkboard during her mini lesson.

> Researcher: You are writing in which language?
> Dora: Somali.
> R: How do you know it is Somali?
> D: My mother told me.
> R: Is there a difference writing in Somali and in French?
> D: Different.
> R: How is it different? I thought it might be the same. But you say it is different.
> D: Writing with cursive letters [letters attached] it is not same as writing in French
> R: And how do we write in French?
> R: How do you know that in Somali we write with cursive letters?
> D: My mother told me.
> R: She told you that you had to write that way. Do you see that sometimes in books?
> D: Yes in books in Somali.
> R: Do you have books in Somali at home?
> R: Does your mother read to you in Somali?
> D: Sometimes, she reads to me in English and sometimes in French.
> R: Do you know words in English? Tell me some words you know.
> D: Hello.
> R: Do you know how to write Hello?
> D: No, I cannot write it.
> R: Do you know other words in English?
> D: No.
> R: No. Is English different for you than French?

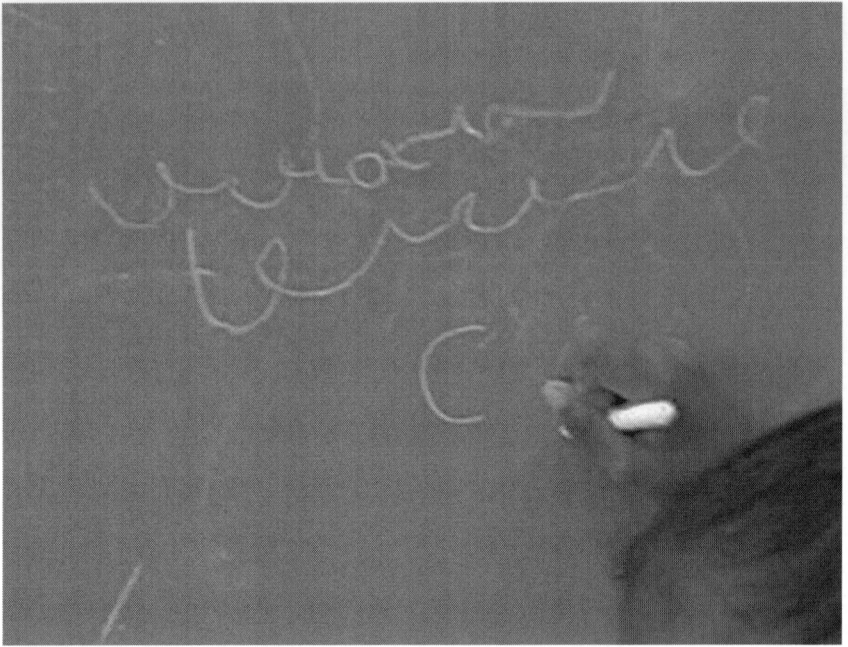

Figure 2 Dora and the mini lesson

D: Yes.
R: Tell me how is it different?
D: Because French is not the same as English.
R: How do you know?
D: I don't know.

In this vignette there is an assemblage of bodies (the school, Dora, the researcher, three languages [Afar, French and English], and the mother . . .). Dora seems to know little English (the example of 'hello' as the only word expressed), yet English is a language of communication with friends in the neighbourhood and siblings. Dora claims that she does not know how to read in either French or English. Yet, in another interview at school, the researcher wrote down five numbers in English (one, two, four, six and eight) and wrote the numbers 1, 2, 9, 10, 4, 6, 8. When asked to match the numbers with the words, Dora got all but one right. Could the number activity in English be a force of becoming, that intensive trajectory, a smoothness emitted out of a striated space? Might there be within the assemblage a relation to the school board/ district policy of communicating in French only, given that the schools are immersed in English language environments (the neighbourhood, television, internet, pop culture)? The question is how the social and political/pragmatic forces at work give rise to continuous nomadic navigation over striated spaces that impact on vectors of becoming-multilingual. The experiences of life that form an assemblage are singular and complex and contribute to sense emerging while reading, reading the world and self. MLT generates a toolbox with a power to affect non pre-given sense that emerges in the actual in terms of how MLT functions and what it produces.

Dora expresses little knowledge of English although French and English are different. When asked why that is so, she answers 'I don't know.' Her mother reads stories in English and when asked in the interview how Dora knows that the story is in English, she says that her mother told her so. Moreover, in this vignette, Dora recognises that French and Afar, a native language, are different in writing. Again when asked how she knows that the writing is in Afar, she says her mother told her so. The question remains what is the relationality of the mother in the assemblage that constructs language territories with Dora. Does mother occupy extensive space in the moment?

Humans, according to DeLanda (2005) occupy extensive spaces. How might parents as part of an assemblage contribute to the striating and smoothing forces of becoming-multilingual, becoming-literate? When helping the children with French (and other languages), the question is what happens when parents reinforce school-based ways of learning to read and write in the home. In this context, how do parents and learning affect the assemblage and how are they affected in the assemblage? The question also suggests what is effected in the relation between the assemblage and reading, reading the world and self. Affect and learning flow through space between the nomad and the sedentary, intensive and extensive, virtual and actual. While space has the potential to create problems, MLT becomes a way to read problems in the space it occupies and to respond through concept creation and sensations. Space is not constituted by humans; space transcends the human knower.

## Vignette Assemblage

In the end, 'We never know in advance how someone will learn . . . There is no more a method for learning than there is for finding treasures' (Deleuze 1994: 165). The vignettes presented have various assemblages going on within them while at the same time being themselves part of broader assemblages. While there is movement that territorialises language and literacies, there is simultaneously speed with lines of flight that disrupt and de/reterritorialise literacies differently. Each repetition releases different affects, and functions differently in terms of concept creation as a response to a problem.

Moreover, in the multilingual settings in this study, nonlinear open systems happen. Language systems become stable and unstable as the forces flow from striated spaces onto smooth spaces and onto striated spaces once more. When smoothing forces (deterritorialisations) are emitted, systems become unstable only to reterritorialise as a stable system in a striated space. MLT as theory-practice enfolds repetition and difference (Deleuze 1994), engendered each time in events that relate to and transform reading, reading the world and self. In addition, MLT as theory-practice connects spatiality, reading and reading the world that produces a reading of self (the assemblage) in relation to a becoming multilingual, becoming-literate in minority language contexts. These continual processes of disruption and stabilisation are a central feature of MLT theory-practice and describe becoming. In becoming, seen as desire (the power of life to act [Colebrook 2004; Deleuze and Guattari 1984]), and an assemblage of experiences with/in reading, reading the world and self transforms conceptualisation of writing systems and conversely, conceptualisation of writing systems transform experiences of reading, reading the world and self. Literacies happen in complex ways as multiplicities that overlap and interweave in a milieu – across languages (French, and others), modes (written, visual, oral, tactile), contexts (home, school, community), disciplines (language, science, math, art), and geographies (Canada, and countries of origin in the case of immigrant families). This study is concerned with MLT, trajectories of reading from virtual, intensive, and to actual space and the opposite movement, from actual, intensive and virtual (affirming 'the independence and immanence of multiplicities' [DeLanda 2005: 86]) and the experience of spatiality. Difference is vital to the process that would explicate how 'different expressions of life unfold different spaces, relations, fields or trajectories' (Deleuze and Guattari 1987: 411). 'Children never stop talking about what they are doing or trying to do: exploring milieus, by means of dynamic trajectories, and drawing up maps of them' (Deleuze 1997: 61).

## Intermezzo

There are two elements that flow from this chapter, perhaps two lines of flight that intertwine in between points: an ontology of reading and MLT as minoritarian.

## Ontology of Reading

What kind of reality/ontology is related to reading? Transcendental empiricism (anti-representation, decentered subjectivity, immanence, interpretosis and relationality) is the backdrop for ontology of reading. Accordingly, reading within MLT is intensive/disruptive and immanent, and relates to MLT's theory-practice in becoming and about becoming. Moreover, reading happens within an assemblage (abstract machines in the virtual and concrete machines in the actual). It also resonates in the power to affect and to be affected. In the virtual, an event or encounter, the relationality of elements in an assemblage and affect are the milieu for reading to emerge in the actual by way of a concept, perhaps a territory, as a response to a problem at hand.

DeLanda (2005) describes a reality that is one of relationality: from actual to intensive to virtual and the converse. While each time there is repetition, the repetition differs. The assemblage configures differently each time. Therefore, the ontology of difference becomes vital to the ontology of reading. Both the ontology of reading and difference relate to how one might live. Deleuze says that 'One [the indefinite] . . . is the immanent contained within a transcendental field' (2001: 30). As such, a life contains only virtuals and the unthought living of potentialities. For Deleuze, 'living consists in difference and its actualisation' (May 2005: 24). If reading relates to how literacies function and what they do/ produce, it does so through becoming, difference and its actualisation in reading, reading the world and self. In Colebrook's words: 'The power to differ expresses itself differently in each of its produced relations, with each effected point or term bearing a power to exceed itself, and to establish a new relation that would then create a new space' (2004: paragraph 16). What is proposed is to approach reading in conjunction with how one might live/what living might consist of, creating a life on a plane of consistency (immanence, difference), and a plane of sensation (affects and percepts), a reading that deterritorialises a problem and sets off on nomadic pathways, experimenting, creating; that actualises differently in each time and space, charged with affection in response to the problem at hand. This is an invitation for literacy educators to engage in concept creation that can be used and seen to work in response to their own problems. In other words: 'Stop! You're are making me tired! Experiment, don't signify and interpret! Find your own places, territorialities, deterritorializations, regime, lines of flight!' (Deleuze and Guattari 1987: 139).

## MLT: Minoritarian

Deleuze and Guattari (1986) put forward three features of the minoritarian: 1) deterritorialisation, 2) political and 3) collective assemblage of enunciation. MLT proposes to be minoritarian, that is, to construct a minority within a majority. In this case, and in this time and space, MLT is a minority within majority literacy theory (i.e., New Literacy Studies, Multiliteracies, New Literacies). Majority literacy theory does not deploy Deleuzian ontology and the features of minoritarian.

*Deterritorialisation*: As was stated earlier, MLT is related to deterritorialisation for it is a theory-practice of becoming and in becoming. Becoming refers to literacies as processes. They are intensive and function to disrupt literacies in striated spaces. MLT's goal is to disrupt stability in order for MLT to fulfil its creative purpose. This might imply that MLT is in constant disequilibrium. When experimentation and creativity in becoming actualise into a concept through MLT, MLT actualises until the next problem prompted by reading, reading the world and self, deterritorialises and MLT is once more involved in becoming. MLT is not static;[5] the concepts produced with the toolbox are created to function in relation to the problem at hand. From the moment a concept is created, it becomes a territory. Therefore MLT has an important goal: to focus on deterritorialising spaces occupied by striation, and the becoming that happens in creating concepts.

MLT's focus is on the singularities of literacies as processes, that is, on becoming and exploring space and trajectories (speed) of the in-betweeness. Colebrook calls for a move away from 'constituted space and systems . . . Accordingly, space will differ within itself according to the lives that occupy it' (2004: paragraph 4). In the context of MLT as minoritarian, both lives and space deterritorialise *in situ* and each time lives and space transform and differ.

*Political*: Literacy education is a social, cultural, political and economic endeavour. Governments are responsible for planning educational policy and curricula. Education speaks in the name of a collective and collective assemblages of enunciations are emitted (Masny 2012). Literacy education becomes one in which one concept of literacy (school-based literacy) is privileged over others, and literacy education proceeds into an overcoding of that concept. Once that happens, the concept becomes fixed in a closed system, in striated space, and is replaced by order-words, or prescriptivism. MLT as minoritarian offers an alternative that eschews privileging one literacy over another, disallowing hierarchical divisions of literacies. MLT disrupts conventional notions of what literacy does and what it produces in order for different concepts to emerge.

*Collective Assemblage of Enunciation*: Deleuze and Guattari (1987) point out that there are no individual assemblages of enunciation; only collective ones overcoded with order-words. However, there are potentialities for collective assemblages of enunciation to be disrupted through lines of flight, becomings, that shoot through overcoded practices. Overcoded practices in literacy can be seen for instance in the ways a government refers to its communities in relation to degrees of literacy/illiteracy. MLT, in reading, reading the world and self, disrupts overcoded practices. Literacy problems happen, and in response MLT explores the immanence of literacies along nomadic pathways to create concepts in conjunction with the power of affect. In the end, MLT as minoritarian relates to what living consists of and how one might live collectively.

## Notes

1. Plugging-in is a concept that Deleuze created in response to reading a book intensively: 'there is nothing to explain . . . to understand . . . to interpret . . . like plugging into an electric circuit' (Deleuze 1995: 8).
2. Virtual and actual are also part of Deleuzian ontology (Semetsky 2009). Both concepts will be presented in relation to MLT and to conceptualisation of space.
3. I acknowledge that allotting a short space to literacy education reifies the complex issues that are important to literacy research.
4. Multiple literacies refer to reading, reading the world and self in different contexts. However, this does not give way to a multiplicity of literacies (such as digital literacy, emotional literacy, financial literacy, and more . . .). This view would provide literacies with a silo effect with each literacy having its own vertical root-like existence. Multiple literacies refer to a univocity (no hierarchy, no divisions), one literacy (a composite and irreducible reading, reading the world and self) *in situ*. In this way, there is neither arborescence nor divisions at work. It is *in situ* that a concept emerges/is created not given.
5. MLT when adopted by educational authorities might become static in the curriculum unless it is used to respond to problems through the introduction of experimentation and creating in smooth space.

## References

Alvermann, D. (2001), 'Researching Libraries, Literacies and Lives: A Rhizoanalysis' in E. St. Pierre and W. S. Pillow (eds), *Working the Ruins: Feminist Poststructural Theory and Methods in Education*, New York: Routledge, pp. 114–29.

Barton, D. and M. Hamilton (2005), 'Literacy, Reification and the Dynamics of Social Interaction' in D. Barton and K. Tusting (eds), *Beyond Communities of*

*Practice: Language, Power and Social Context*, Cambridge: Cambridge University Press, pp. 14–35.

Bonta, M. and J. Protevi (2004), *Geophilosophy*, Edinburgh: Edinburgh University Press.

Colebrook, C. (2002a), *Gilles Deleuze*, New York: Routledge.

Colebrook, C. (2002b), *Understanding Deleuze*, London: Unwin.

Colebrook, C. (2004), 'The Sense of Space: On the specificity of affect in Deleuze and Guattari', *Postmodern Culture*, 15(1) <http://pmc.iath.virginia.edu/text-only/issue.904/15.1colebrook.txt> (accessed 31 October 2012).

Cook-Gumperz, J. (1986), *The Construction of Literacy*, Cambridge: Cambridge University Press.

DeLanda, M. (2005), 'Intensive and Extensive Spaces' in I. Buchanan and G. Lampert (eds), *Deleuze and Space*, Edinburgh: Edinburgh University Press, pp. 80–8.

Deleuze, G. (1990), *The Logic of Sense*, trans. M. Lester with C. Stivale, ed. C. V. Boundas, New York: Columbia University Press.

Deleuze, G. (1994), *Difference and Repetition*, P. Patton, New York: Columbia University Press.

Deleuze, G. (1995), *Negotiations 1972–1990*, trans. M. Joughin, New York: Columbia University Press.

Deleuze, G. (1997), *Essays Critical and Clinical*, trans. D. W. Smith and M. A. Greco, Minneapolis: University of Minnesota Press.

Deleuze, G. (2001), *Pure Immanence: Essays on a Life*, trans. A. Boyman, New York: Zone Books.

Deleuze, G. (2004), 'Intellectuals and Power (an interview with Michel Foucault)' in D. Lapoujade (ed.), *Desert Islands and Other Texts, 1953–1974*, trans. M. Taormina, Los Angeles and New York: Semiotext(e), pp. 206–13.

Deleuze, G. and F. Guattari (1984), *Anti-Oedipus: Capitalism and Schizophrenia*, trans. R. Hurley, M. Seem and H. R. Lane, Minneapolis: University of Minnesota Press.

Deleuze, G. and F. Guattari (1986), *Kafka: Toward a Minor Literature*, trans. D. Polan and R. Bensmaia, Minneapolis: University of Minnesota Press.

Deleuze, G. and F. Guattari (1987), *A Thousand Plateaus: Capitalism and Schizophrenia*, trans. B. Massumi, Minneapolis: University of Minnesota Press.

Deleuze, G. and F. Guattari (1994), *What is Philosophy?* trans. H. Tomlinson and G. Burchell, New York: Columbia University Press.

Denzin, N. and Y. Lincoln (eds) (2005), *The Sage Handbook of Qualitative Research* (3rd edn), Thousand Oaks, CA: Sage.

Eakle, A. J. (2007), 'Literacy Spaces of a Christian Faith-based School', *Reading Research Quarterly*, 42(4): 472–510.

Gort, M. (2006), 'Strategic Codeswitching, Interliteracy, and Other Phenomena of Emergent Bilingual Writing: Lessons from first grade dual language classrooms', *Journal of Early Childhood Literacy*, 6(3): 323–54.

Hagood, M. C. (2009), 'Mapping a Rhizome of 21st century Language Arts: Travel plans for research and practice', *Language Arts, 87*(1): 39–48.

Juzwik, M. M., S. Curcic, K. Wolbers, K. D. Moxley, L. M. Dimling and R. K. Shankland (2006), 'Writing into the 21st Century: An overview of research on writing, 1999 to 2004', *Writing Communication, 23*(4): 451–76.

Leander, K. M. and D. W. Rowe (2006), 'Mapping Literacy Spaces in Motion: A rhizomatic analysis of classroom literacy performance', *Reading Research Quarterly*, 44(4): 428–60.

Masny, D. (2006), 'Learning and Creative Processes: A poststructural perspective on language and multiple literacies', *International Journal of Learning*, 12(5): 147–55.

Masny, D. (2009a), 'Bridging Access, Equity and Quality: The case for multiple literacies', National Conference for Teachers of English and Literacy, Wrest Point Conference Centre. Hobart, Tasmania <http://www.englishliteracyconference.com.au/files/documents/hobart/conferencePapers/refereed/MasnyDiana.pdf> (accessed 20 September 2012).

Masny, D. (2009b), 'Literacies as Becoming: A Child's Conceptualisations of Writing Systems' in D. Masny and D. R. Cole, *Multiple Literacies Theory: A Deleuzian Perspective*, Rotterdam: Sense, pp. 13–30.

Masny, D. (2011), 'Multiple Literacies Theory: Exploring futures', *Policy Futures in Education*, 9(4).

Masny, D. (2012), 'Multiple Literacies Theory: Discourse, sensation, resonance and becoming', *Discourse*, 33(1).

Masny, D. (2012), 'Cartographies of Talking Groups', in D. Masny and D. R. Cole (eds), *Mapping Multiple Literacies: An Introduction to Deleuzian Literacy Studies*, London: Continuum, pp. 93–124.

Masny, D. and M. Waterhouse (2011), 'Mapping Territories and Creating Nomadic Pathways with Multiple Literacies Theory', *Journal of Curriculum Theorizing*, 27(2).

May, T. (2005), *Gilles Deleuze: An Introduction*, Cambridge: Cambridge University Press.

Semetsky, I. (2003), 'The Problematics of Human Subjectivity: Gilles Deleuze and the Deweyan legacy', *Studies in Philosophy and Education*, 22: 211–25.

Semetsky, I. (2009), 'Deleuze as a Philosopher of Education: Affective knowledge/ effective learning', *The European Legacy*, 14(4): 443–56.

Stagoll, C. (2005), 'Event' in A. Parr (ed.), *The Deleuze Dictionary*, New York: Columbia University Press, pp. 87–9.

Street, B. V. (1984), *Literacy in Theory and Practice*, Cambridge: Cambridge University Press.

UNESCO (2008), *The Global Literacy Challenge*, Paris: UNESCO <http://unesdoc.unesco.org/images/0016/001631/163170e.pdf> (accessed 19 August 2011).

Williams, J. (2008), *Gilles Deleuze's* Logic of Sense: *A Critical Introduction and Guide*, Edinburgh: Edinburgh University Press.

Chapter 5

# Affective Literacies:
# Deleuze, Discipline and Power

*David R. Cole*

This chapter explores the philosophy of Gilles Deleuze in order to understand classroom management in terms of the moving power-structure(s)
in the teaching and learning context. The classroom dynamic presents
a form of affective literacy or literacies in the framework of Multiple
Literacies Theory (Masny 2006). This is because the ways in which communication happens in the classroom demonstrates an affective map of
the power flows in that context; in this chapter this power differential is
dealt with through the concept of 'affectus'. The affective interactivity of
literacies in classroom management is complementary to and congruent
with the conceptual framework of this writing. This piece will focus on
the Deleuzo-Guattarian concepts of 'anti-production' (as presented in
*Anti-Oedipus*) and 'order-words' (in *A Thousand Plateaus*), that will be
unpacked and analysed in the specific educational context of classroom
management and as pertaining to teacher education. The two conceptions of desire from *Anti-Oedipus* (1984) and *A Thousand Plateaus*
(1987) will be reconciled in this chapter through the communication of
affective literacies and in the power relationships of affect as affectus.

   Anti-production locates the immovable and yet invisible points in
the socius that Deleuze and Guattari subject to analysis and synthesis
in *Anti-Oedipus*. The primarily Marxian-Freudian concept of anti-
production explains 1) how traces of previous occasions where classroom management strategies have been deployed remain in institutions
of teaching and learning and 2) how classroom management pertains to
desire. Anti-production shows how this 'holding' of disciplinary events
takes place, and provides a bridge between residing in a school, and the
collective memories of the resident population, spreading in the population contagiously. The second concept that acts as a platform in this
chapter for affective literacies, discipline and power is that of the order-
words. Deleuze and Guattari (1987) offered the idea of the order-words

to provide a connection between the 'collective assemblage' and enunciation, or how we use language socially. The order-words 'flow' around places of learning like the routing of electricity in plasterboard walls, and present a means to explain how disciplinary triggers are shared communally and linguistically. This chapter includes scenarios to illustrate classroom management as affective literacies and how to deploy Deleuze and Guattari's concepts in teacher education. It will also show how teacher education and classroom management could be modified from the Deleuzo-Guattarian philosophical perspective, by emphasising that students and teachers competently analyse the affective literacies that are at work in schools and how they impact on teaching and learning. The chapter contends that classroom management is made easier through understanding and applying affective literacies to questions of power (affectus), and by combining an analysis of anti-production with order-words to improve classroom management.

## Classroom Management and Deleuze

Deleuze did not present a theory or model of classroom management during his career. While this should not surprise one, it doesn't mean that his philosophical ideas as a toolbox cannot be used to craft a workable notion of classroom management. In contrast, Guattari was directly influenced by the radical pedagogy of Freinet and Oury, which implies a notion of classroom management through the augmentation of the group to act as subject (see Guattari 1995). It is in the combined works of *Anti-Oedipus* and *A Thousand Plateaus* that Deleuze's philosophical toolbox meshes most closely with the practical materiality of Guattari. However, pre-service students and teachers often have little use for such ideas, as they look for directly applicable models of classroom management that will help them in their chosen profession. It is therefore worth considering the conjunctive aspects between the affective literacies of this chapter, built with the Deleuzo-Guattarian concepts of anti-production and order-words, and classroom management theory at its most open and liberal. The ideas that most readily join with the focus of this chapter are those of William Glasser (1998a, 1998b). This chapter is not a comparative study between Glasser and Deleuze, but it does show how Deleuze's philosophy in compatible with classroom management theory. Glasser was influenced by the constructivism of Dewey, and worked against the dominant paradigm of behaviourism in classroom management. In summary, he proposed that classroom management required educators to satisfy the needs of the students, and these needs are driven by:

1. Survival, safety, security
2. Love, belonging and acceptance
3. Personal power, competency and achievement
4. Freedom, independence and autonomy
5. Fun and learning
   (Glasser 1998a: 5)   !!   not sure !!

Glasser (1998b) proposed that teachers conduct needs analyses to make sure that their pedagogy takes into account the drives as listed above. The problem that most teachers find with this process is that there is not enough time in 'normal' teaching and learning contexts to inquire into students needs to such depth. Glasser's classroom management model is radically student-centred, and this fact could potentially jeopardise both the position of the teacher and the teaching and learning structures that could help with classroom management. However, Glasser's ideas are meant to give the teacher the greatest possible chance of allowing the students to make the right choices in education, and to make classroom management a matter of being a lead teacher, and not a boss teacher (Glasser 1998a). These tactics do resonate with the Deleuzian approach of this chapter, yet if one takes the ideas of Deleuze and Guattari seriously, one cannot straightforwardly fall back into choice theory in terms of classroom management. This is because understanding and working with drives in the classroom does not necessarily imply choice according to Deleuze and Guattari.

One could say that the classroom management model of this chapter is more akin to conducting an orchestra, or like being a DJ at a dance. The teacher must acclimatise and become one with the atmospheres of the class, and through this acclimatisation process work out how to make learning happen. The classroom management plan to be outlined here is a highly disciplined and rigorous practice, which replaces traditional power hierarchies with subtle pulsations in energy and drive. Such a discipline could include some of Glasser's ideas, yet one shouldn't presuppose any needs before one has experienced a particular context. Rather, one should firstly understand how every context is permeated by affective literacies and power through affect.

## Affective Literacies and Power (affectus)

When one goes to a school, college or university for the first time, one may discern affect. This is the atmosphere of the place, which has been produced by the historical and material presence that the institution emits. For example, a school may have been run on military lines, thus the experience of teaching and learning at the institute would seem as if one has entered the army. In an opposing example, a college might specialise in the creative arts; the pedagogic affect that one experiences in the space would in this case be more liberal, open and spontaneous. Affective literacies involve the reciprocal articulation of such affects, and can be bodily, visual, audio or linguistic (see Masny and Cole 2009). Affect in these affective literacies is the act of changing in relation to an encounter with another, in places of teaching and learning. This is due to the power relationships that permeate such institutions as a result of classroom management, discipline and control.

For the purposes of this section on affective literacies and power, I am interested in the notion and Latin term 'affectus', or subjective modulation. In his book *Spinoza: Practical Philosophy*, Deleuze says that affectus is 'an increase or decrease of the power of acting, for the body and the mind alike' (1988: 47). In the terms of this chapter, this increase or decrease in power occurs when the teacher and students experience changes in atmosphere through classroom action and any lines of conflict that are present. According to the philosophy of this chapter, the teacher cannot straightforwardly control the class, but has to assimilate with the prevailing atmospheres in the context and work through the affective literacies that are present. He or she must not attempt to quash or nullify 'affectus', but should try to understand, articulate and work with the presence of affects in the classroom – like moving with an energy field or taking part in a dance. I have elsewhere named this movement with affect in education as the two-role model of affect (Cole 2011). Deleuze expands his definition of affectus by arguing that it is crucially separate from emotion; affectus is simultaneously the physical and nonphysical increase or decrease in a body's power of acting. Deleuze states:

> The *affectio* refers to a state of the affected body and implies the presence of the affecting body, whereas the *affectus* refers to the passage from one state to another, taking into account the correlative variation of the affecting bodies. Hence there is a difference in nature between the *image affections* or *ideas* and the *feeling affect*. (1988: 49)

Put differently, affectus is the material and immaterial elements of change and importantly for educational usages may be understood as *the act of learning*. Affectus is the passage from one state to another, which occurs in relation to affecting bodies, and in the case of classroom management, due to conflict, power and discipline. Affectus is also what theorists such as Hickey-Moody and Haworth (2009), Di Leo et al.

(2002) and McWilliam (1996) have called pedagogy; in other words, affectus is a relational practice through which knowledge is made and transmitted. This relational practice is here transcribed into affective literacies, which are multiple opportunities to work with affectus in an educational context and via the energy penetration of classroom management strategies. The image affections, or ideas, to which Deleuze refers above, are generated by a specific kind of movement in affect. This change involves increasing or decreasing one's *capacity* to act, or the modulation of affectus; and such a plane of action prompts affection or the feeling of affect in the consciousness of the body (see Hickey-Moody 2009), read as a plane of materiality. Affectus therefore differs from notions of subjective change as a contained pedagogy, as affectus is a type of 'non-human' pedagogy, as shall be illustrated in the examples of classroom management below as a machine.

The affective literacies that correspond to affectus and that we are using in this chapter for classroom management are only grounded in terms of interrelated, non-personal connections; and they are necessarily a response to, and part of, becoming in the world (cf. Semetsky 2006). This 'becoming in the world' will be explained below in terms of practical examples in classroom management. One could say that the affectus of affective literacies is a rhythm, and that affectus may be incorporated into transversality (see Guattari 1984). Affective literacies are an articulation of an encounter between form and forces that are non-human and chaotic. In terms of classroom management, affectus necessitates institutional administrators, teachers, computer programmers and students understanding and working with the lines of force and power as they are represented through and in context.

A vital aspect of using affectus and affective literacies for classroom management is to understand that they do not signify closed systems, i.e., functioning only in classrooms. Teachers and students should be able to explore the affective economies of learning in community spaces, in and out of schools. For example, the multiple and complex processes of political activism on the Net make for excellent affective literacy activities and engagement in today's wired and globalised classrooms (see Pullen and Cole 2009). Understandings of power are often reversed and subtly questioned and renegotiated on the Net, and teachers need to engage with these movements of power that regularly take place in mediated environments. Such understandings and articulations can take one into a new vision of society that permeates educational institutions and the requisite classroom management of these spaces. Affective literacies connect with power and classroom management in that the new worlds that are emerging due to Net connectivity are relayed into action. Teachers need to be up to date with these cultural shifts, and engage through affectus with contemporary group dynamics, Net hierarchies and protocols that are currently emerging in post-industrial societies. This is also the nexus of what Masny calls 'creative process', or research that is about 'confronting teaching as unknowability and learning as literacies or [the] different ways of becoming [that are] involved in uncontrollable and uncontrolled ways of "reading-learning"' (2006: 148).

## Anti-Production

Affective literacies that foreground power as *affectus* are importantly involved with desire. The idea at this point is that the teachers and students working through affectus – moving with the classroom management situation by pertinently attending to the contextual and situational power relationships affectively – necessarily tap into the desires of the host population and any group dynamics. There may be censors and problems with this scheme in education, if, for example, the children and teachers are not allowed to talk overtly about sexuality or violence. The other major drawback with this idea might be the complexity of the desires involved; if, for example, the local community is mired in poverty or it is suffering due to alienation, then the specific understandings of this situation and the desires that living in poverty or as an outsider generate may create insurmountable problems for the educator (see Anyon 2005). However, these examples of desire in education draw us closer to understanding Deleuze- and Guattari's concept of 'anti-production'. Desire is not enjoined with lack according to Deleuze and Guattari, although one could say that educational desiring-production is imbricated with circuits of anti-production, as the desire for continual learning production leads to the habitual repetition of concepts such as 'lifelong learning'. This is because it could be argued that lifelong learning is a containment strategy of post-modern capitalism and does not lead to revolutionary change (cf. Wallin, forthcoming).

Furthermore, the operations of anti-production in education can be seen in the political economies of schools, colleges or universities. Capitalist surplus value incorporates students and teachers in enveloping circuits of educational production to make money from learning ('edu-debt'). To exemplify the conjunction between surplus value, capitalism and anti-production (edu-debt), one could say that in a culture driven by semiotics, there is always more to learn. In an age of rapidly developing computerised information technologies, there are always new computer skills to be mastered and new software programs and gadgets to be bought and managed. In a system of global educational rankings, there is always progress to be made; there is always another scale upon which one can compare performance. This exteriorising surplus capitalist economy drives education into processes of interminable production and debt (see Lazzarato 2006). Anti-production can be detected in the ways that the labour of teachers and students never catches up with the motility of surplus value. The educational containment by surplus value is commensurate with the functioning of capitalism, which ensures the interconnected nature of production through anti-production at all levels of the social assemblage (Deleuze and Guattari 1984).

Therefore, one must include anti-production in terms of the affective literacies, affectus and classroom management described in this chapter. One could say that anti-production produces an atmosphere of 'unrealisation' in the classroom, as the potential of the teenagers and teachers is often thwarted by the societal processes of capitalism and desiring-production that swirl through teaching and learning contexts. There is an important political message attached to 'anti-production', which states that the ways in which the youth are socialised in contemporary society often gives them unrealistic expectations as to what they can achieve. The lure of fast cars, glamorous models and luxurious lifestyles is communicated through advertising and film, and a gap between material needs and desire is created as a function of living and being schooled under the sign of capitalist endeavour (see Darder et al. 2009).

There are serious consequences of anti-production in terms of classroom behaviour and the management skills necessary to deal with such a situation. Deleuze and Guattari do not give a straightforward solution to the behavioural and adaptive problems produced by anti-production, yet by theorising anti-production as being liminal with desire, one may begin to recognise the complexities of the situation. If one goes too far in the direction of capitalist endeavour in one's pedagogy, and tries to utilise the desires that capital produces, the resulting knowledge work can be contrived and artificial – except perhaps if one makes money through teaching and learning! Contrariwise, if one ignores contemporary capitalist society, one may come across as being a dinosaur only interested in knowledge for scholastic or purely scientific purposes. This chapter suggests that there is a middle way that may be gleaned from a detailed understanding of Deleuze and Guattari's notion of anti-production. This middle way takes capitalist production and explores and explicates the desires that flow through its processes – good and bad. Such a strategy should demonstrate the value of knowledge in contemporary society, while providing engaging and dynamic lesson plans.

For example, in terms of anti-production in education, one may analyse the reasons for the 2008 Global Financial Crisis (GFC) with the students, but not in a purely analytical or statistical fashion. The educator and group will draw social and cultural consequences from the facts of the GFC, as well as understanding how this event has ramifications for the global financial system in the future. Anti-production is being used here purposefully and with the intention of dealing with potential behavioural problems associated with the striations of desire caused due to economic collapse. The last element of this chapter's concept construction to better understand affective literacies, power and discipline in the classroom involves language and Deleuze and Guattari's account of order-words.

## Order-Words

> It is in this sense that language is the transmission of the word as order-word, not the communication of a sign as information. Language is a map, not a tracing. (Deleuze and Guattari 1987: 77)

When teachers implement classroom management techniques, they invariably use language. Therefore, one must take into account language use in addressing the question of power and discipline in the classroom. In *A Thousand Plateaus*, Deleuze and Guattari deploy the notion of 'order-words', which is taken from a non-normative approach to linguistics. This means that the 'order-words' are immediately drawn away from mainstream linguistics, because the latter is interested in fixing language by according primacy to constants and a secondary role to variation. In contrast, Deleuze and Guattari had a reversed take on constants and variations within the systems of language. In their terms, variations are primary, and exist on a virtual plane, as one can never fully predict how a word will be actualised in advance. Such actualisation of words depends entirely on the context, and in the terms of this chapter, on behaviour management situations involving affect, anti-production, discipline, power and conflict.

Deleuze and Guattari were interested in the multiple and criss-crossing relations that are possible between the statement and the act. These relationships, though complex, are importantly political for Deleuze and Guattari, and the political nature of language becomes integral to their account. For example, when a teacher asks/directs/tells a student to do something, this is a statement that is politically empowered by and through the context of teaching and learning, and is potentially empowering in terms of the learning that could take place and any ensuing group dynamics – as well being disempowering if the statement fails in its intent (see Cole 2009). All behaviour management statements have a political and relational dimension according to this schema, which can be analysed by understanding the 'order-words'.

The language that we are primarily concerned with in classroom management is about command, instruction and its reception. With the desired action of learning stemming from speech, transformations in the agent must occur accordingly. Deleuze and Guattari refer to this context of change as 'incorporeal transformation' (1987: 92). An example of such a change could be when a teacher reprimands a student for disobeying the class rules. The physical bodies of the teacher and child have not altered in the exchange, hence the notion of incorporeality in this context. Yet by making such a statement about power in the classroom, i.e., reasserting the class rules, the relationships of bodies in the particular context and the overall form of the classroom 'assemblage' are altered. The statement of 'rule adherence' turns into an act, that of compliance or defiance on the part of the student(s). This particular type of transformation has social implications that alter the bodies it affects, i.e., those of the teacher, the student, the cohort and anyone who is listening or who hears about the speech act. One could say that the statement and reinstatement of class rules is an immanent act, actualised once the teacher is in a particular time and space that is related to the context of being a teacher and that implies a previously defined role of what it means to be a 'good teacher' (see Rogers 1998) who can manage the class. Yet the realisation of the political and pragmatic level of the order-words also allows the teacher to question the presuppositions inherent within the order-words, i.e., the statement and reinstatement of the school rules.

Classroom management through language and the class rules is a social activity. The social character of language is, according to Deleuze and Guattari, the 'transmission of order-words, from one statement to another or within each statement in so far as each statement accomplishes an act and an act is accomplished in the statement' (1987: 72). Order-words therefore importantly demonstrate a social order through language. They may concern directions, commands, instructions, questions, requests or promises that are linked to statements by a 'social obligation'. Order-words are part of a matrix that codes, possesses and potentially enhances or restricts action. For example, order-words can be the instruments of the state that defines education in a particular territory and in a certain manner (see Masny 2005). In the context of this chapter, the order-words of the state will refer to previously defined, normatively correct and acceptable behaviours in the context of teaching and learning.

The recognition and analysis of the order-words used in classroom management by the state is therefore a potentially subversive activity, and one that can undermine governmentally dominant forms of control through social acquiescence and quietism. Deleuze and Guattari affirm that in addition to the order-words, language consists of indirect discourse, which refers to speaking in a received, 'passed on' or clichéd style. In the case of indirect discourse, it may not be clear who is speaking or where the words have come from. Indirect discourse has a collective style because of its generalised form (see Grisham 1991). The order-words of classroom management situations relate to and bleed into indirect discourse as the teacher typically lives in society, interacts with the media, and deals with groups of students who also live in society. Therefore, dominant forms of socialisation and normalisation can be transmitted through indirect discourse as much as through the order-words, and teachers should be aware that clichéd and colloquial forms of language can be detrimental to working with knowledge because of the conditioning and coding that lies in indirect discourse.

In corollary, language is a set of statements and propositions, order-words, implicit and explicit presuppositions, indirect discourse and incorporeal transformations that make social processes. For Deleuze and Guattari, the primary role of language, contra traditional linguistics, is neither to inform nor to communicate, but to produce order-words according to an overriding and dominant social reality. Therefore, language has a negative status in Deleuze and Guattari's analysis, as their philosophical approach to understanding language continually undermines the potential homogenisation inherent within communication (see Roy 2008). Their approach is one that invites experimentation and the creation of new language. If one uses cliché or mindlessly restates the rules without sensitivity or empathy to a particular context, one is immediately caught out by the ideas of Deleuze and Guattari.

To take their notion of 'order-words' seriously for classroom management purposes, one must be able to take apart socially dominant forms of language use, and be able to ask searching questions about their purposes and grounds. The consequence of applying the order-words in this chapter opens up the use of language in education as a means to comprehending contextual and practical adaptations in teaching and learning – and as they happen affectively. This is not to tell teachers how to speak, or what to say in order to control an unruly class. Rather, the challenge here is to continually analyse the typical order-words of control, e.g., 'be quiet' 'sit down', etc., in order to get to a level of language production and reception that achieves affective auto-reflexivity in moments of classroom management and disciplinary crisis.

## The Classroom Management Machine

This chapter proposes a means to understanding classroom management in terms of: affective literacies, which focus affectus as power, anti-production and the order-words. The responses to classroom management situations below demonstrate how the non-human pedagogy mentioned in terms of affectus may be figured. This is because the classroom management ideas in this chapter are a machine, and not a matter of experience, judgement or subjectivity. The proposal here is that this amalgam of elements from the work of Deleuze and Guattari helps to deal with classroom management situations. This link to the practical and immanent life of education may be illustrated by thinking through the responses that an 'affective literacies (affectus)-anti-production-order-words' machine produce:

### Examples of Classroom Management[1]

1. *A student approaches you and tells you that he has ADHD (Attention Deficit Hyperactivity Disorder). He can't take the test within the time allotted, can't turn in assignments on time, or can't take notes, etc. He is requesting special consideration. Other students in the class overhear your conversation and start to whisper among themselves.*

This example very well illustrates how affectus, anti-production and order-words are connected to classroom management. The teacher should choose their response to this situation carefully, as the wrong tone, and the reproduction of order-words related to learning conformity, could augment a potentially disastrous situation. The teacher needs to grant special consideration for this student, while not being seen to give special privilege to one student's needs. The best way to handle this case would be in a neutral context, without the other class members being present, where the problems that this student is experiencing may be discussed in full, and affective literacies may be achieved between student and teacher. These literacies would articulate the student and teacher's perspectives on ADHD and the consequences in the teaching and learning context. These affective literacies would help to establish a sound working relationship between the student and teacher for the future, and also deal with the anti-production of submitting this student to uniform assessment processes.

*2. You've assigned online discussion groups. You are reviewing their postings and discover inappropriate language and sexual references to you and/or other students.*

These postings are clearly not acceptable; yet show how educational practice relates to societal tendencies that have been dealt with in this chapter through anti-production. These postings should not be addressed in an overly judicious or moralistic manner, or by assigning the order-words of reprimand to the (unknown) subjects. Rather, the postings should be discussed with the class members, not in terms of reprimand or punishment, but to articulate the affects that have been scribed as forms of affective literacies. Offensive and obscene material should not be simply castigated or nullified in education; but worked through and shown how it communicates hurt (affectus). This example of turning a classroom management and potentially conflictive situation into a pedagogic process, demonstrates how to conjoin affectus, anti-production and the order-words. The authors of this material should understand that online environments are not neutral, but they are engaging with affective literacies that are connected to the anti-production of contemporary society and the order-words of control.

*3. John recently began teaching at college. In the fourth week of the term, he administered the first exam. Mary, a bright student, was a 'no-show' and had also missed the previous week. After the exam, John telephoned her at the number she had provided on her student profile. A middle-aged man answered the phone. John identified himself as Mary's teacher and asked for her. The man identified himself as Mary's father, told John that Mary was not home, then asked the nature of the call. John replied that Mary had missed the test and went on to speculate about its impact on her grade.*

It would be best if John did not discuss Mary's grade with her father, and this is because of the affectus that would be produced by such an exchange. John needs to arrange a time and date to speak to Mary in person and to ask her what has happened. Speaking to her father in the first place would potentially damage the relationship that John has established with Mary and therefore make communication harder in the future. This example shows how discussing matters with parents can influence the affective literacies necessary to make classroom management work. Furthermore, Mary's father could pass on order-words connected to grading (simply put: A = good, E = bad), and this might also impact on the anti-production of grading, in terms of Mary's likelihood not to benefit from future assessment results.

4. *You are presenting a new concept to your class. You've worked very hard to organise your presentation and find the material very interesting. However, the energy level in the class is very low. The students appear to be falling asleep and are not interested in the lesson.*

One should not overtly demonstrate one's disappointment in the students' reaction to one's material – however interesting one might think it to be, and this is an example of affectus in the classroom. Such disappointment could lead to further and increased disruption and a potential split between your ideas about the material and that of the cohort, or eschewed affective literacies. Rather, one needs to take time out from the prescribed curriculum and examine the reasons for the lull in energy. Maybe the students just need a break or a change in the presentation of the material. Furthermore, they could be experiencing 'information overload' and need a more interactive teaching and learning environment. This example shows how order-words can be multimodal and not only instructive or directing knowledge work, and that anti-production has to be engaged with affectively.

5. *A student comes to class who is obviously on drugs or drunk.*

This is a delicate situation that should be treated carefully. According to the affective literacies of this chapter, one should not immediately reprimand the student, or make an example of them, as this could provide a basis for an irrational outburst or enflamed situation (affectus). Rather, one should start the lesson off as had been planned, and when the rest of the class has become engrossed in the focus of the learning, one should address the student personally and ascertain the details of the intoxication (affective literacies). Once this interaction has been achieved, the student should either be asked to leave the class, or reminded of the class procedures that will happen during and after the lesson; and they will have to remain within these parameters to successfully negotiate the teaching and learning context. One could say that the teacher is working with affective literacies in terms of building relationships, anti-production in terms of the impact of intoxication, and the order-words in terms of not using language to express reactive indignation to drug/alcohol use.

6. *Many of your students come from different cultures with different ethnic and linguistic backgrounds. You have been lecturing and students are complaining that they cannot understand you or follow your logic.*

The linguistic diversity of student backgrounds will add to the richness of the educational experience, and is an important part of the affective literacies addressed in this chapter. However, this situation can lead to the increased possibility of misunderstandings and subsequent conflict and disruption (affectus). Therefore, the teacher must take time to create specific sessions that aid inter-cultural literacy (by using affective literacies), and by avoiding the order-words and clichés connected to cultural differences. These pedagogic actions may include looking at the different languages represented in the cohort and showing what different cultures bring to the particular knowledge field that is being studied. No group should be highlighted as being in particular need of help, as this can lead to the anti-production of that group; cultural diversity will be complemented and included in knowledge work on an everyday basis by deploying affective literacies.

7. *Marina finds spelling and grammar errors in your sentences on the board with embarrassing consistency, and she comes around after class to give you her critical opinion of the course. When she's in class, you feel like you're being constantly monitored.*

Making spelling and grammar mistakes will attract criticism. However, the relationship between yourself and Marina needs to be addressed. This situation would be best handled outside of the class when she has come to complain, and affective literacies may be constructed mutually. One needs to be able to handle personal criticism as a teacher, yet if it is ill directed or a cover for a different problem, this also needs to be looked at. In this case, Marina has suggestions that will help with the running of the class and these suggestions should be used. If Marina has a social difficulty, this should be addressed and suggestions made to help, e.g., a change of seating plan, less or more group work, a different means to discursive pedagogy in the lessons (e.g., using an IWB).

The aspect of changing teaching and learning patterns involve affective literacies by thoroughly discussing the pedagogy, anti-production in terms of the culture of the classroom, and the order-words in terms of the terminology used when changing practice.

8. *Patrick is critical and outright insubordinate in class, always challenging your information and interpretations on the basis of readings from the textbook. Though he often remembers the text incorrectly, you sometimes start to wonder if it was in fact you who failed to master the material.*

Patrick's behaviour needs to be addressed as soon as possible in this situation as it is an ongoing problem. This means that the ways in which he is reacting to your pedagogy need to be examined in terms of the affective, relational and anti-production consequences. One could counter Patrick's claims by stating that it is healthy to consider if one has mastered the material of the lesson, as this should lead to increased knowledge and engagement with the topic. However, it is unhealthy to feel belittled by a student. The power relationship (affectus) between you and the student should be addressed; the teacher may be put back in tune with the knowledge field that they are exploring, so one can deal with any critical remarks that arise during the lesson and Patrick is less inclined to make outbursts. Patrick's manner should be explored through whole class engagement with knowledge and the objects of inquiry, and not through a 'power war' with Patrick or by using order-words, as this could lead to a narrowing of affective literacies and intensification in the impact of the conflict.

9. *Teri had a class in the past similar to yours, and constantly compares your instruction to her other experience. Inevitably, your class always comes up short in her eyes.*

Comparative pedagogy could be a positive aspect of the lesson. Yet if this process is initiated with a negative intent, using order-words and anti-production, the outcome will be negative. This is why the teacher should lead an affective literacies session to show how knowledge can be shared and transmitted via different means. For example, the teacher could introduce the use of ICTs, or change the affectus and power relationships by asking students to lead sessions. The point here is not to get caught in one circuit of pedagogy that can lead to anti-production. This example shows how affective literacies, anti-production and the order-words are a form of non-human pedagogy, as the reciprocal relationships that develop with knowledge are not personal, but straddle non-human divides between participants in the teaching and learning context.

10. *Clearly disappointed in her test grades, Kathryn always challenges your grading of the tests. In an effort to seem accommodative, you once relented on strict scoring for one minor point, but this has only emboldened her, and she now calls openly for you to 'be more fair' with the grading.*

The point here is not to completely hand over one's pedagogy and educational experience to the anti-production and order-words of examinations. Exams are important and highly valued by society and schools; however, they can also lead to anti-production as they delimit educational possibilities. The teacher needs to make this point for Kathryn through affective literacies and affectus. Kathryn has become embroiled in the minutiae of the exam result rather than seeing the overall and broader picture of the lessons as an experience. While one has to engage with the marking of exams, the affective literacies here should direct the conversation outwards and to the bigger picture, for example, to the content, knowledge and purpose of the lessons, rather than always going inwards and to the exact reasons for a mark.

## Conclusion

Deleuze did not theorise society in disciplinary terms in the same way as did, for example, Foucault (1995). Yet, one may see from the examples above how the classroom management machine has potentially strong consequences in terms of power and discipline in the classroom. The affective literacies operate constantly in the teaching and learning context, especially because society has given education a high priority, and therefore the affect of teaching and learning lives on beyond the time accorded to the actions of teaching and learning – and this enhances both anti-production and the order-words. Deleuze (1995) speaks of the 'control society' in his later statements about social processes and the ways in which the technologies of the self have evolved recently to monitor and define how one should behave and think in any context. This chapter should not add to the impression of a control society, by enhancing classroom management to increase normatively determined modes of behaviour. Rather, the affective literacies, anti-production and order-words work together to unleash behavioural constraints from the ways in which teaching and learning is currently orchestrated in education.

Certainly, there are resonances in this philosophy with alternative modes of education that prioritise the acts of learning and look to diminish the traditional effects of schooling such as conformism, power-lessness, subjugation under the sign of capital, etc. (e.g., Reimer 1971). Yet, this chapter also points to a new way of performing the work of classroom management, one that is stimulated and stimulating due to the action of affectus (power), understands anti-production, and works with order-words to creative effect. The mode of classroom management proposed here sits within the currently defined ways of doing education, yet ceaselessly looks to overturn and remodel these processes. This work is immanent now, and should be acted upon by teachers, pre-service students and teacher trainers alike in terms of their practice of teaching and learning.

## Note

1. I would like to acknowledge the Central Florida University (CFU) teacher-training unit for supplying these examples of classroom management.

## References

Anyon, J. (2005), *Radical Possibilities: Public policy, Urban Education, and a New Social Movement*, New York: Routledge.

Cole, D. R. (2011), 'The Actions of Affect in Deleuze: Others using language and the language that we make . . .', *Educational Philosophy and Theory*, 43(6): 549–61.

Cole, D. R. (2009), 'The Power of Emotional Factors in English Teaching', *Power and Education*, 1(1): 57–70.

Darder, A., M. Baltodano and R. Torres (eds) (2009), *The Critical Pedagogy Reader* (2nd edn), New York: Routledge.

Deleuze, G. (1988), *Spinoza: Practical Philosophy*, trans. R. Hurley, San Francisco: City Lights.

Deleuze, G. (1995), *Negotiations*, trans. M. Joughlin, New York: Columbia University Press.

Deleuze, G. and F. Guattari (1984), *Anti-Oedipus: Capitalism and Schizophrenia*, trans. R. Hurley, M. Seem and H. R. Lane, London: Athlone.

Deleuze, G. and F. Guattari (1987), *A Thousand Plateaus: Capitalism and Schizophrenia*, B. Massumi trans., London: The Athlone Press.

Di Leo, J., W. Jacobs and A. Lee (2002), 'The Sites of Pedagogy', *Symploke*, 10(1–2): 7–12.

Glasser, W. (1998a), *Choice Theory: A New Psychology of Personal Freedom*, New York: Harper Perennial.

Glasser, W. (1998b), *Choice Theory in the Classroom* (revised edn), New York: Harper and Row.

Grisham, T. (1991), 'Linguistics as an Indiscipline: Deleuze and Guattari's pragmatics', *SubStance*, 20(3), Issue 66: 36–54.

Guattari, F. (1984), *Molecular Revolution: Psychiatry and Politics*, Harmondsworth: Penguin Books.

Guattari, F. (1995), 'La Borde: A Clinic Unlike Any Other' in *Chaosophy*, ed. S. Lotringer, New York: Semiotext(e), pp. 28–46.

Foucault, M. (1995), *Discipline and Punish: The Birth of the Prison*, A. Sheridan, trans., New York: Random House.

Hickey-Moody, A. (2009), 'Little War Machines: Posthuman Pedagogy and its Media', *Journal of Literary and Cultural Disability Studies*, 3(3): 273–80.

Hickey-Moody, A. and R. Haworth (2009), 'Affective Literacies' in D. Masny and D. R. Cole (eds), *Multiple Literacies Theory: A Deleuzian Perspective*, Rotterdam: Sense, pp. 79–93.

Lazzarato, M. (2006), 'The Concepts of Life and the Living in the Societies of Control' in M. Fuglsang and B. M. Sorensen (eds), *Deleuze and the Social*, Edinburgh: Edinburgh University Press, pp. 171–90.

Masny, D. (2005), 'Multiple Literacies: An Alternative or Beyond Friere', in J. Anderson, T. Rogers, M. Kendrick and S. Smythe (eds), *Portraits of Literacy Across Families, Communities, and Schools: Intersections and Tensions*, Mahwah, NJ: L. Erlbaum Associates, pp. 71–84.

Masny, D. (2006), 'Learning and Creative Processes: A Poststructural Perspective on Language and Multiple Literacies', *International Journal of Learning*, 12(5): 147–55.

Masny, D. and D. R. Cole (eds) (2009), *Multiple Literacies Theory: A Deleuzian Perspective*, Rotterdam: Sense.

McWilliam, E. (1996), 'Pedagogies, Technologies, Bodies' in E. McWilliam and P. G. Taylor (eds), *Pedagogy, Technology and the Body*, New York: Peter Lang, pp. 79–87.

Pullen, D. and D. R. Cole (eds) (2009), *Multiliteracies and Technology Enhanced Education: Social Practice and the Global Classroom*, Hershey, PA: IGI Global Publications.

Reimer, E. (1971), *School is Dead*, Harmondsworth: Penguin Books.

Rogers, B. (1998), *You Know the Fair Rule and Much More*, Hawthorn, Victoria: ACER.

Roy, K. (2008), 'Deleuzian Murmurs: Education and Communication' in I. Semetsky (ed.), *Nomadic Education: Variations on a Theme by Deleuze and Guattari*, Rotterdam: Sense, pp. 159–71.

Semetsky, I. (2006), *Deleuze, Education and Becoming*, Rotterdam: Sense.

Wallin, J. J. (forthcoming), 'Remachining Educational Desire: Bankrupting Freire's Banking Model of Education in an Age of Schizo-Capitalism' in D. R. Cole (ed.), *Surviving Economic Crises Through Education*, New York: Peter Lang, pp. 229–46.

# Chapter 6

# Deleuze and the Virtual Classroom

*Christopher M. Drohan*

## Collateral Learning

Recently, I asked students in my 'Media and Current Events' course to reflect upon the power of television in contemporary society. In one particularly candid essay, a student commented that television had always been one of the most essential parts of her family life and upbringing. As far as she could remember, the living-room television was always on in her home. It served as a conversational rallying point for all family members as they interacted with each other throughout the day. In this way, she looked at the television as an element of stability in her life – a dependable constant that helped mediate familial differences and conflict. She even went so far as to call it her first 'teacher', and talked about how in light of the respect and admiration her parents had for television news-casters and celebrities, it bore a profound measure of authority in her home. She came to regard it as the most important source of 'true information' she had access to in her youth, her most 'reliable' gauge of worldly affairs.

With mixed feelings of horror and disbelief, I – as an educator – began to imagine how alien my overwhelmingly 'traditional' classroom must seem to this pupil. In an effort to give my student's confession some context, I recalled Postman's distress at facing the daunting task of teaching the 'Sesame Street generation'. Writing in the early 1980s, he described a culture remarkably similar to that recalled by my student:

> Parents embraced 'Sesame Street' for several reasons, among them that it assuaged their guilt over the fact that they could not or would not restrict their children's access to television. 'Sesame Street' appeared to justify allowing a four- or five-year-old to sit transfixed in front of a television screen for unnatural periods of time . . . At the same time, 'Sesame Street' relieved them of the responsibility of teaching their pre-school children

how to read – no small matter in a culture where children are apt to be considered a nuisance . . . Its use of cute puppets, celebrities, catchy tunes, and rapid-fire editing was certain to give pleasure to the children and would therefore serve as an adequate preparation for their entry into a fun-loving culture. (Postman 1985: 142)

Postman's use of the word 'unnatural' here smacks of metaphysical bias, as if the world of television was something super-imposed upon the 'natural' world, a portal into a false dimension, sucking children in one at a time.[1] And yet, Postman is very quick to point out that despite being 'unnatural', television is 'nothing but educational'. What it teaches is the 'television style of learning', which is 'hostile to what has been called book-learning, or its handmaiden, school-learning'. Television does not encourage students to love school or anything about school. It encourages them to 'love television'. Borrowing Dewey's term, Postman calls this kind of learning, 'collateral learning', that teaches 'children to do what television-viewing requires of them' (1985: 144).[2] He even goes so far as to call television a 'curriculum', that has no 'prerequisites', and includes no 'perplexity', and avoids 'exposition like the plague' (1985: 145–8).

Although Postman speaks to the pedagogical value of television, his tongue-in-cheek criticisms equally apply to all the other electronic devices we currently use to entertain and educate ourselves. Any teacher who attempts to use laptops, electronic tablets, or any other popular computerised technology in the classroom today is well aware of the ways in which they can distract students as much as they can facilitate learning. Each of these devices encourages its own form of 'collateral learning', that can be just as entertaining and engaging as television – if not more so.

Accordingly, as educational institutions begin increasingly to demand that teachers incorporate computerised technology into the classroom, we should explore what it is exactly that they are inviting into the learning environment, and what it is that these devices 'require' our students 'to do'. Applying Postman's logic, each kind of electronic device comes with its own collateral curricula, which would then be competing – supposedly – alongside the class' academic one. In what follows, we aim to explore some of the broader implications of the electronic classroom, and some of the philosophic implications of 'wireless' education in particular. Throughout, we will make use of the pedagogical models put forth by Deleuze, McLuhan and Postman, combining and building upon their ideas in order to explore the concept of 'virtual learning' that is being popularly embraced by today's academy.

## The Act of Learning Versus the Content of Learning: A Difference in Kind

We shall begin our central argument by drawing a difference in kind between the act of 'learning' and the significant 'knowledge' that it arrives at. This difference is conceptualised in detail by Heidegger in his book, *What is Called Thinking?*, and can best be summarised by the following analogy:

> We shall never learn what 'is called' swimming, for example, or what it 'calls for', by reading a treatise on swimming. Only the leap in the river tells us what is called swimming. The question, 'What is called thinking?' can never be answered by proposing a definition of the concept *thinking*, and then diligently explaining what is contained in that definition. (Heidegger 1972: 21)

As a former swim instructor, I can certainly identify with Heidegger's reasoning here. I recall the endless frustration of trying to teaching young swimmers how to make and coordinate the motions of the formal strokes, each of which involves a variety of complex and counter-intuitive bodily motions that need to be individually catered to different body types. No matter how many times I would demonstrate a stroke or show my students the individual motions that comprise it – on land and in the water – these visual representations were never enough to impart its act to them. Only by breaking the stroke down into its component motions, and slowly and repetitively getting my pupils to make these necessary motions in the water, would their muscles and minds begin to understand it.

In *Difference and Repetition*, Deleuze returns to Heidegger's swimming analogy and offers some further insight into the acts of learning and thinking. In the case of teaching someone to swim, the instructor's demonstrations and abstract representations of its motions function as 'signs' of its act, the meaning of which must be individually decoded by the students in the water.[3] In this way, learning 'takes place not in the relation between a representation and an action (reproduction of the Same) but in the relation between a sign and a response (encounter with the Other)' (Deleuze 1994: 22). Between the instructor's representation of the stroke and their acting it out there is an intense relation of the pupil's body to the teacher's signs, a delicate and complicated series of student responses and instructor feedback in words, gestures, facial expressions and/or any other means of communication available.

For instance, in order to teach the difficult whip-kick used in the breast and elementary strokes I would often have to physically manipu-late a student's ankles and feet with my arms in order for the motion to be felt and understood. In these moments, our bodies worked symbioti-cally together in a feedback loop of my arm movements and their leg movements until the two became synchronised, I released their feet, and they propelled themselves away from me using the correct kick. Quite literally, a 'flow' was created between my arms and the student's legs, mediated and singularly bound by the water surrounding them and the shared desire for the swimmer to whip-kick on their own. Deleuze explains this kind of flow:

> The movement of the swimmer does not resemble that of the wave, in par-ticular, the movements of the swimming instructor which we reproduce on the sand bear no relation to the movements of the wave, which we learn to deal with only by grasping the former in practice as signs. That is why it is so difficult to say how someone learns: there is an innate or acquired prac-tical familiarity with signs, which means that there is something amorous – but also something fatal – about all education. (Deleuze 1994: 23)

Although Deleuze would not formally speak of 'flows' in his writing until his collaborations with Guattari, already we see their concept pre-ceded by this literal example. This poetic anecdote is notable not only for its existential beauty, but for the fact that it exemplifies several key ideas that are essential to Deleuze's overall conception of pedagogy. Let us consider these briefly in relation to the analogy of swim instruction.

## I. *The Act of Learning Imparts a Flow of Signs*

In the learning act, the pupil receives a set of unfamiliar signs that they are then required to adapt their being to in order to understand. Signs may literally be emitted from anything in the world (e.g., a teacher, a book, nature, etc.).[4] 'Innately', we are all existentially (i.e., 'fatally') predisposed towards interpreting and understanding signs – regardless of whether or not these understandings are 'amorous' or harmful to our subjective desires. Appearing outside our subjective understandings, signs imbue the student with curiosity, their foreign nature gripping the student with apprehension or even fear as they struggle to make sense of the sign's place in the world in relation to their own.[5]

Gazing into the black depths of the water, the aspiring swimmer understands that the water is a powerful existential challenge, and perhaps even a sign of death. As they take the plunge, their flesh encounters the unfamiliar signs of the water and its currents, as the swim instructor bombards them with signs of the critical motions that will help them navigate it. It is then up to the student to struggle to make sense of these disparate signs and to pull them together into the coherent and significant understanding of floating and moving in the water. Although not all signs are as powerful and threatening as these first signs and encounters with water, every sign involves this kind of delicate 'juggling' of previously unrelated signs into a synchronised ballet of consistent thoughts and actions.[6]

## II. *The Signs of Learning are Problematic and Require an Apprenticeship to Establish Their Meaning*

In so far as a sign is not immediately understood by a student, it concretely embodies an existential problem for them – namely, that the sign has no place in the world as they know it:

> Signs 'cause problems' through their disorienting shock, forcing thought to deal with experiences that disrupt the common, coordinated functioning of the senses and faculties . . . Through this encounter with signs, thought discovers a problematic field of differential relations and singular points that exists both within and without (the reminiscence field of Marcel-madeleine-virtual Combray being like the fluid sensori-motor field of swimmer-sea). (Bogue 2003: 337)

Deprived of any sort of general knowledge of its significance, the student must play-around with the sign, subjectively considering it in a variety of different relations to their own experiences and memories of the world until a general set of principles have been established for it. Deleuze calls this act of 'searching' for the meaning of a sign an 'apprenticeship'. Surrendering to its *otherness*, we move with the sign through the world until we significantly understand its place therein. Given the ever-changing nature of the world, the path towards understanding the sign is fraught with all sorts of difficulties and 'regressions'. In this way the sign represents a complex and essential problem for the apprentice, one that that is made all the more difficult by the fact that the sign can have infinite significance.[7]

For example, one does not need to be a swim instructor to recognise that the sign and problem of water has infinite manifestations, and that it is more than just a question of drowning, floating, or swimming. Water's problems are many: flooding, evaporation, dehydration, freezing, pressurisation, etc. Likewise, the general ways in which we deal with these problems are endless. For instance, the threat that water poses to our mortality can be dealt with in any number of ways: swim strokes, personal flotation devices, watercraft, changes of state, hydraulics, etc. When someone is tossed in the water, they respond to its mortal signs with a plethora of different emotions, movements and thoughts. As they struggle in the surf, the closer these get to the essence of the water they are immersed in the closer they get to the point where they can float and navigate its currents freely, and use water's powers in a myriad of ways.

## III. *The Signs of Learning are Virtual and Essential*

Borrowing from Bergson, Deleuze calls each sign's essential problem a 'virtual' object.[8] It was Bergson that showed us that each one of us bears a 'virtual past' that exists alongside our voluntary and involuntary memories (Bergson 1991: 133). This pure past resides immaterially and subconsciously within us, remaining 'real without being present'. 'Real' because it determines our concrete memories, but 'not present' because the actual past has disappeared in time and the origins of these images no longer exist. For instance, the same pure memory can affect one with different memory images depending on the circumstances in which it is recalled, as these memories vary according to our reasons for soliciting them and the context in which they are remembered. Concrete memory is therefore composed of *signs* of the pure past, which signify its presence without making it absolutely signified.[9]

Likewise, as we learn we encounter problematic signs towards which we then apply our memories and past learning so as to make sense of them. Upon the encounter with a sign, the exact nature of the problem it represents remains inherent within it, but as of yet unsignified. Accordingly, each sign corresponds to a virtual image of itself that is real but not presently articulated in a coherent form. Only after we have studied the sign and 'apprenticed' to its meaning are we then able to represent this image relative to our other worldly understandings.[10] So, on the one hand, the sign presents a concrete image of itself that signifies our own problem trying to understand it and its place in the world. On the other hand, and at another level, this concrete image of the sign represents a virtual, immaterial and amorphous meaning that we must struggle to figure out.

Using the words of Proust, Deleuze observes that the sign and its problem together signify an 'essence' that is 'real without being actual, ideal without being abstract', and which has the power to captivate our senses and imaginations through the insignificant production of its eventual sense (Deleuze 2000: 60). This essence inheres within all the materials it expresses, but is not signified completely by any one of them. It is 'pure matter which is entirely distinct from the matter of the common things that we see and touch but of which . . . they too had seemed to me to be composed' (Proust 2003: 270). This sign is rather searched *through* all of these 'common things' and expressed significantly *by* all of them simultaneously, so that its truth is multifarious, inter-subjective, multi-worldly, infinite and utterly 'schizophrenic'.[11]

In this way, every essence is always expressed at two different ontological levels. On the one hand, it represents ideal essences and powers that are entirely virtual, inhering within matter and inscribing forms in it, though remaining 'inaccessible to the senses' (Massumi 2002: 133).[12] On the other hand, there are the sensed, material expressions that correspond to these essences, the concrete modes of materiality that correspond exactly to these virtual truths:

> For each of our impressions has two sides: 'Half sheathed in the object, extended in ourselves by another half that we alone can recognize' (III, 891). Each sign has two halves: it *designates* an object, it *signifies* something different. The objective side is the side of pleasure, of immediate delight, and of practice. Taking this way, we have already sacrificed the 'truth' side. We recognise things, but we never know them. (Deleuze 2000: 27)

Beyond the comfort of a world filled with familiar objects, Deleuze is showing us how to question and extend our thoughts and worlds. He calls upon us to seek a higher significance for every object and relation that we recognise, to look for their 'truth', their essential 'difference' from all other things.[13]

## IV. *Learning Bridges the Concrete with the Virtual, the Significant with the Infinite*

Following Deleuze, we call 'learning' that process of engaging the essence and power of signs and apprenticing to their 'truth'. In this way every classroom represents the space in which this apprenticeship takes place, the engagement of teacher and pupil within a virtual field that exists alongside and perpendicular to their significant actions and thoughts. Regardless of the means through which the instructor tries to teach and the student tries to learn, and regardless of the media involved in this communication, a space of learning is first and foremost a virtual space wherein insignificant essences and powers become signs – both to the teacher and student. Concurrently and symbiotically, teacher and student confront these unknown signs together, sharing their respective knowledge of the world in the delicate exchange of these signs through a space that is virtual and insignificant for them both.

The swimming pool is a poignant example of this exchange, for in few other classrooms are the stakes as high. As the student in the water struggles to stay afloat and not drown, the instructor likewise hurls as many signs as they can at them to impart their ability to swim. With the prospect of death on all sides, the two are united in the insignificant and virtual space of the water's power (e.g., to kill, to support, to propel, etc.). This power is expressed as the concrete strokes and gasps of the swimmer, the concrete words and gestures of the instructor: 'Learning to swim . . . means composing the singular points of one's own body . . . with those of another shape or element, which tears us apart but also propels us into a hitherto unknown and unheard-of world of problems' (Deleuze 1994: 192). In the end, either the problem of the water is resolved, and the swimmer begins to float on their own, or the power of water proves momentarily insurmountable, and the exchange of signs fails to resolve in a significant understanding of the liquid medium at hand. The swimmer sinks, at which point the instructor's superior understanding of water allows them to dive in and rescue the student, whose exhausted body has folded into and become a mere sign of the water's power and flow.

## V. *The Effect of Teaching is Virtual (i.e., Insignificant) and 'Collateral'/'Heterogeneous'*

Effectively, the learning process is entirely virtual and insignificant, even though it is surrounded by significance (e.g., the concrete problem(s) the student faces; the teacher's various instructions; and the student's many attempts to articulate a meaningful expression to address the problem(s) at hand – regardless of whether these expressions are verbal, gestural, or thought). Although navigated, explored and apprenticed to with significant actions and thoughts, the signs and problems of pedagogy reside in the insignificant becoming of the teacher and student together in relation to a problematic situation, the object of which is concretely given, but the essence of which cannot be signified until the apprenticeship is complete.

Returning to the analogy of swimming, Deleuze calls this virtual and insignificant essence of the problem its essential 'Idea',[14] the significance of which is built around its insignificant and as of yet 'unconscious' meaning:

> To learn to swim is to conjugate the distinctive points of our bodies with the singular points of the objective Idea in order to form a problematic field. This conjugation determines for us a threshold of consciousness at which our real acts are adjusted to our perceptions of the real relations, thereby providing a solution to the problem. Moreover, problematic Ideas are precisely the ultimate elements of nature and the subliminal objects of little perceptions. As a result, 'learning' always takes place in and through the unconscious, thereby establishing the bond of a profound complicity between nature and mind. (Deleuze 1994: 165)

The student and teacher wrestle with a problematic idea in a virtual space shared by their bodies and minds. The student 'grasps that which can only be sensed', assembling the teacher's empirical signs and significations into 'little perceptions' that build upon each other into broader ideas (i.e., significant actions and thoughts) that slowly begin to synchronise to the rest of their respective understandings. At the point at which the teacher and student begin speaking or acting similarly, they begin building a solution to the 'profound' problem they face with an equally 'profound' harmony of their minds and bodies to the 'natural' and problematic world around them.

## VI. *Learning is Proactive, not Passive*

Fundamentally, the virtual problem of a sign is a problem of communication – not just between teacher and pupil – but of teacher, pupil *and* the 'natural' world surrounding them (Deleuze 1994: 165). The significant knowledge the teacher wishes to impart to the student passes through the media of communication they share as a series of amorphous signs. These signs are then perceived by the student, whereupon the student interprets and constructs a personal significance for them relative to the world they know. Every effective teacher realises that the information they wish to impart to their students is always impeded by two variables. First, the media of communication itself, which contains its own concrete limitations and virtual relations in excess of the teacher's intentions. Second, the fact that the teacher must translate their own actions and thoughts into the medium of communication, which necessarily turns the significant understandings they are trying to teach into signs of that medium for their students.

A seasoned teacher is well aware that they must lead their students by signs so as to allow them to excogitate their own understandings of them: 'We learn nothing from those who say: "Do as I do." Our only teachers are those who tell us to "do with me," and are able to emit signs to be developed in heterogeneity rather than propose gestures for us to reproduce' (Deleuze 1994: 23). Merely 'reproducing' the thoughts and actions of a teacher does nothing to help a student extend their own ability to create in and with the world around them. Rote learning of any kind turns a student into a passive receptacle for information, the proverbial 'robot' or automaton that gets programmed by their teacher in an educational model designed to teach them subservience instead of wisdom.[15] Just as there is a difference in kind between amorphous signs and the meaningful significations they become, likewise there is a difference in kind between teaching with signs and teaching with significant actions or thoughts. The former challenges the pupil to extend their knowledge into thoughts, actions and worlds that are completely novel to them, while the latter merely reinforces patterns of thought and behaviour already acquired. We will denote education based on engaging and interpreting signs 'proactive learning', because the student must extend their thoughts and actions into new territories, effectively 'producing' new meanings and understandings. While education that is based on memorising and repeating the generalised thoughts or actions of a teacher or institution we will call 'passive learning', as in this model the student is required to passively submit themselves to the order of thoughts and actions prescribed by the teacher, school and curricula.

## Virtual Learning

Now that we have explored Deleuze's concept of the virtual in relation to his concept of pedagogy, let us turn towards the contemporary classroom so that we can compare his concept of 'virtuality' to that which is being promoted in the academy. 'Virtual classrooms' have quickly become a staple of contemporary academia, the ubiquity of which is a testament to the power of their concept – a concept which has proliferated and entrenched itself with remarkable speed and effect. Here in Canada, post-secondary institutions are rapidly working together to elevate this educational form to become a new standard of academic learning and excellence.[16]

One can consider the rising popularity of virtual classes as the beginning of a new epoch in post-secondary education.[17] The academy has been split into two great camps, two great classes directly facing each other: 'virtual' and 'physical'. This divide is as much 'material' as it is 'metaphysical'. 'Material', in the sense that virtual distance-ed and online classes subtract themselves from the infrastructure of the post-secondary institution (e.g., the physical classrooms, gymnasiums, student centres, etc.). They represent a change in the very media of teaching itself, a shift from classrooms of an extended, physical space of three dimensions towards the two-dimensional screens of today's digital-visual devices. 'Metaphysical', in the sense that they challenge the sanctity of these physical institutions, as if the spirit of academia which was lodged in them has suddenly taken flight, emerging in the wired and wireless computerised devices of the students and teachers of the school.

In this way, the very concept of the academy is changing, split by the simulacrum of itself that it has created. And yet the sense in which post-secondary education is becoming 'virtual' remains ambiguous, the term 'virtual' latching itself on to a host of different meanings: virtual class-rooms, virtual campus tours, virtual residencies, virtual libraries, etc. This list is by no means exhaustive; rather it just shows how many key functions of academia have been incorporated into 'virtual learning'. Moreover the diversity of these functions attests to the symbolic nature of the virtual in general. When applied to contemporary academia, the word has no specific meaning, rather it represents the interface of these disparate senses, the blanket term by which they come together and form alternative, electronic modes of education.

From a Deleuzian perspective, it should be clear that the 'virtuality' of teaching should not be contrasted with the 'real', but should be looked at as an essential part of the lesson at hand. All learning is virtual in the sense that pedagogues, pedagogical institutions and pedagogical tech-nologies impart signs to students who in turn must interpret and make sense of them in both thoughts and actions. This process is 'virtual' because the significant pedagogical programme must be transmitted to some degree through insignificant signs. The student then interprets these into their own significant understandings, so as to create a new image of thought and action from the essence of what is taught. At every step of the way, regardless of the medium of teaching, there are concrete effects and affects that accompany this exchange, such that the empirical 'reality' of the 'virtual' is never in doubt.

Nonetheless, despite the fact that all teaching involves virtual exchanges, there are concrete differences between classrooms that are conducted in-class and those that are taught 'virtually' online. So-called 'virtual' learning experiences often bear the added sense of being some-what 'fake', 'imitative', or 'simulacral'. Within this paradigm, virtual education is seen as more of a simulation or approximation of either a 'real world' or classroom learning experience. It's not that the 'virtual' exercise is not real, rather that it fails to impart the necessary skills required for understanding and dealing with the concrete situation it purports to represent. For example, many pilots today 'learn' to fly in a flight-simulator. Typically this simulator is assembled out of various aspects of an actual mechanical flight (e.g., a real cock-pit is used, complete with instruments that look and mechanically function just like an aircraft's). Nonetheless there are certain flight variables that these simulators simply can not imitate, like the turbulence and vibrations of an actual flight. Regardless of how well an aspiring pilot does in virtual training, no responsible teacher would ever let them go straight from the simulator to a solo flight. Although there is a good chance they might fly a plane without incident, an experienced pilot knows that there are still many variables that they must learn through supervised flight instruction before they can be left on their own.

It is not that virtual education is different in kind from lived experience; rather, that it only imitates it to a certain degree. Thus, the media of every modern classroom must therefore be judged according the degree to which it 'simulates' the kind of experience it purports to represent. In turn, the question of today's virtual classroom becomes a question of the media of communication used within each class as well as the space of the classroom itself and whether both are sufficient catalysts for a high degree of simulation. Extending the sense of this question, we ask: 'What kind of collateral learning comes with a digital classroom instead of a concrete one?'; 'What kind of collateral learning is gained by having a group do their project online instead of in person?'; 'Does this space, and the teaching media within it, facilitate effective learning?'; 'What kind of an "encounter with signs" is facilitated by this lesson in this space?'; etc.[18] In order to explore these questions in more depth, I would like to combine Deleuze's concepts of pedagogy and the virtual with some of McLuhan's reflections on the state of contemporary education.

## A 'Classroom Without Walls'

McLuhan speaks of a 'classroom without walls', acknowledging that 'most learning occurs outside the classroom'. McLuhan makes this observation in respect to the 'sheer quantity of information conveyed by press-mags-film-TV-radio' and other mass media forms that bombard us with 'worlds of illusion' and 'new and unique powers of expression'. His concern was that students, when faced with this spectacle, might not have the 'judgment and discrimination' needed to sort through this information 'intelligently' (McLuhan 1957). On the one hand, there is nothing particularly novel about this statement. For those of us privileged enough to have access to formal education, the fact of the matter is that we nonetheless spend the majority of our lives working, living and learning outside of structured classes. However, what is fascinating about this fact is the challenge it presents to the contemporary pedagogue.

Teachers today are well aware that the difference between 'education and entertainment' is null and that today's students expect their education to be delivered to in forms of content and media that are fun and easy to digest and use, respectively. The modern educator asks, 'How do I, as a teacher, engage my students in the technology they are familiar with, speaking in the content they are fluent in, in such a way as to lure them into unfamiliar signs and new bodies of content?' In other words, how does a teacher access the 'classroom without walls' from within their walled or online classrooms? At every moment there is a collateral classroom working in parallel to the classroom at hand, an invisible, 'virtual' learning space that the teacher must reconcile with in order for their lessons to be taught.

As a professor, one of biggest things I struggle with is managing the 'virtual' lives of my students when they are in class. In the effort to build students' technological literacy, my school mandates that every class incorporate laptops or other personal digital devices into the classroom. As a polytechnic institution, this seems logical. Subsequent to graduation, the majority of our students will venture out looking for employment in positions that undoubtedly will require them to work regularly with applied computer technology. Having computers in the classroom is seen as a necessary part of preparing them for this kind of workspace, along with the challenges of organising, communicating and time-managing their work in and through these devices. Nonetheless, whenever I try to get a class to collectively participate in a laptop activity, the outcome is always problematic to say the least.

To begin with, most of my students are extremely adept at using their computers, and spend a great deal of their time outside the classroom socialising and entertaining themselves with them. In other words, they have all amassed a fantastic amount of collateral learning with these devices, such that inevitably the lessons of my 'concrete' classroom must compete for attention within the 'virtual' learning spaces my students have already created within these devices. Relative to the space my students encounter in their computers, my concrete class appears to move in slow motion, effectively becoming more of background layer to the intense graphics and sounds of the digital space they've already created. In this way the concrete classroom is to the digital one what elevator music is to a lobby: a 'white noise' that in no way engages one's actual attention.

Relative to the spectacle of a pupil's digital device, the modern classroom is nothing more than a lounge, an informal stop between substantial digital business meetings. These encounters take place in-between classes, at which point students can get on with what most of them consider to be their 'real' learning, that is, the exchange and reservation of digital conversations, software and media files without the added censorship of their teachers. For my students, the 'modern' classroom is anything but. They survey their classes through the lenses of their digital devices, which partake in an informational community that is universal and ubiquitous, shuffling information at speeds that approximate light's. Whether with an email, text, or chat, these students silently connect with their peers in their own virtual classrooms that happen in parallel to mine.

Furthermore, in classrooms where PDAs and WWANs are present, there is no piece of significant information that teachers can teach at their students that is not already available somewhere on the web. In fact, even the teachers will be constantly checking in with the web in order to fact-check their own answers or verify a student's comments. Whereas teaching in the twentieth century was a matter of rote memory and verifying facts, digital wireless networks have rendered these ency-clopaedic functions obsolete, instead shifting the focus of the classroom towards the skills necessary for extracting this knowledge from digital networks most efficiently. Data retention is therefore supplanted by data recovery, which revolutionises both the teleology and the techniques of pedagogy itself.

The point at which the device occupies the student's entire attention span is effectively the point at which the teachers' authority is usurped, and the concrete space of their classroom dissolves. Today's media-savvy youth spin technological circles around their pedagogues; this, in turn, means that the teacher's role becomes no more than that of a disciplinarian. More often than not, the teacher in a modern computer-enriched classroom functions like a web-administrator, patrolling their classroom for 'unacceptable' applications of these devices above and beyond the assigned lesson or task. In this way, many teachers are becoming the front line of a new state bureaucracy of digital monitors, more concerned with classroom control (i.e., the 'do as I do' of passive education) than proactive education. However, there is no necessary reason why technology imbued classrooms have to proceed in this dys-functional way. Many teachers out there are fully capable of keeping up with their digital pupils and working symbiotically with them.

In so far as the new digital devices are techniques for communicating and sharing information, the contemporary teacher cannot 'teach at' today's techno-savvy students, but must 'teach with' them. Just as the 'shop' or 'home economics' teacher of old would circulate around the class critiquing and guiding their student's manual creations, today's teacher has the opportunity to facilitate their class in and through remarkable technologies, like some digital guru or informational DJ. Yet for this to happen, and for the dynamics of the classroom to return to a state of proactive learning, our understanding of the concept of a classroom must be drastically revised. As we begin to build new, 'virtual' classrooms, we need to clarify where this imperative comes from and how it will change the idea of teaching as an apprenticeship.

## The Medium is the Lesson

In the same way that Postman uses Dewey's concept of 'collateral learning' to describe how television viewers must radically adapt their attention spans, ideas and consumer habits in order to be able to watch, understand and enjoy television, likewise every student must embody a particular style and discipline of learning in the presence of their teacher and the classroom at hand. Regardless of the teacher's intended message – and the student's interpretation of it – collaterally and simultaneously the student is taught a whole host of extraneous behaviours and understandings that dwarf the teacher's message.

Towards these digital, extraneous learnings, one is reminded of Marshall McLuhan's most famous adage, 'the medium is the message'. As a corollary of this principle, McLuhan recognised that regardless of what a teacher's or any other broadcaster's intended message is, the audience receives more of an education from the teaching or broadcasting medium itself than what passes through it:

> For the 'content' of a medium is like the juicy piece of meat carried by the burglar to distract the watchdog of the mind. The effect of the medium is made strong and intense just because it is given another medium as 'content'. The content of a movie is a novel or a play or an opera. The effect of the movie form is not related to its program content. The 'content' of writing or print is speech, but the reader is almost entirely unaware either of print or of speech. (McLuhan 1994: 18)

There are two very important pedagogical observations contained in this passage. First, that the content offered by the teacher, just like the content offered by a television, is nothing more than the proverbial 'meat on a stick'. Despite the best intentions of pedagogues and the curricula they implement, and regardless of whatever lessons they deliver to their students, the more important message is that of the medium through which they deliver said content. Although subconscious (i.e., 'virtual'), arguably students learn more through the infrastructure of the classroom and school itself than they do through the lessons taught within. Class content takes a back-seat to the medium of the classroom itself.

This leads us to McLuhan's second important point: that the content of every medium is another medium. Deleuze and Guattari would quickly make the Hjelmslevian point here that as much as the content of one medium is another, likewise both are expressions of each other. All media forms are caught in these co-dependent 'double-articulations', as one expresses the content of another and vice-versa:

> The first articulation chooses or deducts, from unstable particle-flows, metastable molecular or quasi-molecular units (*substances*) upon which it imposes a statistical order of connections and successions (*forms*). The second articulation establishes functional, compact, stable structures (*forms*), and constructs the molar compounds in which these structures are simultaneously actualised (*substances*).

Thus:

> It is clear that the distinction between the two articulations is not between substances and forms. Substances are nothing other than formed matters. Forms imply a code, modes of coding and decoding. Substances as formed matters refer to territorialities and degrees of territorialisation and deterritorialisation. But each has a code *and* a territoriality; therefore each possesses both form and substance. (Deleuze and Guattari 1987: 40–1)

For instance, consider the medium of the average physical classroom. In this space the teacher forms the 'substance' of their students just as much as the student's behaviours and responses form the 'substance' of the teacher's lesson. Both serve as the 'content' of each other. Likewise, at the molar, administrative level, the teacher – as the 'substance' of the academy's educational 'content' – is dependent upon the 'form' of the classroom (its students, administration, infrastructure, etc.) in order to conduct their lessons. Contrariwise, the classroom's 'substances' are nothing without the energy and charisma of the teacher's *formative* lessons. Extending this line of thought, we quickly realise that the classroom is rife with co-dependencies of this kind: teacher-student, teacher-administration, student-administration, teacher-teaching space, student-teaching space, teacher-technology, student-technology, etc. Every class is a complicated network of these overlapping double-articulations that run from the macro-level of school, state and economic bureaucracies down to the micro-level of student-teacher dynamics, classroom technologies, and even such incidental things as the temperature and lighting in the room. All of these relations serve to shape the style and effectiveness of the learning space, shaping the virtual limits of what can be taught there and how it can be taught.

Even online instruction – which is an obvious attempt to create a 'classroom without [concrete] walls' that can engage students in a technological format and level of convenience they are used to – cannot shed these double-articulations. Despite eliminating the specific place and time of many classes, their are limits, borders and digital walls that are erected about these classes just like concrete ones. Likewise, although online classes spare the school's administration the costs and difficulties of amassing the cumbersome infrastructure of the traditional classroom (i.e., walls, chalk-boards, desks, chairs, etc.), instead this has become the responsibility of the students themselves. The infrastructure of the school is 'subjectivised' and 'privatised' in so far as the burden is put on the student directly to find their own space, desk, computer, etc., through which they can access these online classes.[19] Far from dissolving the gross infrastructure of the traditional classroom, the online class merely displaces it, consequently displacing the concrete space of the modern classroom from the institution into the living-spaces of its students and teachers. Thus, the virtuality of the modern class is more of a function of rendering the infrastructure of the institution virtual, and not that of the specific classroom materials, lessons, or attitudes.

As school administrators continue to displace the infrastructure of the school into computer technology, the role of the teacher also comes into question. One begins to wonder if these machines could do the teaching independent of them, and if an automated computer program could supplant the role of the teacher in a class. Not only is the 'content' of teaching made obsolete by the spectacle and collateral learning of today's computer technologies, but the role of the teacher disappears as well when all a teacher has to offer is a chimera or simulation of the information and entertainment therein. As schools, administrations and curricula align themselves with the kind of representational and passive learning espoused by mass media's most popular forms of content delivery, the signs of proactive learning disappear, as do the purveyors of them – teachers.

Whereby the medium of teaching determines the quality of an apprenticeship with the signs of proactive learning, let us conclude this chapter by saying that now, more than ever, we need to critically evaluate the myth and the role of the virtual in our classrooms today. Deleuze has already begun this work, and his research shows us that philosophers of education need to realise that the virtual is more than just matter of retaining the 'essence or effect' of the classroom in a different form (e.g., McLuhan's 'classroom without walls'); it is also a matter of encouraging students to engage in the 'effective' (from the meaning of the middle-English word, 'virtuall') production of signs and their 'immanent' essences in the concrete (Peirce 1902). In this sense, education is more a matter of creating forms than of discovering them in a lesson and memorising their significance.

In turn, this necessitates highly technical – and technological – classrooms, whereby both teacher and student can explore and extend problems and signs together. Yet this also requires a new kind of teacher, one that is capable of being at home in the 'collateral' worlds of their students so as to encourage and lead them into new and 'profound' realms of understanding. The age of passive teaching is over, as rote learning is better administered by the World Wide Web than by any individual. Proactive learning demands educators who can help their students make sense of the glut of information they face in the electronic worlds they grapple with.

Finally, we should note that etymologically the term virtual comes to us from the Latin word 'vertu', which interestingly emphasises the 'virtue', 'goodness' and 'excellence' of the word, and the tendency of that which is virtual to become that which is ethical (Peirce 1902). Deleuze's concept of virtuality abounds with these overtones, and as he equates learning with an apprenticeship with signs he simultaneously offers us a different way of living and sharing our worldly experiences. His apprenticeship with the virtual essences of signs calls for a different kind of classroom, one that is more experimental than ideological, more pragmatic than disciplinary.

In their article, 'Deleuze, Ethical Education, and the Unconscious', May and Semetsky show that Deleuze introduces a number of 'concep-tual shifts' in the philosophy of education, and that this '*ethical* dimen-sion' is part and parcel of his ontology. Deleuze's revolution is fourfold:

First, it proposes a broader inquiry into who we *might* be. Second, it proposes that it is what we do *not* know, rather than what we do, that is of educational significance. Third, it asserts that much of our world, as well as our learning, are unconscious rather than conscious. This postulate accords with Deleuze's larger ontology, in which there is more to this world than appears to common sense in immediate experience. And fourth, it proposes education as committed to experimentation rather than the transmission of facts or inculcation of values. (May and Semetsky 2008: 143)

Upon these principles, Deleuze sets up his own kind of 'classroom without walls', a classroom of 'life' wherein teachers and students work through problematics together, symbiotically building their abilities together. This kind of teaching completely overthrows the 'traditional model' of 'the teacher who knows, the student who doesn't, and the material to be known'. Instead, this triumvirate structure reformulates itself according to 'the teacher who learns, the student who investigates, and the material that appears' (May and Semetsky 2008: 148). It is because Deleuzian pedagogy proceeds by signs that both teacher and student are able to learn new thoughts, actions and conceptualisations of both:

> One cannot teach the truly new in its newness, but one can attempt to induce an encounter with the new by emitting signs, by creating problem-atic objects, experiences or concepts. Hence, the pedagogy of signs entails first a critique of codes and conventions, an undoing of orthodox connections, and then a reconnection of elements such that the gaps between them generate problems, fields of differential relations and singular points. Such teaching, however, is itself a form of learning, for it proceeds via an encounter with signs and an engagement with problems. To teach is to learn, finally, since for Deleuze genuine teaching and learning are simply names for genuine thought. The goal of teaching and learning is to think otherwise, to engage the force of that which is other, different and new. What Deleuze details in his accounts of learning and teaching is that dimen-sion of education that inspires all true students and teachers, the dimension of discovery and creation within the ever-unfolding domain of the new. It is also the dimension of freedom, in which thought escapes its preconceptions and explores new possibilities for life. (Bogue 2004: 341)

When we, as educators, are asked – or commanded – to make our class-rooms more 'virtual', we should keep in mind this notion of educational 'freedom' that Deleuze promotes and interprets as an opportunity to erase the divide between collateral learning and our 'classes'. Virtual education is an opportunity to use the new technologies that are flood-ing our classrooms to extend our lessons outside of the classroom walls, and to thrust ourselves into the greater world outside the institutions we are faced with. In the spirit of Deleuze, we begin by introducing ourselves and our students to new challenges and problematics that will allow us 'to *experiment* in practice' with what we 'might make of [ourselves] and the world' (May and Semetsky 2008: 150). Relentlessly, teachers and students must push the frontiers of new modes of sharing information so as to acquaint our minds and bodies with the new signs and problems therein. In this spirit, the rigid classroom of old becomes a frenzied workshop of shared desires, and a playground of signs waiting to be discovered; while pedagogy is brought back to its classic ideals: teachers as mentors; an academy of friends.

## Notes

1. Cf. the character of Mary-Anne in *Poltergeist*, the film version of which hit theatres two years before Postman's book (dir. Tobe Hooper, USA: Metro-Goldwyn-Mayer, 1982).
2. For more on Dewey and the particular role that every medium plays in shaping one's learning experience, see Semetsky's detailed juxtaposition of Dewey and Deleuze in Semetsky 2006.
3. In the early twentieth century, many English pools would have frog aquariums on deck as the frogs' swimming motions were used to illustrate the most popular stroke of the period – the breast-stroke (Sprawson 2000: 22–3).
4. As Deleuze and Guattari remark, 'the world begins to signify before anyone knows *what* it signifies; the signified is given without being known. Your wife looks at you with a funny expression. And this morning the mailman handed you a letter from the IRS and crossed his fingers. Then you stepped in a pile of dog shit. You saw two sticks on the sidewalk positioned like the hands of a watch. They were whispering behind your back when you arrived at the office. It doesn't matter what it means, it's still signifying' (Deleuze and Guattari 1987: 112).
5. A detailed account of the existential crisis posed by the sign can be found in Drohan 2009: 23–9.
6. In his article 'Semiosis and the Collapse of Mind-Body Dualism', Andrew Stables reiterates this point saying, 'Each act of a teacher, be it instruction, explanation, question or whatever, is then both an invitation and a threat. It invites the student to develop her worldview in some way. Indeed, it might be said that each teaching gesture is a (more or less) controlled challenge to the student's self-identity, for the very act of presenting a new piece of information or asking someone to undertake a new activity is a way of telling them their world is not quite as it was before: that what they thought was right is not quite right, or that their ways of doing certain things before will not be quite the same in the future' (Stables 2009: 27–8).
7. In *Proust and Signs*, Deleuze spends an entire chapter describing how everyone that searches signs 'does not know certain things at the start, gradually learns them, and finally receives an ultimate revelation. Necessarily then, he suffers disappointments: he "believed," he suffered under illusions; the world vacillates in the course of apprenticeship. And still we give a linear character to the development of the Search' (Deleuze 2000: 26).
8. For a complete synopsis of this concept in relation to education, see Daignault 2008: 43–60.
9. The whole passage is worth quoting in full: 'That the past does not have to preserve itself in anything but itself, because it is in itself, survives and preserves itself in itself – such are the famous theses of *Matter and Memory*. This being the past in itself is what Bergson called the virtual. Similarly in Proust, when he speaks of states induced by the signs of memory: "Real without being present, ideal without being abstract." It is true that, starting from this point, the problem is not the same in Proust and in Bergson, it is enough for Bergson to know that the past is preserved in itself . . . While Proust's problem is, indeed:

how to save for ourselves the past as it is preserved in itself, as it survives in itself? . . . Let us note Proust's reaction: "We all possess our memories, if not the faculty of recalling them, the great Norwegian philosopher says according to M. Bergson . . . But what is a memory which one does not recall?"' (Deleuze 2000: 58–9).

10. For a concise explanation of '*real virtuality*', see DeLanda 2002: 33–8.

11. 'Schizophrenic' relates to the analytic model of the self. Deleuze and Guattari arrive at a different unconscious populated by independent flows of desires – a 'desiring machine' (see Deleuze and Guattari 1987: 18).

12. Massumi's phenomenological account of the virtual offers a number of enlightening 'parables' of sense to illustrate this idea.

13. 'Essence is not only particular, not only individual, but is individualizing. Essence individualizes and determines the substance in which it is incarnated, like the objects it encloses . . . This is because essence is in itself difference' (Deleuze 2000: 48). For an extensive account of this principle in relation to Deleuze's broader 'Spinozist' ontology, see Drohan 2010: 257–8.

14. In contrast to the significant ideas that follow from our apprenticeship. The difference between essential 'Ideas' and significant 'ideas' (represented visually by a difference in the case of their first letters) appears for the first time in *Difference and Repetition*. A full account of this can be found in Drohan 2009: 120–6.

15. As early as 1979, Lyotard recognised that in the 'postmodern' classroom, education was being treated by many as a form of 'capital' and learning as a commodity: 'It is not hard to visualize learning circulating along the same lines as money, instead of for its "educational" value or political (administrative, diplomatic, military) importance; the pertinent distinction would no longer be between knowledge and ignorance, but rather, as is the case with money, between "payment knowledge" and "investment knowledge"' (Lyotard 1999: 6). When educators are given the imperative to implement computerised learning into the classroom, a similar sentiment is at work. Justified by the pretext that this will better prepare students for the workplace, instead we are effectively seeing students treated as mere human capital, that – much like the machines they are using – are simply being programmed for optimal working conditions. In this framework, the teacher functions much like a site or network administrator, ensuring that the school's program (read 'curriculum') is effectively downloaded (read 'learned') and implemented by the classroom's machines (read 'students'), and that 'ineffective programs' and 'machines' (read 'misbehaviour' and 'students', respectively) are culled from the room.

16. This alliance already has a name, 'Canada's Virtual University', which is currently accredited by nine public universities. See: www.cvu-uvc.ca/partners.html

17. One Philosophy professor at York University has even gone so far as to declare it to be a 'change [that] will dwarf in scope and impact that of the massive building phase of the red-brick university campus developments that followed the Second World War' (Phillips 2009). The article was quickly castigated by one of Phillips' peers (Pettigrew 2009).

18. This last question comes from Deleuze who says that in order for one to learn, one must 'constitute' the 'space of an encounter with signs' (Deleuze 1994: 23). In other words, every classroom must be capable of admitting a large number of these encounters and of tolerating a high degree of experimentation in the effort of its students to understand them.

19. For more on the relation between cyber-technologies and 'social subjection' see Deleuze and Guattari 1987: 456–8.

# References

Bergson, H. (1991), *Matter and Memory*, New York: Zone Books.

Bogue, R. (2004), 'Search, Swim and See: Deleuze's apprenticeship in signs and pedagogy of images', *Educational Philosophy and Theory*, 36(3).

Daignault, J. (2008), 'Pedagogy and Deleuze's Concept of the Virtual' in I. Semetsky (ed.), *Nomadic Education: Variations on a Theme by Deleuze and Guattari*, Rotterdam: Sense, pp. 43–60.

DeLanda, M. (2002), *Intensive Science and Virtual Philosophy*, New York: Continuum.

Deleuze, G. (1994), *Difference and Repetition*, trans. P. Patton, New York: Columbia University Press.

Deleuze, G. (2000), *Proust and Signs: The Complete Text*, trans. R. Howard, Minneapolis: University of Minnesota Press.

Deleuze, G. and F. Guattari (1987), *A Thousand Plateaus: Capitalism and Schizophrenia*, trans. B. Massumi Minneapolis: University of Minnesota Press.

Drohan, C. M. (2009), *Deleuze and the Sign*, New York: Atropos Press.

Drohan, C. M. (2010), 'To Imagine Spinoza: Deleuze and the Materiality of the Sign', *The Philosophical Forum*, XLI(3): 257–8.

Heidegger, M. (1972), *What is Called Thinking?*, Toronto: Harper and Row Publishers.

Lyotard, J-F. (1999), *The Postmodern Condition: A Report on Knowledge*, Minneapolis: University of Minnesota Press.

McLuhan, M. (1957), 'Classrooms Without Walls', *Explorations*, 7 (May).

McLuhan, M. (1994), *Understanding Media: The Extensions of Man*, Cambridge, MA: MIT Press.

McLuhan, M. (1999), *The Medium and the Light*, Toronto: Stoddart.

Massumi, B. (2002), *Parables for the Virtual: Movement, Affect, Sensation*, Durham, NC: Duke University Press

May, T. and I. Semetsky (2008), 'Deleuze, Ethical Education and the Unconscious' in I Semetsky (ed.), *Nomadic Education: Variations on a Theme by Deleuze and Guattari*, Rotterdam: Sense.

Peirce, C.S. (1902), 'Virtual', in *Dictionary of Philosophy and Psychology*, ed. James Mark Baldwin, New York: Macmillan.

Pettigrew, T. (2009), 'Debunking the Virtual University Myth', *McLeans.ca*, 7 October <http://oncampus.macleans.ca/education/2009/10/07/debunking-the-virtual-university-myth> (accessed 20 September 2012).

Phillips, P. J. J. (2009), 'Enjoy Your Last Days on Campus: Another forecast of changes coming to university education', *University Affairs*, 5 October <www.universityaffairs.ca/enjoy-your-last-days-on-campus.aspx> (accessed 20 September 2012).

Postman, N. (1985), *Amusing Ourselves to Death*, Toronto: Penguin Books Canada.

Proust, M. (2003), *In Search of Lost Time Vol. VI: Time Regained*, New York: The Modern Library.

Sprawson, C. (2000), *Haunts of the Black Masseur: The Swimmer as Hero*, Minneapolis: University of Minnesota Press.

Stables, A. (2009), 'Semiosis and the Collapse of Mind-Body Dualism' in I. Semetsky (ed.), *Semiotics Education Experience*, Rotterdam: Sense, pp. 21–6.

# ASSEMBLAGE III: MATHEMATICS AND SCIENCE

# Chapter 7

# Philosophical Problematisation and Mathematical Solution: Learning Science *with* Gilles Deleuze

## David Holdsworth

Education theorists (e.g., Masny and Cole 2009; Semetsky 2005, 2006, 2008) have taken up the thought of Gilles Deleuze as the inspiration for an approach to pedagogy that recognises the complexity of the learning experience and that creatively takes us towards its limit. In this essay, I begin from the observation that Deleuze's remarks about the master-pupil relation and about learning are often embedded in a context where he is discussing mathematics. Although there is no truly standard view about what mathematics is, and how we learn it, it is typically taken to be intimately connected with both numbers and geometry. In this sense it is typically taken to be *about* something. Moreover, it is taken to be fundamental for *science as such*. We learn quite early in school to differentiate numerals (signifiers in a language) from numbers (abstract signifieds in the world), thus inaugurating a sequence of lessons that leads to a representational conception of mathematical objects in the popular and professional imagination. This conception of mathematics extends to the *standard view* of representational theories in science *as such*. Although it is essential not to treat science in general to be the same as mathematical science, the focus in this research has been on formal aspects of scientific practice.

This chapter addresses the ways in which mathematical and scientific practice in the twentieth century has taken us to the limits of formal language – limits that can be thought of as transcendental, both in the semantic sense of Ludwig Wittgenstein, and the pragmatic sense of Karl-Otto Apel (1980). But this ascent to the principles is, at the same time, a descent into the consequences – it is both ironic and comedic in Deleuze's sense – for it is only at the limit of mathematical abstraction that we learn to theorise the concrete. Here we discover the mathematical simulacrum – the axiomatic space of objects that have no original, although they exhibit all the structure of those *experienced* objects that motivated the axiomatisation in the first place.

At the level of these experiences there is already a kind of reflexivity entering into the mathematical practice itself; like all forms of reflexivity, this takes us beyond the limits of formal language to complexity as such, which cannot be *thought* mathematically or reduced to numerical/ geometrical models.[1] As we learn from Deleuze, this encounter with complexity is productive and takes us beyond the limits of either the Platonic or the Hegelian dialectic[2] to a political space in which we encounter the forces of creative intensity.

I develop my arguments in three aspects: First I observe that in *Difference and Repetition* (Deleuze 1994) Deleuze's remarks about *apprenticeship* and *learning* often occur in the context of discussions of mathematics. Second, I interpret Deleuze's general views about the *dialectic of the problem* and the *mathesis universalis* to show that, for Deleuze, differential notions that are properly mathematical arise in a variety of scientific contexts, reinforcing the view that, despite the *univocity of being*, mathematical and scientific practices are actualised *plurivocally*. Third, I trace one development in modern mathematics that illustrates the ascent to the limits of *the mathematical proposition* where we encounter the *folding* of logic (arithmetic) and geometry. I argue that no specific pedagogic strategy is called for to promote Deleuzian scientific education over and above that being promoted already by the philosophy of nomadic education (Semetsky 2006, 2008) or multiple literacies theory (Masny and Cole 2009).

The chapter concludes with a reflection on the pedagogic consequences for the teaching of *mathematical science*. It is proposed that, contrary to recent innovations in mathematical pedagogy, as well as orthodox approaches that return to the rote learning of techniques, experimental methods are possible and desirable at all levels of mathematical science-learning, including the teaching of higher algebra. It is argued that to be consistent with a Deleuzian conception of the *mathesis universalis*, science teaching must abandon its dominant (and contradictory) dispositions, on the one hand, to valorise the concrete, while, on the other hand, treating abstraction as the ultimate expression of Truth. The resultant challenge for science education is to develop a pedagogic strategy that is adequate to Deleuze's interpretation of *mathesis* as a universal science of life.

## Preliminary Reflections on Mathematical Education

There are many difficulties in coming to terms with the implications of Deleuze's thought for science education: First, there is a difficulty differentiating questions about the importance of mathematics within Deleuze's thought as sources of his ideas and questions that can be raised about the philosophy of mathematics and mathematics itself. On the one hand, it is clear that mathematical theories – perhaps most notably those of Bernhard Riemann – were indispensible as sources of key Deleuzian concepts such as the concept of *multiplicity*. But these appropriations are filtered through Henri Bergson and others and appear within Deleuze's thought in philosophically transformed ways that are not to be confused with the ideas of a mathematical scientific practice, about which Deleuze has a great deal to say. Second, those passages where Deleuze speaks directly of *apprenticeship* and *learning* arise often in contexts where he has been talking about mathematics:

> The exploration of ideas and the elevation of each faculty to its transcendent exercise amount to the same thing. These are two aspects of an essential apprenticeship or process of *learning*. For, on the one hand, an apprentice is someone who constitutes and occupies practical or speculative problems as such. Learning is the appropriate name for the subjective acts carried out when one is confronted with the objectivity of a problem (Idea), whereas knowledge designates only the generality of concepts or the calm possession of a rule enabling solutions. (1994: 164)

The most conspicuous occasion where we find an explicit remark in *Difference and Repetition* about teaching is embedded within an extended passage that reflects Deleuze's views about mathematics:

> The theory of problems is completely transformed and at last grounded, since we are no longer in the classic master-pupil situation where the pupil understands and follows a problem only to the extent that the master already knows the solution and provides the necessary adjudications. (1994: 180)

The specific context in which this remark occurs is an extended discussion of Niels Abel and Évariste Galois as the illustration of a 'revolution more considerable than the Copernican', in which the relationship between problem and solution is reversed. Under Deleuze's interpretation, 'instead of seeking to find out by trial and error whether a given equation is solvable in general, we must determine the conditions of the problem which progressively specify the fields of solvability in such a way that "the statement contains the seeds of the solution"' (1994: 180). Deleuze goes on to say that

> the group of an equation does not characterise at a particular moment what we know about its roots, but the objectivity of what we do not know about

them. Conversely, this non-knowledge is no longer an insufficiency but a rule of something to be *learnt* which corresponds to a fundamental dimension of the object. (1994: 180, original emphasis)

We find within this account many aspects of Deleuze's general take on *problems and solutions*. Problems (Ideas) are themselves multiplicities whose reality resides within the structure of the virtual. Like Heidegger's *question*, problems do not evaporate with the discovery of solutions; more importantly, they are *not propositional*. As Deleuze and Guattari say in *What is Philosophy?*: 'All types of propositions are *prospects*, with an information value' (1994: 138).

According to Deleuze, with Abel and Galois 'the mathematical theory of problems is able to fulfil all its *properly dialectical requirements*' (1994: 180). That is, it does not arise out of a negation that collapses non-knowledge back into the identity of the concept, and the *recognition* of propositional content. Indeed, it opens up to what can be learned by any student who encounters mathematical problems. Deleuze goes on immediately to observe a tendency within modern mathematical practice to treat group theory and set theory as fundamental to mathematical understanding. Acknowledging that there is here, in the history of mathematics, a kind of break that can be fitted into a sequence from analytic geometry to differential calculus to group theory, he remarks that this is not what matters.[3]

What is important for Deleuze is rather 'the manner in which, at each moment of that history, dialectical problems, their mathematical expression, and the simultaneous origin of their fields of solvability are interrelated' (1994: 181). What is important is not the moment in the history of mathematics when differential calculus is created and later accounted for in group-theoretic and algebraic terms, but the generic philosophy of difference that this episode both makes visible and enables us to articulate. And so Deleuze says: 'There is as yet nothing mathematical in these definitions. Mathematics appears with the fields of solution in which dialectical Ideas of the last order are incarnated, and with the expression of problems within these fields' (1994: 181).

It is not only mathematics, but the problematic/dialectic itself which is differential, giving rise in a variety of actualisations of other scientific fields of inquiry. He says:

Herein lies the adventure of Ideas. It is not mathematics which is applied to other domains but the dialectic which establishes for its problems, by virtue of their order and their conditions, the direct differential calculus corresponding or appropriate to the domain under consideration. In this sense there is a *mathesis universalis* corresponding to the universality of the dialectic. (1994: 181)

Seen through a Deleuzian lens, then, there is no specific insight to be brought to mathematical and scientific education that is not already carried by a problematic/dialectical approach to education in general. If this is right, then a paper on Deleuze and science education must set its practical objectives elsewhere than the articulation of a new pedagogic strategy for mathematics and science. Its objective must be to show that, from a Deleuzian point of view, the teacher of mathematics must *learn* by inviting the student to *do with me*. It must be a nomadic education of participation (cf. Semetsky 2008; Semetsky and Delpech-Ramey 2011).

## Tracing the Mathematical Proposition I: The Question of Being

In this section, I suggest that science education must go hand in hand with a reflection on the nature of mathematical and scientific practices while taking into account questions with regard to the 'enclosure of the school' (Deleuze 1988a). We must ask what is being taken for granted about the constitution of propositions, the practical meaning of 'logic', the functioning of negation, the dynamics of information exchange, and so on. For Deleuze:

> Learning may be defined in two complementary ways, both of which are opposed to representation in knowledge: learning is either a matter of penetrating the Idea, its varieties and distinctive points, or a matter of raising a faculty to its disjoint transcendent exercise, raising it to that encounter and that violence which are communicated to the others. (1994: 194)

Throughout his philosophical career, but most conspicuously in *Difference and Repetition*, Deleuze's project was to think difference without collapsing it into identity under a concept – to free difference from what he saw as the constraints of representation and its four 'iron collars': identity in the concept, opposition in the predicate, analogy in judgement, and resemblance in perception.

Deleuze writes: 'The sameness of the Platonic Idea which serves as model and is guaranteed by the Good gives way to the identity of an originary concept grounded in a thinking subject' (1994: 265). This characterises representation, for Deleuze, as the site of transcendental illusion. This is not the only illusion. The second illusion concerns the subordination of difference to resemblance and the way in which it becomes no longer necessary to consider only resemblance of the model to the copy, but possible to compare the sensible to itself while making the identity of the concept applicable to it. The third illusion concerns 'the negative and the manner in which it subordinates difference to itself and "betrays" the power of intensity to affirm difference by subsuming difference within extensity', and, I add, without lifting affirmation itself to the level of consciousness. Later, Deleuze writes:

> Everything, however, is reversed if we begin with the propositions which represent these affirmations in consciousness. For Problems-Ideas are by nature unconscious: they are extra-propositional and sub-representative, and do not resemble the propositions which represent the affirmations to which they give rise. If we attempt to reconstitute problems in the image of or as resembling conscious propositions, then the illusion takes shape, the shadow awakens and appears to acquire a life of its own: it is as though each affirmation referred to its negative, or has 'sense' only by virtue of its negation, while at the same time a generalised negation . . . takes the place of the problem. (1994: 267)

So for Deleuze propositions do represent affirmations, but affirmations are the virtually differentiated positivities of the real, not yet actualised or differenciated as the propositions that represent them, and which cannot be rendered in terms of isomorphic images of resemblance. But isomorphism is a mathematical concept; and even in denying that it applies to the relation between the affirmation and the proposition, we must be careful. How are we to understand the proposition in Deleuze's corpus and how is it different from the proposition in orthodox philosophies – especially philosophies of science?

We can start from a passage from Inna Semetsky's work on the self-organised classroom: In the section on Deleuze's 'non-philosophy' of language (Semetsky 2005) she draws our attention to the requirement for Deleuze of a new means of philosophical expression that exceeds rational thought, to the affirmation that language alone, itself a multiplicity, can be properly said to have structure, and that anything can possess a structure in so far as it maintains even a *silent discourse*. Language is not necessarily linguistic and subject to analysis but exists, along with philosophy itself, in an essential relationship to non-philosophy. Most importantly, the new form of expression that Deleuze will take from Spinoza functions *semiotically* by virtue of the 'triadic logic of included middle' (Semetsky 2003: 28).

But what are propositions? It is useful to turn briefly to the notion of the ontological proposition to gain some clarity on this question. Starting from Deleuze's commitment to the univocity of Being, I shall focus on Deleuze's reading of Spinoza, whose ideas are appropriated by Deleuze and *reversed*. These moments of reversal are crucial to a reading of Deleuze. Following his reversal of Plato, Deleuze will engage with respectful readings of major philosophical figures in order to open up the moment of reversal that will move his own philosophy forward. In Spinoza, Deleuze will find an account of expression which establishes the triadic logic referred to by Semetsky, an account of expression that attributes to it three aspects: substance, attribute and essence, which taken together are the first triad of expression. Substance expresses itself through the attributes. What is expressed is an essence that belongs properly to the substance. Deleuze writes: 'What is expressed has no existence outside its expression, but is expressed as the essence of what expresses it' (Deleuze 1992: 43). There is a second triad of expression (relating attributes, modes and modifications) which is the productive level, and an infinite number of levels beyond that, but what is important for us is the general way in which the complex relations arise between the elements of the expression – that which expresses itself, the expression itself, and that which is expressed. These are the relations of folding and unfolding (implication and explication) that are so important in Deleuze.

The *ontological proposition* of the univocity of Being is of particular importance. In *Difference and Repetition* the ontological proposition is given a specific content and functions to relate three terms – being, difference and sense – determining the complex relations among them within expression. Deleuze writes:

> Substance must itself be said *of* the modes and only *of* the modes. Such a condition can be satisfied only at the price of a more general categorical reversal according to which being is said of becoming, identity of that which is different, the one of the multiple, etc. (1994: 41)

In this way being and difference in Aristotle is reversed and substance and modes in Spinoza is reversed. As a consequence of this reversal univocal Being will be said of difference.

Semetsky's rendering of this in the context of her work in philosophy of education also draws our attention to the complexity of expression:

> Being is . . . *univocal* indeed, but 'because the diagrammatic multiplicity can be realised only and the differential of forces integrated only by taking divergent paths' being necessarily becomes plurivocal when, due to the immanent differences, it happens to be diversified, articulated and enacted in its actual manifestations. (Semetsky 2003: 30; quoting Deleuze 1988a: 38)

It is important to investigate how the *folding* and the *complexity* occur within the ontological proposition itself for Deleuze. We can think of it in terms of three 'perspectives'. The quotation marks are crucial here, since we are precisely required to suspend a binary logic of excluded middle, but it is possible to move towards a better comprehension of Deleuze if we reflect on each pair: 'being and sense' from the 'perspective' of difference; 'being and difference' from the 'perspective' of sense; and 'difference and sense' from the 'perspective' of being. Here are the essential points:

*Being and Sense*: distinct attributes express themselves in numerically distinct modes, expressing their univocal sense.

*Being and Difference*: It is here where we encounter the 'categorical reversal of predication'. Deleuze says 'Being is said in a single and same sense of everything of which it is said, but that of which it is said differs: it is said of difference itself' (Deleuze 1994: 36).

*Difference and Sense*: Difference is itself multivocal from the 'perspective' of being; it can refer to individuating differences within being, it can refer to differenciation/actualisation, or it can refer to extrapropositional processes of differentiation.

I have been emphasising in this section the complexity of the ontological proposition itself, as well as a corresponding complexity to manifestations of propositions as expressions of affirmation in Deleuze. We are particularly interested in plurivocal manifestations in the form of *mathematical propositions*. I will show in the next section that the traditional conception of propositions already gives rise to a trajectory of mathematical development that takes us to the limits of what can be thought about complexity. I argue, in effect, that analytic philosophy meets Deleuze at this point.

## Tracing the Mathematical Proposition II: Frege, Russell

The received view, actively promoted by orthodox mathematical education, is that mathematics is *about* something, for example, that arithmetic is *about* numbers and *geometry* is about space. This *aboutness* of mathematics, despite its predominance in the teaching of mathematics, is not true to the practice and even the sentiment of mathematicians in the last two hundred years.[4] I want to focus, however, on a particular trajectory relevant to interpreting Deleuze and his relation to mathematics and science. There are two objectives in this section. The first is to clarify the treatment of propositions in orthodox approaches to the philosophy of mathematics. Although there was, and still is, considerable disagreement within the orthodox tradition, there is a common acceptance of a representational model, and for this reason the orthodox framework is fundamentally different from a Deleuzian framework. The second objective is to sketch a movement of thought within the orthodox tradition towards a conception of mathematics where we encounter the *mathematical simulacrum*. The mathematical simulacrum arises as a site where 'models' exist in the absence of an ontological original, and do so in such a way that diverse structures are folded together so that it is no longer possible to speak of a particular structure represented by the mathematical theory.

## *Representational Renderings of Propositions*

Russell and Frege treat propositions differently; however, both represent a point of view dramatically different from that of Deleuze. Frege and Russell differed, among other things, on the *question* of whether or not a concept can be the logical subject of a proposition, a question which for Deleuze would be nonsensical. In the Appendix to *Principles of Mathematics*, Russell (1903) discussed in detail the differences between his views and those of Frege. One issue that cannot be ignored is the difference in usage by Russell of 'concept', and by Frege of '*Begriff*', but this much can clearly be said – that concepts cannot be the subject of propositions for Frege, whereas Russell (in the period prior to roughly 1905) believed that we can predicate something of concepts in a sentence. For Frege, concepts belong to the field of references; a concept is the referent of a grammatical predicate. Russell, on the other hand, regarded concepts as constituents of propositions, which in turn are the referents of sentences.

From the point of view of Deleuze, this entire debate is ill-founded and can only be understood in the context of the principle of the propositional function. It is this that is the target of Deleuze and Guattari (1994) in their chapter on 'Prospects and Concepts' where it is argued that the propositional function is to be seen as a reduction of philosophy (that which creates concepts) to science (that which produces functions). So we see here clearly how far removed Deleuze (and Guattari) are from the Frege/Russell tradition, a tradition that is still embedded in ontology of identity and an epistemology of reference.

## The Emergence of Mathematical Simulacra

In the *Essay on the Foundations of Geometry*, Russell (1897) developed his views on geometry within a broadly Kantian framework, but one that was revisionist. Whereas Kant had taken for granted that logic was that described by Aristotle and geometry that described by Euclid, in his *Essay* Russell takes exception to this view. He specifically develops in detail the resources of the new *projective* geometry, arguing that it is the projective structures that are *a priori*, not the structures of Euclid nor the structures of the new non-Euclidean geometries, such as that of Riemann. In this way he made the more general non-metric spaces fundamental to the *a priori* of space. Hence it is clear that some notion of logic as a fundamental presupposition is at work in his *Essay*.

By 1903, when Russell wrote *Principles of Mathematics*, his views on *modern* logic had become more explicit. Indeed, the opening sentence of *Principles of Mathematics* offers us a definition: 'Mathematics is the class of all propositions of the form "*p implies q*", where *p* and *q* are propositions containing one or more variables . . . and neither *p* nor *q* contain any constants except logical constants' (Russell 1903: 3). Shortly thereafter, on page 10, we are given a definition of logic: '(Symbolic or formal) logic is the study of the various general types of deduction', going on to point out that since Boole's 1854 *Laws of Thought* the subject had undergone 'considerable technical development'. Indeed, on page 4, Russell had asserted that the Kantian doctrine (that all mathematics is grounded in intuition) could now be definitively refuted because all of mathematics could be deduced from these developments.[5]

There seems to have been, from the beginning of Russell's projects, throughout the period from 1897 to 1903, a mutual interdependence between logic and geometry. The *Essay* must take logic for granted in order to assess the general non-metrical features of geometry, and the *Principles* (anticipating the *Principia*) took the Boole/Peano analysis of logic for granted, an analysis that depends ultimately on the non-metrical properties of spaces reduced to sets and classes. So I ask: can this be understood as an example of something like a Deleuzian (or Heideggerian) fold?

My thesis is that it can be so understood, an understanding that can be discovered most clearly in the subsequent history of both logic and geometry. I must limit myself here to this formal assertion, reinforced by reference to the development of algebraic logic (Lawvere 1972) and algebraic geometry (Grothendieck 1961) – the development of what John Bell has called *synthetic differential geometry* (Bell 2000). My claim is this: that these developments, at the end of extensive research in various branches of algebraic topology and algebraic logic, filtered through the development of axiomatic treatments of category theory (Herrlich and Strecker 1973) and topos theory (Goldblatt 1979), enable us to rethink the relationship between mathematics and structure.

To see this in general intuitive terms we need only consider an example at the level of *category theory*. In category theory we talk about the assemblage of mathematical objects and structure-preserving morphisms between the objects characteristic of a particular structure, such as the structure of a topological space, or the structure of a partially ordered set. The theory is equipped with a generalised notion of equivalence in terms of which 'it can be shown' that the category of $T_0$-topologies is equivalent to the category of partially ordered sets (for example). And yet, the formal languages that articulate these two kinds of structures are of different orders. So, in a sense, one and the same 'theory' is a theory of radically different structures. My thesis is that we can understand the mathematical expressions of logic/sets and topology/geometry in the same way, thus providing a rigorous way of saying, using the resources of contemporary axiomatic mathematics, that these structures are fundamentally implicated within each other, even though they are explicated in experience in fundamentally different ways (see also Holdsworth 1979). It is in this sense that contemporary axiomatic theory takes us to the limit of our capacity to theorise structure.

## Questioning at the Limits of Complexity

In 'Ideas and the Synthesis of Difference', Chapter IV of *Difference and Repetition*, Deleuze says that modern ontology is inadequate. It is clear that what he means by 'modern ontology' is cognate to that of Heidegger, and specifically that aspect of Heidegger's thematisation of post-metaphysical thought that characterises questioning and the question as something that is never eliminated at the point of its answering. On page 195, just before he addressed the inadequacy of modern ontology, Deleuze had said of the ontology of the question: 'Far from being an empirical state of knowledge destined to disappear in the response once a response is given, the question silences all empirical responses which purport to suppress it, in order to force the one response which always continues and maintains it.' By way of explaining the inadequacy of this ontology of the question, Deleuze acknowledges that although this modern ontology does play upon indeterminateness as an objective power (agreeing with his notion of the indeterminate within the problematic field), it will 'introduce a subjective emptiness which is then attributed to Being, thereby substituting for the force of repetition the impoverishment of the already said . . .' (1994: 196). Even more importantly, Deleuze writes:

> Sometimes it even manages to *dissociate the complex*, thereby entrusting questions to the religiosity of a *beautiful soul* while relegating problems to the status of external obstacles. However, what would a question be if it were not developed under the auspices of those problematizing fields alone capable of determining it within a *characteristic science*? (1994: 196, emphasis added)

If the practice of mathematics is a science characteristic of the problematising field of thought about structure, taking us to the limits of the mathematical simulacrum where multiple structures can be thought simultaneously without any one structure as the one *about* which we are thinking, then it seems a small step to see this as the limits of complexity, that is, the point beyond which we encounter *the complex as that which cannot be thought from the inside.*

Consider the branch of science thought to be *about* complexity itself. It is helpful to consider here John Protevi's (2006) presentation of complexity theory and chaos theory. I emphasise two aspects of Protevi's paper: First, we must be clear that in the case of chaos theory we are interested in the growth of unpredictable behaviour from simple rules, whereas complexity theory is concerned with the emergence of relatively simple functional structures from complex dynamics and, conversely, the development of new and different levels of complexity in a system. Second, when we talk about *complexity theory* or *chaos theory* we do not mean, strictly speaking, a mathematical theory as such. To understand how complexity theory explains, for example, the *emergence* of functional structures, there are three components, or what Protevi calls linked concepts. Namely: (1) those concerning the system being modelled; (2) those in the dynamical model; and, (3) those in the mathematics used to construct the model. The point is that mathematics (specifically, the mathematical theory of manifolds in the sense of Riemann) is only one aspect of the *theory*.

Within the framework of interconnected concepts it is possible to provide an account of diachronic emergence as well as a specific notion of chaos while invoking the mathematical theory of manifolds as a shared resource. At the level of the category of manifolds it is not possible to say that the mathematical theory itself is about either complexity or chaos, but in the context of divergent characteristic sciences it is relevant to both. The mathematical theory of manifolds brings us to the limits of complexity as such. At the level of the *mathematical category* the systems of objects being studied are not about particular structures, but take us abstractly to the limits of structure beyond which we encounter a generic notion of complexity – that which apparently cannot be thought.[6] The specific mathematical category of manifolds also encounters that limit, but in the context of an active questioning within the problematic fields of complexity and chaos themselves as mathematical practices within these characteristic sciences. Thus, chaos and complexity become folded (implicated) within the mathematical simulacrum (the category of manifolds), and unfolded (explicated) across the diverse scientific practices characteristic of the problematic fields of interest.

I have focused in the last two sections on a demonstration that mathematical science in the twentieth century has forged a path, without deviating from its commitment to the primacy of formal representational language, to interpretations of *theories* that anticipate aspects of Deleuze. It should be emphasised, however, that I intend neither to reconstruct Deleuze for analytic philosophers, nor to correct aspects of Deleuze's project.[7] I seek only to identify a site where Deleuze and the analytic tradition encounter each other. I turn now to the implications of this for science education.

## Formulating Questions in Practice and in Teaching: Learning Science with Deleuze

How can we imagine an educational strategy that prepares students to think about mathematics and science in an open, experiential way, taking seriously the multivocity of scientific practice implied by the Deleuzian perspective; and how would we teach higher mathematics, and mathematical science, to such students at the university level? In order to address these (and other) questions, a broader framework of education theory would be required emphasising 'Deleuze's relational dynamics of experience and his triad of affects-percepts-concepts' (Semetsky 2009). The exact relationship of this triad to the general underlying triad difference-being-sense (foregrounded in this essay) will reveal much about the learning of science.

Deleuze begins to articulate aspects of a method in *Bergsonism*, introducing a sequence of 'rules' (1988b: 15):

First Rule: *Apply the test of true and false to problems themselves. Condemn false problems and reconcile truth and creation at the level of problems.*

This is followed by one of Deleuze's most forceful remarks about schooling:

> We are wrong to believe that the true and the false can only be brought to bear on solutions, that they only begin with solutions. This prejudice is social . . . Moreover, this prejudice goes back to childhood, to the classroom: It is the school teacher who 'poses' the problems; the pupil's task is to discover the solution. In this way we are kept in a kind of slavery. (Deleuze 1988b: 15)

> Second Rule: *Struggle against illusion, rediscover the true differences in kind or articulations of the real.*
> Third Rule: *State rules and solve them in terms of time rather than of space.*

Deleuze does not give us much insight into how these rules can give rise to a pedagogic strategy in general, much less one for teaching mathematics and science. By way of an initial gesture towards finding tactical elements of such a strategy, I want to conclude by considering an influential book on category theory where we are invited to think about principles of advanced mathematics in terms of *slogans*. It may well be that these slogans can be seen as the Foucauldian *statements* of mathematics, the transverse multiplicities that unite the *seeable* and the *sayable* at the level of practice that Deleuze found so congenial. Here are the slogans:

> Slogan I. Many objects of interest in mathematics congregate in concrete categories.
> Slogan II. Many objects of interest to mathematicians are themselves concrete categories.
> Slogan III. Many objects of interest to mathematicians may be viewed as functors from small categories to Sets.
> Slogan IV: Many important concepts in mathematics arise as adjuncts, right or left, to previously known functors.
> Slogan V. Many equivalences and duality theorems in mathematics arise as an equivalence of fixed subcategories induced by a pair of adjoint functors. (Lambek and Scott 1986: 4, 5, 6, 15, 18)

Although these 'slogans' use terminology that is accessible only to a specialist in categorical logic, the thrust of them should be intuitive. If Lambek and Scott are right to think that a student of categorical logic is best served by a list of such slogans (and much follows the presentation of each slogan in terms of detailed mathematical expression), then this can only be because the student is exposed to the *problematic field* of the subject in terms that are accessible to them by virtue of their experience! It is clearly required that we imagine something similar at each stage of experience as pupils come to terms with number and space throughout their learning within a variety of characteristic sciences. There is a practical challenge here that reaches almost to the level of a paradox – we might call it the new 'paradox of learning'.[8] A Deleuzian philosophy of education will need to 'teach' its students to discover the *concrete* at the limits of *abstract* practice. Deleuze himself is a kind of model. His own understanding of mathematics and complexity science was clearly profound. But he found within these mathematical frameworks a philosophical significance that transcends the mathematical practice. He saw, for example, in Riemann's mathematical multiplicities a philosophical notion that was 'bigger' than the structure of manifolds as formal systems.

So students of mathematics in particular and science in general must have the capacity for both concrete and abstract activities. All learning, including science, involves the complex play of the triad of affect, percept and concept if that learning is to be Deleuzian, but this does not obviate the need to handle difficult symbolic material. *The learning of science is, at the same time, a becoming-philosopher and a becoming-interdisciplinary.* Interdisciplinary learning with Deleuze, however, is not just a negotiation among diverse practitioners. Ultimately it emphasises what diverse practices have in common, practices as apparently dissimilar as literary theory and mathematical physics (Holdsworth 2006).

My arguments in this paper have moved in two directions: (1) the ascent to the limit of formal mathematical expression where we encounter complexity as that about which something can be said, but that cannot be thought (from the inside); (2) the descent from higher algebra to the level of elementary experience with number and space, where questions are posed within experience, and problems, as the *sense* of these questions, are encountered. Deleuze is a helpful guide *with* whom we can learn a great deal about mathematics, about the importance of mathematical concepts in the processes of philosophical problematisation, and the ways in which solutions are to be encountered, even when they themselves take the form of a mathematical proposition.

These considerations about mathematical practice and the learning of mathematics call for little of a strategic nature that is not already being explored by multiple literacies theory or nomadic education. This is not to say that a more pragmatic paper, informed by a Deleuzian perspective, could not be written on techniques of science education; however, it would be tactical rather than strategic. The question at the level of educational practice is how to *see* and *articulate* the mathematical statement/slogan as a Foucauldian/Deleuzian diagram. Early in Deleuze's career he wrote an introduction to Jean Malfatti de Montereggio's study of *mathesis* where he says that 'mathesis will be fulfilled only in a true medicine [that is, science] where life is defined as knowledge of life, and knowledge as life of knowledge' (Deleuze 2007: 143). At the end of his life he wrote *Pure Immanence: Essays on A Life* (Deleuze 2001).

Much remains to be said as we move from the dialectic of the problematic in mathematics and science to the *mathesis* of life and from the ontological proposition to the implication/explication of affect/percept/concept, but there is a unity to Deleuze's own life that motivates an attempt. With Deleuze we learn not only how to engage with characteristic sciences without reducing concepts to functions – we learn also to *think* without 'entrusting questions to the religiosity of a *beautiful soul*' (Deleuze 1994: 196, quoted above), but, at the same time, without losing respect for the *beautiful mind* of the accomplished philosopher.[9]

## Notes

1. My thesis here is that complexity as such cannot be theorised in the sense that it cannot be represented. Although complexity theory captures aspects of the complex, it does not represent it.
2. Deleuze's objection to Plato – that which will give rise to a reversal – concerns the way in which Plato collapsed difference back into identity through the four figures of the Platonic dialectic: 'the selection of difference, the installation of a mythic circle, the establishment of a foundation, and the position of a question-problem complex' (Deleuze 1994: 63). But neither will Deleuze turn to Hegel, whose dialectic treats difference as the negative. Deleuze will turn to Nietzsche, through his particular interpretation of the eternal return, and a recuperation of the *simulacrum*.
3. All the same, I will discuss developments in the recent history of logic and geometry that emphasised the appearance of what John Bell (2000) has called *synthetic differential geometry*. These are the mathematical structures where we encounter differentials synthetically, a notion I take to be consistent with Deleuze's differential philosophy.
4. One can cite multiple examples, from Poincaré's work on topology (arguably a precursor to twentieth-century French enlightenment thought from Bachelard to Foucault), to Bourbaki. It depends, of course, on how we read them since one could say that topology is *about* connectedness in non-metric spaces, and Bourbaki, to be sure, were dedicated to showing that mathematics is *about* structure.
5. This claim appears in the 1903 book notwithstanding the logical paradoxes that were to delay the publication with Alfred North Whitehead of the *Principia Mathematica* until 1911.
6. It should be emphasised that this notion that complexity *cannot be thought as such* can be asserted only with respect to orthodox notions of thought as cognition. It is not intended to preclude a notion of 'thought from the outside', as developed by Foucault in his reflections on Blanchot (Foucault 1990), or Deleuze, especially as found in his sympathetic reading of Foucault (Deleuze 1988a).
7. I concur with James Williams (2006) in his critique of DeLanda (2002).

Rendering Deleuze for an audience of analytic philosophers necessarily misses the broader insights of Deleuze's appropriations from formal theories. I also concur with what Williams says in his critical introduction and guide to *Difference and Repetition* that Deleuze's treatment of representation would benefit from 'debate with the Fregean analytic tradition' (Williams 2003: 39).

8. See Semetsky 2009 for a lucid account of the Socratic paradox as found in Plato's *Meno*. Semetsky models Deleuze's affective non-thought on the complex, Gaussian, plane, hence arguing, in a way, that complexity can render itself to unorthodox representation albeit not in the system of Cartesian coordinates of analytic geometry. Her model confirms the priority, for Deleuze, of the presentations of the unconscious, unthought, versus conscious, conceptual, commonsensical representations as cognition.

9. *A Beautiful Mind*, dir. Ron Howard, USA: Universal Pictures, 2001.

# References

Apel, K. O. (1980), *Towards a Transformation of Philosophy*, trans. G. Adey and D. Frisby, London and Boston: Routledge and Kegan Paul.

Bell, J. L. (2000), 'The Incredible Shrinking Manifold: Spacetime from the Synthetic Point of View', presented at the University of Western Ontario, Conference on Spacetime, London, Canada <http://publish.uwo.ca/~jbell/The%20Incredible%20 Shrinking%20Manifold.pdf> (accessed 2 September 2011).

DeLanda, M. (2002), *Intensive Science and Virtual Philosophy*, London and New York: Continuum Books.

Deleuze, G. (1988a), *Foucault*, trans. S. Hand, Minneapolis: University of Minnesota Press.

Deleuze, G. (1988b), *Bergsonism*, trans. H. Tomlinson and B. Habberjam, New York: Zone Books.

Deleuze, G. (1992), *Expressionism in Philosophy: Spinoza*, trans. M. Joughin, New York: Zone Books.

Deleuze, G. (1994), *Difference and Repetition*, trans. P. Patton, New York: Columbia University Press.

Deleuze, G. (2001), *Pure Immanence: Essays on A Life*, trans. A. Boyman, New York: Zone Books.

Deleuze, G. (2007), 'Mathesis, Science, and Philosophy – Introduction to Etudes sur La Mathése ou Anarchie et Hièrarchie de la Science', trans. D. Reggio, *Collapse*, *III*: 141–55.

Deleuze, G. and F. Guattari (1994), *What is Philosophy?*, trans. H. Tomlinson and G. Burchell, New York: Columbia University Press.

Dukic, V. (2011), *Ontology and (non)-Ontology: Deleuze, Heidegger and the Being of the Question*, Trent University, MA Thesis, unpublished.

Foucault, M. (1990), 'Maurice Blanchot: The Thought from Outside' in J. Mehlman and B. Massumi (eds), *Foucault – Blanchot*, New York: Zone Books, pp. 9–58.

Goldblatt, R. (1979), *Topoi: The Categorial Analysis of Logic*, Amsterdam and New York and Oxford: North Holland Publishing Company.

Grothendieck, A. (1961), *Catégories fibrées et descentes*, Paris: Séminaire de Géometrie Algèbrique de l'Institut des Hautes Etudes.

Herrlich, H. and G. Strecker (1973), *Category Theory*, Boston, London and Sydney: Allyn and Bacon.

Holdsworth, D. G. (1979), *A Functorial Semantics for Quantum Logic: Towards a Realist Interpretation of Logical Structure in Quantum Theory*, University of Western Ontario, PhD Thesis, unpublished.

Holdsworth, D. G. (2006), 'Becoming Interdisciplinary: Making Sense out of DeLanda's Reading of Deleuze', *Paragraph*, 29: 139–56.

Lambek, J. and P. J. Scott (1986), *Introduction to Higher Order Categorical Logic*, Cambridge, London and New York: Cambridge University Press.

Lawvere, F. W. (1972), *Toposes, Algebraic Geometry and Logic: Lecture Notes in Mathematics, Volume 274*, New York, Heidelberg and Berlin: Springer-Verlag.

Masny, D. and D. R. Cole (2009), *Multiple Literacies Theory: A Deleuzian Perspective*, Rotterdam and Boston: Sense.

Protevi, J. (2006), 'Deleuze, Guattari and Emergence', *Paragraph*, 29: 19–39.

Russell, B. A. W. (1897), *An Essay on the Foundations of Geometry*, Cambridge, London and New York: Cambridge University Press.

Russell, B. A. W. (1903), *Principles of Mathematics*, New York: W. W. Norton.

Semetsky, I. (2003), 'Philosophy of Education as a Process-philosophy: Eros and communication', *Concrescence: The Australasian Journal of Process Thought*, 4: 23–34.

Semetsky, I. (2005), 'Not by Breadth Alone: Imagining a Self-Organised Classroom', *Complicity: An International Journal of Complexity and Education*, 2: 19–36.

Semetsky, I. (2006), *Deleuze, Education and Becoming*, Rotterdam: Sense.

Semetsky, I. (ed.) (2008), *Nomadic Education: Variations on a Theme by Deleuze and Guattari*, Rotterdam: Sense.

Semetsky, I. (2009), 'Deleuze as a Philosopher of Education: Affective knowledge/ effective learning', *The European Legacy: Toward New Paradigms*, 14(4): 443–56.

Semetsky, I. and J. Delpech-Ramey (2011), 'Educating Gnosis/Making a Difference', *Policy Futures in Education*, 9(4): 518–27.

Williams, J. (2003), *Gilles Deleuze's Difference and Repetition: A Critical Introduction and Guide*, Edinburgh: University of Edinburgh Press.

Williams, J. (2006), 'Science and Dialectics in the Philosophies of Deleuze, Bachelard and Delanda', *Paragraph*, 29: 98–114.

# Chapter 8

# From Brackets to Arrows: Sets, Categories and the Deleuzian Pedagogy of Mathematics

*Rocco Gangle*

The movement of the swimmer does not resemble that of the wave. (Deleuze 1994: 23)

## Teaching Universals: Mathematical Pedagogy

What would it be to conceive the teaching and learning of mathematics in a Deleuzian spirit? It would be among other things to invent new modes of practice linking mathematics to other forms of thought and experience. It would mean coming to terms with the unique and explicit place of *mathesis* in Deleuze's thought as a whole, from the earliest studies of mathematical 'esotericism' and the key role of differential calculus in *Difference and Repetition* to the later collaborations with Guattari and the final, unfinished project on sets (*'Ensembles'*). Throughout this development, a rejection of *mathesis* understood as mere measurement is coordinated with an orientation towards creative genesis and the overcoming of any facile division between abstractive and materialised processes. Certainly Deleuze recognised a privileged place for mathematics within philosophy, but always in a quite unorthodox sense as a 'dialectics' or *mathesis universalis* that would slip across historically sedimented distinctions between physics, chemistry, alchemy, art, magic, philosophy, science and life (Semetsky and Delpech-Ramey 2011). For Deleuze, mathematics in the usual sense would be only a one-sided and restricted presentation of a much more general practice or combination of practices. The present aim is to unfold certain *pedagogical* consequences of this understanding of universal *mathesis*.

The highly compressed yet crucial discussion of mathematics and philosophy in Chapter IV of *Difference and Repetition* concludes by arguing for a 'dialectics' as distinguished from a 'metaphysics' of differential calculus in particular (Deleuze 1994: 178). It is this distinction of 'dialectics' and 'metaphysics' that then underwrites Deleuze's interpretation of what is generally taken to be mathematics in the scholarly arena as merely the field of solutions relative to a more extensive, real and positive dialectical field of problems (1994: 179). Deleuze acknowledges the influence of the mathematician Albert Lautman in characterising the dialectical nature of a *problem* according to three coordinated aspects: 'its difference in kind from solutions; its transcendence in relation to the solutions that it engenders on the basis of its own determinant conditions; and its immanence in the solutions which cover it' (1994: 178–9). Difference, transcendence and immanence: these constitute the dialectic through which a problem is simultaneously related to and distinguished from its solutions. This in turn defines the relation of problems to 'symbolic fields' of expression:

> Just as the right angle and the circle are duplicated by ruler and compass, so each dialectical problem is duplicated by a symbolic field in which it is expressed ... Mathematics, therefore, does not include only solutions to problems; it also includes the expression of problems relative to the field of solvability which they define, and define by virtue of their very dialectical order. (Deleuze 1994: 179)

For Deleuze, mathematics therefore does not merely apply to the world as a theory to one of its possible models, but rather motivates a dialectical apprenticeship to the world as a lived, experimental practice: *mathesis*. This process of apprenticeship corresponds to a 'universal sense' of mathematics that would be opposed to the 'precise sense' in which mathematics – and particularly differential calculus – would be restricted to a mere 'instrument'. For this reason, 'there is no difficulty with any supposed application of mathematics to other domains' (Deleuze 1994: 181). Deleuze in this way rejects the dualist 'application' model of the relationship of mathematics to the world in favour of an immanent or structural 'incarnation' of mathematical Ideas. Indeed this latter conception ensures the genuine universality of mathematical thought:

> Ideas always have an element of quantitability, qualitability and potentiality; there are always processes of determinability, of reciprocal determination and complete determination; always distributions of distinctive and ordinary points; always adjunct fields which form the synthetic progression of a sufficient reason ... In this sense there is a *mathesis universalis* corresponding to the universality of the dialectic. (Deleuze 1994: 181)

Throughout Deleuze's work, the relationship between mathematics and philosophy is linked to themes of apprenticeship and semiotics. In this light, it becomes clear that philosophical *mathesis* (at the very least in its restricted sense) must consider the ways mathematics is actually learned and created, that is, appropriated, extended and transformed over time. In this way, a concern for mathematical pedagogy arises naturally even within the purely theoretical engagement of Deleuze's philosophy with respect to mathematics. Practical questions of mathematical pedagogy (in the broad sense of teaching and learning) are already intrinsic to Deleuze's philosophy of *mathesis*.

We know that apprenticeship to mathematics in the usual sense is not an abstract affair, but rather involves an array of concrete practices with overdetermined histories: classroom pedagogical techniques, textbook conventions, forms of mathematical notation, and so forth. We are all engaged in this practical apprenticeship to one degree or another in our ordinary and professional lives, from balancing a chequebook or interpreting statistical data to invoking the structuralist methods of Lévi-Strauss. And because of its immense practical importance, learning mathematics remains a central pillar of general educational training at all levels, from elementary through undergraduate, in both public and private schools. Yet despite this practical importance, the theoretical results of contemporary mathematics remain largely unknown even among the educated general public and are considered at any rate almost wholly politically neutral.

Although mathematics is the scientific domain where strict universality is taught, it is difficult to imagine a cultural-political struggle over mathematics curricula with stakes presumed as great as those in biology (evolution), history (national history canons and standardisations), economics (neo-liberal versus socialist or Marxist models) or even physics (creationist/Big Bang cosmologies). There can be little doubt that claims to universal truth in science and more generally in the application of rational method are at the heart of the legacy of the Enlightenment as well as the various strains of its contemporary defences and critiques. Yet strangely, the universality of mathematical truth in particular is seldom questioned or even discussed in detail in such investigations. Consider, for instance, the almost total absence of detailed investigations into mathematics in a thinker as otherwise broadly concerned with the genealogy of modernity as Foucault. This general disregard seems to be related directly to how the abstractness of mathematics is understood. Because mathematical truth is usually thought to be purely abstract, its methods of study and exploration are often considered to be relatively inert. These latter are thought to become practically (and politically) relevant only through their diverse applications in the 'real world'.

Yet in Deleuze's thought, *mathesis* and apprenticeship coordinate an equally theoretical and practical intersection of mathematics and philosophy. It is clear that the universal and apodictic knowledge of mathematics is necessarily mediated by particular persons, historical institutions, contingent techniques and conventional notations. The rigour of Deleuzian immanence requires that these seemingly irreconcilable aspects of mathematical apprenticeship be conceived interdependently. Are there specific mathematical tools and techniques that will allow us to do this?

Over the past several decades, a unique branch of mathematics called *category theory* has emerged as a powerful generalisation of mathematical structures that among many other things allows various domains of mathematics to be understood in their determinate and determinable relationships to one another. In what follows, I argue that what it might mean to teach and learn mathematics in a Deleuzian philosophical spirit may be demonstrated through category theory's structures and methods, in particular through their instigation of rigorous as well as creative forms of diagrammatic exploration. With respect to the set-theoretical foundations that have dominated mathematics since the early twentieth century, category theory today offers new directions and a distinct vision of mathematical reality. This vision broadly accords with Deleuze's dialectical conception of *mathesis*, and this accord in turn helps to illuminate the Deleuzian notions of practical apprenticeship and diagrammatics. What thus emerges in what follows is a clear path towards a powerful and transformative Deleuzian mode of mathematical teaching and learning.

## Rival Math-Images: Categories Versus Sets

We cannot presume acquaintance with the relevant mathematics and will try to introduce the necessary concepts with as much clarity and rigour as possible. We will begin by contrasting category theory with its better-known cousin, set theory. These two branches of mathematics represent quite distinct approaches to mathematics and offer two differing conceptions of mathematical truth, what in a Deleuzian spirit we will call divergent *math-images*. These, we argue, correspond in important ways to Deleuze's central contrast between the rival 'images of thought' in *Difference and Repetition*.

As is well known, in *Difference and Repetition* Deleuze (1994) distinguishes between two forms of thinking that condition or could condition philosophy, the one ordered through representation and the other structured through difference and repetition. These contrasting images of thought are distinguished by Deleuze in his introduction according to their respective orientations towards *generality* on the one hand and *repetition* on the other, each of these orientations implying in turn its own form of philosophical practice:

> *Generality* presents two major orders: the qualitative order of resemblances and the quantitative order of equivalences. Cycles and equalities are their respective symbols. But in any case, generality expresses a point of view according to which one term may be exchanged or substituted for another. *The exchange or substitution of particulars defines our conduct in relation to generality* . . . *Repetition* as a conduct and as a point of view concerns non-exchangeable and non-substitutable singularities. Reflections, echoes, doubles and souls do not belong to the domain of resemblance or equivalence; and it is no more possible to exchange one's soul than it is to substitute real twins for one another. If exchange is the criterion of generality, theft and gift are those of repetition . . . *To repeat is to behave in a certain manner, but in relation to something unique or singular which has no equal or equivalent.* (Deleuze 1994: 1, emphases added)

What do these two orientations of thought have to do with the teaching and learning of mathematics? In particular, how may the apodictic universality of mathematical truth be coordinated with a form of thought devoted to the 'theft and gift' of 'something unique or singular which has no equal or equivalent'? General representations make up the terrain of our most familiar, reflexive image of thought, particularly of mathematics. Yet philosophy on Deleuze's understanding is, or should be, oriented towards repetition and singularity. The difficulty for Deleuze thus rests not only in carefully distinguishing the two images of thought, but more importantly in finding ways to express the image of difference and repetition in appropriate ways. The basic method of philosophy shifts accordingly for Deleuze from reflection or recognition to practical relation.

This question is at once pedagogical and philosophical. As Durie has emphasised, 'a delineation of the relation between maths and philosophy in the case of the singularity that is Deleuze precisely poses philosophy a *problem* – the problem of how to *become relational*' (2006: 183). In category theory, mathematics itself becomes relational. In fact, category theory reveals the effectively relational essence of all mathematics by providing a purely relational milieu for examining structural mappings and translations across various mathematical terrains. By distinguishing category theory from its older and more famous cousin, set theory, we will be able to bring this relational character of category theory into clearer view. In addition, the contrast of these two highly general mathematical fields will open up avenues for thinking quite broadly of the connections – Deleuzian and no longer Kantian in spirit – between 'pure' and 'practical' mathematical reason.

Category theory is a recently evolved branch of mathematics investigating the structured relations between certain abstract structured systems called categories. It is usefully contrasted with set theory in so far as both of these forms of mathematics provide highly general frameworks within which all other fields of mathematics may be conceived and formalised. Set theory is often described as a 'foundation' for mathematics, and category theory is sometimes portrayed as an alternative or rival foundation. Yet ultimately the inner dynamics of category theory mitigate against thinking in terms of foundations at all. Category-theoretical 'foundations' are in fact best understood as a rigorous un-grounding or non-foundation. It is this aspect of category theory that links it naturally with a Deleuzian conception of mathematics and a possible Deleuzian pedagogy. In what follows, the mathematical specialist will be asked for leeway allowing for a partially intuitive (as opposed to formal) introductory presentation of this often highly technical material. It is presumed that the expert will be competent at reading between the lines where necessary. At any rate, several excellent mathematical introductions to category theory exist, particularly those of Lawvere and Schanuel (1997), Awodey (2010), and, for the more ambitious, MacLane (2010). We are concerned here with mathematical pedagogy first and foremost, although strictly mathematical considerations are by no means foreign to such concern. The justification for our somewhat mixed procedure will hopefully become clear in the final section.

Set theory originates with the ground-breaking work of Georg Cantor at the beginning of the twentieth century. Cantor (1955) already emphasised that the essential character of a set is to gather dispersed individuals into the unity of a single collection. Such a collection abstracts away from any particular qualities of its elements or any relations they may share. A set of green things is not green, for instance. It is this that finally guarantees the univocity of set theory. Set theory concerns one kind of thing, sets, defined solely by their elements and nothing else. Indeed, set theorists generally restrict themselves to the ordinal series of sets built up from the empty set (as well as subsets of these). In this way, sets are treated simply as sets of other sets, with the important exception of the empty set itself – {} – which is the unique set with no elements whatsoever. Every set is thus uniquely determined by the elements that belong to it.

The standard notation of set theory represents this well. A set is represented by placing a collection of elements (or some expression designating such a collection) between curved brackets: {a,b,c} or {x: 0<x<1}. This notation captures quite naturally the operation of gathering or collecting by separating off and isolating. What is listed inside the brackets is inside the set; what is not between the brackets is not in the set. The abstract dynamics relating such sets were axiomatised by Zermelo in 1908, with later modifications by Fraenkel. The axioms of the resulting standard Zermelo-Fraenkel set theory are assertorical – they make existence claims. Among other things, they guarantee that when certain sets exist, certain other sets exist as well. For instance, if the sets {a} and {b} exist, then the 'paired' set {{a},{b}} also exists. In this way, larger and more complex sets may be built up from smaller sets. Indeed, all the sets needed for standard mathematics may be built up in this way from the empty set alone, which thus serves as a kind of atomic formal foundation for set-theoretical mathematics as a whole – as Badiou (2007) in particular has emphasised and exploited to great effect.

Given the system of sets regulated by the Zermelo-Fraenkel axioms, all the objects and structures of mathematics may then be represented by specific codings of sets. For example, the natural numbers with zero (0, 1, 2, 3 . . .) may be represented by the finite ordinal series of sets in which each successive term is simply the collection of all the terms that precede it ({}; {{}}; {{},{{}}}; {{},{{}},{{},{{}}}} . . .). Such notation is clearly impractical, and set-theorists generally make speedy recourse to substitutions ('When we mean '{{},{{}},{{},{{}}}}', we will write '3' instead'). Integers, rational numbers and reals become definable in similar ways, by building up increasingly complex objects. The elegance of set-theoretical foundations for mathematics stems primarily from what might be called their univocity. Vastly different kinds of mathematical objects and structures (numbers, functions, groups, vector spaces, formal proofs and so on) may be represented by one and the same kind of object: sets. More specifically, all *relations* between mathematical objects are themselves treated as (generally larger and more complicated) objects. Everything is a set, including relations between sets.

In category theory, by contrast, the primitive components of the theory are of two distinct kinds: *objects* and *arrows*. Just as with sets, the basic intuition is conveyed quite well by the standard notation. An arrow is specified by a letter (conventionally lowercase) and is understood to go *from* exactly one object (usually represented by an uppercase letter) *to* exactly one object. Thus 'f: A→B' signifies that the arrow called 'f' goes from the object designated 'A' to the object designated 'B'. The object at the tail of the arrow is called the arrow's *domain*, that at the head or point of the arrow its *co-domain*. An arrow may go from an object to that very same object, in which case the domain and co-domain coincide, for instance in the arrow x: A→A.

In contrast to sets, in which objects (sets) are determined internally, the objects and arrows that make up a category are determined entirely relationally or structurally. In effect, the arrows of a category take precedence over its objects. As we will see, this ultimately entails a diagrammatic form of representation in which multiple, co-determining relations are exposed simultaneously. However, several axioms restrict the possible relations among the arrows, thus guaranteeing a minimum of structure common to any category whatsoever. Unlike at least some of the axioms of Zermelo-Fraenkel set theory, these axioms of category theory are relatively easy to grasp in an informal and intuitive fashion. We summarise them here:

1. Axiom of Composition: If the co-domain of any arrow, say *f*, and the domain of some other arrow, say *g*, consist of the same object, then there is a uniquely determined arrow, called the *composition* of *f* and *g*, which goes from the domain of *f* to the co-domain of *g*. In other words, given an arrow *f*: A→B and another arrow *g*: B→C, there always exists exactly one arrow uniquely determined by *f* and *g*, written *gf* ('*g* following *f*') that goes from A to C, that is, *gf*: A→C. It may be helpful to think of this *composition-arrow* as binding *g* to *f* to form an extended pathway, one which goes directly from A to C and in a certain sense absorbs the mediating function of the object B.

2. Axiom of Associativity: In any category, the order of compositions does not matter when composition-arrows are themselves composed. In other words, if arrows *f* and *g* compose (according to the specifications of the previous axiom) and arrows *g* and *h* do as well, then the composition of all three arrows taken together, *hgf* ('*h* following *g* following *f*'), is a single and unique unambiguous arrow. Formally, $(hg)f = h(gf)$.

3. Axiom of Identity: Every object in a category is equipped with an *identity arrow*. This arrow goes from that object to the very same object. For instance, given an object A, the identity arrow will take the form *i*: A→A. This identity arrow composes with other arrows so as to leave them invariant – formally, $ix = x$ and $xi = x$ for any arrow *x*. In other words, identity arrows function as inert or static transformations, much like multiplying any variable or formula by 1 in basic algebra ($1x = x$). In category theory, the identity of a particular object is thus determined as one specific form of relation.

If set theory reduces relations to objects by building up larger and more complex sets, category theory treats objects of whatever kind from a specific *relational perspective* such that the relations involved satisfy the above axioms. Any system that does so is a category. In this way category theory considers its objects solely in terms of some particular kind of relation they may have to one another (as well as, importantly, the relations of these relations). While the mathematical 'universe' of sets is composed of exactly one kind of object: sets; every category in the 'universe' of categories is made up of its own characteristic duality of object *and* relation: the category of sets *and* functions between them, of groups *and* group homomorphisms, of topological spaces *and* continuous maps, and so on. Such dualities may be relatively abstract (as in these examples) or, on the other hand, quite concrete. For instance, any given collection of people, say the attendees at a particular academic conference, form various categories based naturally on certain of their many relational properties. Among these, for example, would be the category whose objects are the given attendees and whose arrows represent the relation 'is the same age or older than'. In this category a single arrow goes from A to B if and only if attendee A is the same age or older than attendee B. The reader may easily check that the category formed in this way satisfies the axioms specified above.

Perhaps the clearest illustration of the contrast between these two math-images is provided by comparing the set-theoretical notion of *function* with its category-theoretical analogue. Roughly, a function may be understood in general as the assignment to each and every element of a given set (the function's *domain*), of a single value drawn from some other set (the function's *range*). Such functions, or mappings, are ubiquitous in mathematics and often have an intuitively 'operative' structure which may be expressed with a formula, for example the 'double-the-input' map $f(x) = 2x$. Regardless of any such internal structure, however, all functions are represented formally in set theory as sets of ordered pairs (subject to certain restrictions) where every ordered pair <x,y> is itself represented by the set {{x}, {x,y}}. For instance, the function $f(x) = 2x$ as applied to the natural numbers will be represented as follows (with the conventional numerals '1', '2', '3' ... substituting here for the headache-inducing series of brackets indicated above): {{{1},{1, 2}},{{2},{2, 4}},{{3},{3, 6}} ...}. In other words, the function $f(x) = 2x$ will be expressed in set theory as one particular set that is composed of infinitely many other sets, each of which has exactly two elements which in turn encode one element each of the function's domain and range. This form of representation is clearly sufficient to uniquely determine the function. But the intuitive and pedagogically useful picture of a mathematical function as an operational assignment or transformation of terms ('take any number and double it') is forsworn in favour of an encoded hierarchy within a single, complex, static object. In short, for set theory a function is just another object, another set.

In contrast, when functions are treated in a category-theoretical manner, it is in the context of the role they play in a specific category where they retain their essentially relational difference from the objects they relate, namely sets. Thus functions serve as the arrows of the particular *category of sets and functions*. In this category, the objects are understood to be all possible sets and an arrow between two objects represents a possible function from the one set into the other. Thus in this category an arrow f: A→B represents some unique function that maps elements of the set A onto (some) elements of the set B. In general, then, there may be many arrows between any two objects, since there are many possible functions between any two (non-empty, non-singleton) sets.

In distinction from set theory, there are no means within the category of sets and functions for ascertaining directly the elements of a given set or the 'ordered pairs' constituting a particular function. In effect, individual sets and functions are treated within their co-determined category as 'black boxes' indiscernible in themselves. They become distinguishable only through reference to their particular locus in the whole system (precisely, the category) constituted by the ways the various arrows (in this case, functions) *compose* with one another. Rather than a function being conceived as an isolated mapping whose internal structure would be represented by a set of ordered pairs, a function is conceived here by category theory simply as a uniquely determined arrow linking a domain object to a co-domain object within a specified category. Any internal structure it may have is determined solely by the category's system of arrows in so far as the compositions of these latter are necessarily regulated by the category theory axioms. It is these interactive or 'pragmatic' relations-of-relations alone that determine both the category as a structural whole *and* the particular elements composing that structure (in this case, particular sets and functions). While set theory determines functions by *concretising* them into objects, category theory determines them by *abstracting* them into components of meta-relational compositions.

For this reason, category theory finds its natural expression in structural diagrams. The objects of a category may be represented by 'free-floating' letters and the arrows of the category by arrows connecting those letters to one another (or a single letter to itself). In particular, it is often convenient to formulate a category-theoretical problem or result in terms of what is called a *commutative diagram*. A diagram of objects and arrows is said to *commute* when, roughly, all apparently distinct pathways of however many intermediate head-to-tail arrows from any designated object to another are treated as one and the same. A nice intuition of this is given by picturing the arrows gluing or zippering themselves together along any such pathways.

We will take a very simple example, and the basic point should become clear. Here too the potential usefulness of this rigorous diagrammatic method for mathematical teaching and learning should begin to become evident. In Figure 1, the arrows marked *f*, *g* and *h* constitute a commutative diagram if and only if the composition arrow *gf* ('*g* following *f*') – which, it should be recalled, necessarily exists in any category – is identical to *h*. In an informal and intuitive sense (though not thereby an insignificant one) either (1) the reader of the diagram may trace the path from A to B along *f* and then from there to C along *g*; or (2) the reader may go directly from A to C along *h*. In either case (1) or (2) within the perspective of the category, the 'same thing' has been done. If the reader takes a moment to 'complete' the diagram in Figure 1 by adding the requisite identity arrows (inert 'loops' from A to A, B to B, and C to C), what results is a simple but quite interesting fully fledged category, the abstract category called 3.

Such a general, abstract diagram may be specialised into a particular category – for instance, into the category of sets and functions we have just discussed. Here we develop the pedagogical utility of the diagrammatic expressive power of category theory through a specific example, that of the composition of functions. See Figure 2. This diagram is

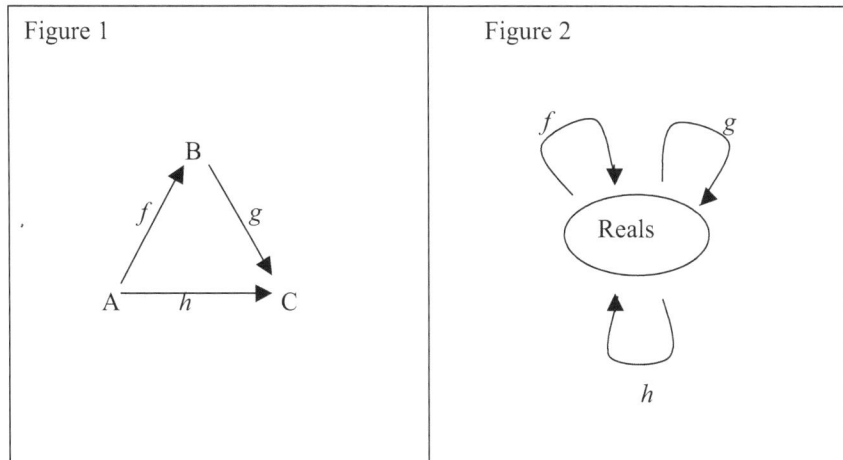

Figure 1

Figure 2

meant to render the same triad of relations as in Figure 1. Figure 1 and Figure 2 do not resemble one another, but this does not prevent the second from preserving – or, in Deleuzian terms, repeating – the inner relational structure of the first. As a diagram 'in' the category of sets and functions, the objects of the diagram in Figure 2 represent sets and the arrows represent functions between sets. In this particular case, the diagram has only one object, which represents the set of real numbers (as indicated). The three objects A, B, and C which are distinct in Figure 1 are thus identified in Figure 2: A = B = C = the set of real numbers. The arrows $f$, $g$, and $h$ then represent functions from the reals into the reals, in other words, real-valued functions of real numbers. If we then specify the three functions as follows: $f(x) = x^2$, $g(x) = 2x$, $h(x) = 2x^2$, then the abstract composition-relation we noted in Figure 1, namely $h = gf$, is realised here concretely as the composability of functions of real numbers, $g(f(x)) = h(x)$.

In a pedagogical context, students may thus be shown quite concretely how the relations of Figure 1 transfer over to Figure 2. Arrows and their pathways may be traced with eyes and fingers. In this way, category theory's diagrammatic form of presentation provides a direct intuition of how, in particular, the composition of set-functions works. More importantly, this direct intuition involves no loss of formal rigour. In general, the formal (diagrammatic) mode of expression immanent to category theory lends itself in a variety of ways to informal and intuitive understanding as well as abstract technicality and exactness. The transition from informal to formal comprehension is, as it were, built into the formalism itself.

This example of set-function composition also hints at what is ultimately the most powerful aspect of category theory, namely its capacity to move smoothly from one level of abstraction to another. The 'structure-preserving map' from Figure 1 to Figure 2 is what category theorists call a *functor*, that is, a higher-order analogue of a function between sets. A functor maps the objects and arrows of one category into the objects and arrows of another such that the roles of identity-arrows and composition-arrows are conserved across the mapping. Through functors, category theory is able to investigate not only relations within categories but, more abstractly, relations between and across heterogeneous categories themselves. In this way it becomes evident that the category-theoretical difference between objects and relations is itself (categorially!) relative. There are very many distinct categories, all of which must satisfy the axioms listed above, and so thereby fall naturally into various determinate relations with one another. These relations in turn may obtain at highly varied levels of abstraction. Thus, relations in one category may become objects in another, or the relations between categories may themselves form a higher-order category. It is this flexibility with respect to the 'form' and 'matter' of mathematics (expressed as the constitutive categorial difference between objects and arrows) that gives category theory its expressive power and broad relevance for all known mathematics.

Commutative diagrams are especially effective instruments for representing relations of relations. Yet even when a diagram does not commute, its system of explicit arrows and connected pathways still offers a highly useful instrument for exploring the necessary entailments and immanent possibilities of its presented relations. It is always possible to compose arrows according to the stipulations of the basic category theory axioms, and a novice category theorist readily learns how to test out new arrows by adding them directly to the diagram and then tracing out – with finger or eye – the compositional consequences. As one works on successive problems, one accumulates a toolbox of strategies in the form of self-instructed diagrammatic habits. In general, the relationship between the theoretical and the practical appears within the domain of mathematics in terms of the difference between object and operation. In contrast to set-theoretical objectivism, the relations comprising category theory are always doubly articulated, at once objective and operative while yet preserving the difference between these two modes, thus giving rise to concrete methods of mathematical exploration and experimentation as well as formal expression. Whereas sets lend themselves naturally to conceptual interpretation in terms of a distinction between form and substance, categories correspond more closely in this respect to the Hjelmslevian difference between content and expression advocated by Deleuze and Guattari: 'between content and expression, there is neither a correspondence nor a cause-effect relation nor a signified-signifier relation: there is real distinction, reciprocal presupposition, and only isomorphy' (1987: 502–3). It is primarily *this* difference between set-theoretical and category-theoretical approaches that opens potentially Deleuzian lines in mathematical teaching and learning.

## Diagrammatic Teaching and Learning

Come on, my reader, and let us construct a diagram to illustrate the general course of thought . . . (C. S. Peirce, 'Prolegomena to an Apology for Pragmaticism' [1906])

Among mathematicians, category theory (especially via its important sub-branch, *topos theory*) is increasingly seen as a viable alternative to set theory as the standard register for mathematical foundations. Yet this debate over set-theoretical versus category-theoretical foundations for mathematics is for the most part a matter for specialists. It may seem to have little to do with the way mathematics is actually taught and understood at non-specialist levels, say high-school algebra or undergraduate statistics. But it is at these levels that the standard, abstract math-image is propagated most broadly through the social body, and it is here that conceiving of the rival math-images of sets and categories in terms of Deleuze's philosophy more generally becomes especially helpful.

When Deleuze contrasts generality on the one hand with difference and repetition on the other he is distinguishing two possible approaches to the relation between problems and solutions, two different ways of understanding how problems and solutions are coordinated. This means that if one is looking for some specific difference marking Deleuzian solutions as opposed to general or representational solutions, one would be looking in the wrong place. The relevant difference is not to be found in the result so much as in the total approach to the process of posing and resolving problems. In this light, the relatively abstract and specialised differences between sets and categories become relevant to even the most elementary forms of mathematical inquiry. What set theory and category theory offer us from this perspective are two contrasting ways to approach and to make one's way through the diverse problematic terrain of the mathematical universe. The fact that these two approaches to mathematics constitute extremely rigorous, abstract and highly developed fields in their own right does not preclude but rather motivates their positive relevance for understanding mathematical practices at all levels, even those of a middle-school student encountering algebra for the first time or a humanities scholar trying to grasp the basic group-theoretical underpinnings of structuralism. In cases like these, if we examine the situation from a Deleuzian perspective, we should attend less to the simple fact of success or failure ('Did the student learn to solve the equation?' 'Has the scholar correctly understood the axioms of group theory?') than to the process of apprenticeship whereby new techniques and habits are cultivated by the learner in his or her encounter with the unfamiliar material. The aim is not so much the production of correct solutions as the immersion at a suitable depth within the right problems. From such a perspective the importance of background assumptions and the general savour of the mathematical intuitions at work in the labour of apprenticeship become particularly acute.

In this way the difference between sets and categories comes to matter on at least two distinct levels – a rigorous mathematical level on the one hand with all its attendant technicalities and formalisms and, on the other, an ordinary intuitional level of concrete practice and learning. More importantly, the difference between sets and categories is especially relevant for conceiving of the multiple relations *between these two levels themselves*. It is with respect to this latter point that the decisive pedagogical advantages of categories become apparent. As we have seen, category theory is intrinsically relational and, even more strongly, *trans*lational – this is reflected in its theoretical underpinnings, its distinctive methods, and even its explicit notational conventions (arrows, not brackets). When confronted with the challenge of teaching mathematics, teachers find themselves caught up in the dynamics of a maieutic process that must work to induce abstraction and formal rigour in minds often disposed otherwise. In the face of this deeply Socratic (and Platonic) problem, a broadly categorial approach presents itself to mathematical pedagogy as a naturally coordinated instrument of practice and theory, creative apprenticeship and formal rigour.

Here the diagrammatic mathematics of category theory intersects with the extensive philosophical diagrammatics of Deleuze. In the later collaborations with Guattari, especially *A Thousand Plateaus* (1987) and *What is Philosophy?* (1994), diagrammatics extend and clarify the earlier notion of dialectics as *mathesis universalis* in *Difference and Repetition*. When in *A Thousand Plateaus* Deleuze and Guattari (1987: 484–8) distinguish metric from non-metric multiplicities in mathematics, it is in order to illustrate their more general concern with the difference between smooth and striated spaces. And if smooth spaces provide a natural environment for the deterritorialising power of *abstract machines*, it is because these latter are *diagrammatic*, that is, they operate 'by *matter*, not by substance; by *function*, not by form' (Deleuze and Guattari 1987: 141). In this way, mathematics at this later stage of Deleuze's thought tends to be folded in with a generalised semiotics in a strongly Peircean spirit, closely linked to a diagrammatical *mathesis* that incorporates and intensifies the earlier notion of 'dialectics'.

Much of the secondary literature on Deleuze and educational theory has emphasised this Peircean aspect of Deleuze's thought (Semetsky 2004, 2007; Bogue 2004; Bogue and Semetsky 2010), and indeed, Peirce's semiotics and pragmatism provide a natural framework for thinking of Deleuzian pedagogy in general. Peirce's emphasis on diagrams as a form of abstract yet material experimentation helps to give concrete content to Deleuze's understanding of philosophy as the method of 'transcendental empiricism'. Given the difference between set-theoretical and category-theoretical mathematics as outlined above, we may now specify this connection in terms of the pedagogy of mathematics in particular. A Deleuzian path in the philosophy of mathematics that draws upon Peirce's semiotics and the later collaborations with Guattari tends to interpret mathematical truth in terms of the dynamics of signs. Such an approach has been charted by Rotman (2000) among others. In many ways category theory lends itself to such an approach, but more importantly it also promises a rigorous mathematical underpinning to the sort of generalised semiotics found in Peirce's late writings and the Deleuzo-Guattarian work. Not only does semiotics help us to understand mathematics, but mathematics – specifically category theory – may help us to understand the breadth and power of semiotics and diagrammatics (Mullarkey 2006).

In *Difference and Repetition* Deleuze links the processes of learning and apprenticeship – which cannot be modelled adequately by merely mimetic reproduction – to the practical employment of signs:

> The movement of the swimmer does not resemble that of the wave; in particular, the movements of the swimming instructor which we reproduce on the sand bear no relation to the movements of the wave, which we learn to deal with only by grasping the former in practice as signs. (1994: 23)

Deleuze's point here is that thought's embodied encounter with the world remains irreducible to any merely representational role. The practical employment of signs exceeds – and may in fact be hindered or misled by – the power of signs to represent theoretical objects. Every actual encounter generates concrete, practical relations and cannot be understood apart from the specific relational nexus in which it occurs. Representations, on the other hand, tend to draw solely upon internal determinations (like those of individuated 'essences') at the cost of contextual singularity.

When we learn, we immerse ourselves in an unfamiliar relational nexus so as to test out and experiment with practices which, over time, become habits and positive affects. The practical apprenticeship to signs converts the passive and dispersed relations of encounter into the consistent and active potentialities of realised concepts. Category theory abstracts away from the intrinsic or non-relational properties of objects in a given domain and instead studies the system of relations (and relations of relations) that defines those objects with respect to one another, in their interdependence. In this way, categories provide a theoretical milieu for investigating the very structure of apprenticeship as a translation and transformation of practical relations. Viewed through the lens of category theory, mathematics as a whole becomes a rich field of more and less abstract modes of practical experimentation – not transcendent representations, but immanent translations across varying levels of abstractness and concreteness, relationality and objectivity.

As Krömer (2007) points out, category theory makes use of the inter-translatability of mathematical objects and operations. Instead of reducing operations to objects, category theory takes the *difference* between object and operation to be constitutive of mathematical objects themselves. This broadly pragmatic orientation allows category theory to shift naturally across variable contexts. Category theory is in this respect more, rather than less, abstract than set theory, yet for this very reason it more readily respects singularity. A set fixes the identity of its constituent elements, while a category translates the identity of its constituent objects into a mere (auto-)relational property that may translate across indefinitely many contexts. That mathematics is a universal science thus does not imply that mathematics cannot engage the singular and the non-exchangeable. Category theory offers rigorous diagrammatic techniques for doing precisely this. In this respect, the mathematics of category theory offers a natural connectivity with both Deleuze's philosophy of mathematics on the one hand and his more general notion of philosophy as semiotic apprenticeship on the other.

From a Deleuzian perspective, a category-theoretical approach to mathematical teaching and learning involves multiple advantages. Among these, two in particular bear emphasis by way of conclusion. First, the mathematics of category theory is intrinsically a *conceptual* mathematics, as is suggested by the title of the fine introduction to categories by Lawvere and Schanuel (1997). The usual restriction of mathematical study and knowledge to mere quantification neglects its intrinsically conceptual dimension, which in category theory is expressed logically without becoming logicist. Mathematical categories map smoothly into the domains studied and classified by conceptual structuralisms of all kinds, and smooth transition into more rigorous theorisation of such structures (even within the humanities) is greatly facilitated by elementary category-theoretical techniques, such as the composition of arrows.[1] Secondly, the methods and expressive forms of category theory lend themselves readily to student experimentation. Diagrams in general function as abstract machinic laboratories for relational experimentation (Stjernfelt 2007). Students – particularly students of mathematics – need such laboratories if their experimentations in and with the universal are to be genuine opportunities for creative apprenticeship and not merely programmes of mimetic subservience to established orders. These two dimensions, conceptuality and experimentation, are in turn naturally integrated within category theory itself. As students work, even informally, with diagrammatic expressions of conceptual relationships, they find themselves producing experimental structures as well as mappings within and between structures. The techniques and habits category theory cultivates help such students to see that these relations themselves may always become new material for investigation and experimentation, for further *mathesis*.

## Note

1. With the assistance of a spring 2011 Davis Foundation grant at Endicott College, I was able to study the use of category-theoretical techniques in undergraduate humanities study, focusing in particular on late medieval and Renaissance philosophy. While the restricted sample size of the experiment made definitive conclusions impossible, initial results indicated highly positive student evaluation of the effectiveness of diagrammatic learning as well as improved comprehension of the interdisciplinary material.

## References

Awodey, S. (2010), *Category Theory*, Oxford and New York: Oxford University Press.

Badiou, A. (2007), *Being and Event*, trans. O. Feltham, New York: Continuum.

Bogue, R. (2004), 'Search, Swim and See: Deleuze's apprenticeship in signs and pedagogy of images', *Educational Philosophy and Theory*, 36(3).

Bogue, R. and I. Semetsky (2010), 'Reading Signs/Learning from Experience: Deleuze's pedagogy as becoming-other' in I. Semetsky (ed.), *Semiotics Education Experience*, Rotterdam: Sense, pp. 115–30.

Cantor, G. [1897] (1955), *Contributions to the Founding of the Theory of Transfinite Numbers*, trans. P. Jourdain, New York: Dover.

Deleuze, G. (1994), *Difference and Repetition*, trans. P. Patton, New York: Columbia University Press.

Deleuze, G. and F. Guattari (1987), *A Thousand Plateaus: Capitalism and Schizophrenia*, trans. B. Massumi, Minneapolis: University of Minnesota Press.

Deleuze, G. and F. Guattari (1994), *What is Philosophy?* trans. H. Tomlinson and G. Burchell, New York: Columbia University Press.

Durie, R. (2006), 'Problems in the Relation Between Maths and Philosophy' in S. Duffy (ed.), *Virtual Mathematics: The Logic of Difference*, Bolton: Clinamen.

Krömer, R. (2007), *Tool and Object: A History and Philosophy of Category Theory*, Basel: Birkhauser Verlag.

Lawvere, W. and S. Schanuel (1997), *Conceptual Mathematics: A First Introduction to Categories*, Cambridge and New York: Cambridge University Press.

MacLane, S. (2010), *Categories for the Working Mathematician*, New York: Springer.

Mullarkey, J. (2006), *Post-Continental Philosophy: An Outline*, London and New York: Continuum.

Peirce, C. S. (2010), *Philosophy of Mathematics: Selected Writings*, ed. M. Moore, Bloomington and Indianapolis: Indiana University Press.

Rotman, Brian (2000), *Mathematics as Sign: Writing, Imagining, Counting*, Palo Alto: Stanford University Press.

Semetsky, I. (2004), 'The Role of Intuition in Thinking and Learning: Deleuze and the pragmatic legacy', *Educational Philosophy and Theory*, 36(4): 433–54.

Semetsky, I. (2007), 'Towards a Semiotic Theory of Learning: Deleuze's philosophy and educational experience', *SEMIOTICA*, 164(1/4): 197–214.

Semetsky, I. and J. A. Delpech-Ramey (2011), 'Educating Gnosis/Making a Difference', *Policy Futures in Education*, 9(4): 518–27.

Stjernfelt, F. (2007), *Diagrammatology: An Investigation on the Borderlines of Phenomenology, Ontology, and Semiotics*, Dordrecht: Springer.

# ASSEMBLAGE IV:
# LIFE, SIGN, TIME

change
rest
being
sameness
difference

# Chapter 9

# Learning the Uncanny

*Joshua Ramey*

Whether it is only one of Plato's thoughts about the ultimate nature of being, and not his only or final thought, the following lines from the *Sophist* suggest that, for all of his overtures to the stability of ultimate reality, even for Plato that reality is not static but dynamic. At *Sophist* 247e, the Stranger says to Socrates:

> I'm saying that a thing really is if it has any capacity at all, either by nature to do something to something else or to have even the smallest thing done to it by even the most trivial thing, even if it only happens once. I'll take it as a definition that *those which are* amount to nothing other than *capacity.* (Plato 1997: 269)

However, we know that Plato tended to domesticate the pluralism inherent in this formula. In the *Sophist*'s subsequent discussion, five particular kinds of being, the so-called 'great kinds', are identified as having the greatest or most general capacity (*dynamis*): change, rest, being, sameness, and a fifth kind, difference, whose difficult status, and apparent identification with non-being, has provoked endless commentary, in particular that by Deleuze in *Difference and Repetition*. Deleuze's disagreement with Plato over the status of difference is central not only to the development of his own ontology, but also to his theory of learning (Deleuze 1994: 64).

For Plato, the potentially open and pluralist conception of being as potency, indicated above, is ultimately ordered by the governance of the transcendentals, and by the dialectical discernment of what can and cannot be, of what is and what is not, by a mind that seeks unity, stability and consistency. Even if being is capacity or potency, knowledge is nonetheless of hierarchy and of discernible, identifiable order. For Deleuze, on the contrary, being is not hierarchically ordered but univocally distributed, and knowledge crystallises in sponse to intensities, rather than in apprehension of self-identical Forms. Intensities are relational entities, events that ramify intersections among disparate processes and forces at many different levels of complexity and organisation among bodies and minds. Because intensities cannot be reduced to the actual materials they organise, Deleuze affirms an incorporeal, imperceptible and intransitive dimension of reality. But against Plato, Deleuze also affirms the ultimate primacy of *difference*, where difference is difference in intensity. Thus Deleuze in some sense naturalises the Platonic ideas by conceiving them not as stable Beings but as pure becomings: singular dynamics of nature from which the forms and contents of nature emerge. An idea, from this perspective, is an intuition of a process of differentiation, a point of view on a dynamic or 'ideal drama' governing a complex flow of temporal iterations.

Unlike Plato, Deleuze gives a *positive* significance to the peculiar instability of the sensible (and of our mutating sensibility) by reading that instability as a *sign* of otherwise imperceptible intensities within the empirical. Deleuze writes:

> It is intensity or difference in intensity which constitutes the peculiar limit of sensibility. As such, it has the paradoxical character of the limit: it is the imperceptible, that which cannot be sensed because it is always covered by a quality which alienates or contradicts it, always distributed within an extensity which inverts or cancels it. In another sense, it is that which can only be sensed or that which defines the transcendent exercise of sensibility, because it gives to be sensed, thereby awakening memory and forcing thought. (Deleuze 1994: 236–7)

In other words, Deleuze takes what for Plato were *interruptions* in the circuit of ideal communication between the Soul and the Forms as both the provocation of thought and the ultimate constituents of being. Rather than situate mind at a remove from the uncanny in sensation, the difficult in emotions, or the paradoxical in thought, and far from contrasting the instability of sensation with the stability of the idea, Deleuze positions the genesis of thought itself in dramatic encounters with imperceptible forces: moments when intensities provoke the mind to interpret and to create.

Thus Deleuze argues, in *Difference and Repetition*, that learning is not simply a matter of carrying into action a representation. Rather, it is a matter of linking signs and actions, the multiple points of a body with the multiple signs emitted, for example, by an ocean wave (Deleuze 1994: 23). In learning to swim, we do not so much *imitate* the possible

Constraints led
leary

actions represented by a teacher as *repeat* her actual response to waves we individually face. As Deleuze puts it:

> The movement of the swimmer does not resemble that of the wave, in particular, the movements of the swimming instructor which we reproduce on the sand bear no relation to the movements of the wave, which we learn to deal with only by grasping the former in practice as signs . . . When a body combines some of its own distinctive points with those of a wave, it espouses the principle of a repetition which is no longer that of the Same but involves the Other – involves difference, from one wave and one gesture to another, and carries that difference through the repetitive space thereby constituted. To learn is indeed to constitute this space of an encounter with signs, in which distinctive points renew themselves in each other, and repetition takes shape while disguising itself. (Deleuze 1994: 23)

This is to say, it is in the singularity constituted by the encounter of *a body* with *a wave* that the 'essence' of swimming exists. For Deleuze there is no merely discursive or simply representational content of the concept of swimming from which anything could be learned. On the contrary, the idea of swimming is indexed to *events* (or open series of possible events) in which the distinctive points of bodies might combine with those of various waves. A teacher does not so much represent swimming to us as she *transmits* a differential relation between bodies and waves, a relation that must be repeated differently in the body of each student in order to take effect, in order to count as knowledge. Swimming is thus not a static notion but a dynamic form of becoming modulated across the body of a teacher *through* the body of a student.

In this sense, learning centres on the discovery of problems, not on solutions. The essence of swimming is never a permanent solution to a problem. Rather, swimming introduces a 'problematic field', enabling non-identical repetition within a milieu. The real question is not 'what is swimming?' but '*where* can I swim?' '*when* can I swim?' or '*how long* and *how fast* can I swim?' These are questions determined by the essence of swimming as a virtual, differential power latent in *signs*. As Deleuze explains it:

> To learn to swim is to conjugate the distinctive points of our bodies with the singular points of the objective Idea in order to form a problematic field. This conjugation determines for us a threshold of consciousness at which our real acts are adjusted to our perceptions of the real relations, thereby providing a solution to the problem. Moreover, problematic Ideas are precisely the ultimate elements of nature and the subliminal objects of little perceptions. As a result, 'learning' always takes place in and through

— but what obat in a 'Olympic pool.

*yep – CLP.*

the unconscious, thereby establishing the bond of a profound complicity between nature and mind. (Deleuze 1994: 165)

What is the character of this unconscious complicity? In a word, it is *creative*. In a certain sense, for Deleuze, every perception is a new creation, and learning happens when a new mode of existence comes into being in response to the inherent novelty of perception itself.[1] Although the inertia of habit and the fixations of memory (and the obstacle of trauma) generally interfere with the development of the potencies implicated in every moment, every mode of life is a form of becoming that actualises virtual potencies, creating new assemblages of bodies and sense. Learning takes place in this context, and happens through a kind of participation in the as-yet-unknown. Learning is a *projection*, a conjecture towards the sense of a virtual Whole of sense (i.e., Swimming itself) that is never completed or directly intuited, but ramified over multiple iterations (Deleuze 1994: 109).

The possibility of continuing to swim is the possibility of different bodies continuing to swim otherwise, differently. Thus the idea of swimming is virtual with respect to its various actualities. However, the virtual aspect of an act of swimming is not its vague or inexact character, but the fact that the potencies of swimming cannot be hierarchically ordered: every iteration, each refraction of the virtual matters equally. Deleuze writes:

> far from being undetermined, the virtual is completely determined. When it is claimed that works of art are immersed in a virtuality, what is being invoked is not some confused determination but the completely determined structure formed by its genetic differential elements, its 'virtual' or 'embryonic' elements. The elements, varieties of relations and singular points coexist in the work or the object, in the virtual part of the work or object, without it being possible to designate a point of view privileged over others, a centre which would unify the other centres. (Deleuze 1994: 209)

Despite manifesting a definite genetic structure, the virtual is not static but *problematic*, in the sense that it *enables* or in some sense provokes a question: how is *this* actuality related to its intensive, germinal and embryonic conditions? If it is the vocation of thought to discover the genetic elements of reality, then it is incumbent upon thought to encounter the singular potencies latent in each case, and thus conceive ideas without governing hierarchy.

But what such encounter demands is that the mind and the body remain open to the deliverances of certain kinds of experiences that are generally categorised under the name of the *uncanny*. F. W. J. Schelling defined the uncanny as all that which should have remained hidden, but has been brought to light.[2] That is to say, the uncanny is the familiar suddenly made strange, the everyday when it takes on the numinous aura of the otherworldly. Throughout his oeuvre, Deleuze's privileged examples of the birth of thought can all be characterised as in some sense uncanny, from Hamlet's encounter with his father's ghost in *Difference and Repetition*, to the uncanny logical paradoxes of *The Logic of Sense*, to the uncanny fascinations of literary authors such as Woolf and Kafka catalogued in *A Thousand Plateaus*, to the various uncanny images capable of provoking genuine thought that Deleuze categorises in the *Cinema* volumes. It might be said that, for Deleuze, the uncanny is in some sense the *paradigm* of that from which we learn, at all.

What would it be to learn from the uncanny? If anything, the uncanny seems to indicate the *limits* of knowledge, the limit of what it is possible to know. Perhaps this is why it is our consistent tendency, both in everyday life and in reflective disciplines such as philosophy, to attempt to explain away or *reduce* the uncanny in experience. But, as should be clear from the sketch of Deleuze's ontology given above, a reductive approach to the uncanny would be tantamount to the foreclosure of thought itself, since thought is only thought if it is co-incident with intensity, if it indexes and ramifies the intensive structure of being itself. Thought is only thought to the degree that it participates in the uncanny.

In his later work with Guattari, Deleuze will argue that our resistance to the uncanny has far-reaching ethical and political consequences. Reductive approaches to the uncanny prevent both thought and action by resisting capacities for acting and being acted upon that might be available at as yet unimagined somatic, social and even cosmic levels. In what follows I will illustrate this point by way of a reading of Alfred Hitchcock's *The Birds*, contrasting a Deleuzian perspective on the film with one that might be given from the perspective of a mind particularly disturbed by the uncanny: Sigmund Freud. I will conclude with some remarks about how Deleuze and Guattari formulated a politics that is centred on an affirmation of the uncanny.

## For Love of *The Birds*

In his famous 1919 essay on the subject, Freud catalogues a number of uncanny experiences (Freud 2003: 135). Inanimate objects can be uncanny if they appear to be alive. Conversely, some animate entities are uncanny because, although animate, they appear to be *in*animate. Freud notes that for this reason there is something uncanny about those in epileptic seizures. The mechanical jerking of the body suggests that the living are animated by something dead, or rather undead, as Stephen King would say. But the uncanny is not always the macabre. Synchronicities can be uncanny, because they are events not causally related to one another, but seemingly connected by some unknown principle (Jung 1960: 417–519). And uncanny can be any unexplainable repeated appearance of the same face or series of words or numbers.

In the mythology of many cultures, including Teutonic and Native American folklore, ravens and crows are often linked to the uncanny and to secret knowledge, as well as to initiation rites and to death. Indeed there is a strange numinosity to the almost mechanical rhythm of a crow's movements and noises, as if with this bird we were in the presence not of an organism but an automaton. Perhaps this is what inspired Daphne du Maurier to write a story, and Alfred Hitchcock to make a film, that plays so deeply on our suspicion of some dark and broken sympathy linking the human drama to that of the birds.[3]

An undisputed masterpiece of filmmaking, *The Birds* (1962) opens in Union Square, just outside a San Francisco bird shop, where a lawyer named Mitch Brenner (Rod Taylor) encounters a rich socialite named Melanie Daniels (Tippi Hedren). Mitch recognises Melanie as an elite playgirl whose bad behaviour often lands her in the tabloids. Mitch's condescending attitude towards such a powerfully attractive woman intrigues Melanie, and she follows him in secret out to his weekend haunt, Bodega Bay. In this sleepy seaside town is the house where Mitch spends weekends with his mother, Lydia (Jessica Tandy), and sister, Cathy (Veronica Cartwright). Lydia, who has lost her husband, is disturbed by the presence of Melanie, whom she sees as an intruder. (Lydia had already managed to fend off one potential interloper, Annie Hayworth, whose attachment to Mitch remains so strong that she still lives in Bodega Bay as a schoolteacher). After commandeering a skiff and secretly delivering a pair of lovebirds to the Brenner house, Melanie is attacked by a seagull – the first in a series of attacks that will eventually terrorise and destroy the town. At the film's conclusion, Mitch, Melanie, Lydia and Cathy narrowly escape from the Brenner house, but not before Melanie endures a horrific attack by the birds when she ascends, alone, to the attic. Melanie survives and the quartet escapes, but as they drive away the birds seem to be rallying for another onslaught, and attacks are being reported over the radio at other locations across California. We are left with the suspicion that some aviary vengeance might be hell bent on destroying civilisation itself.

There are several uncanny elements in the film. Obviously the attacks themselves violate what we are familiar with in birds.[4] And the birds themselves, both visually and sonically, are utterly unnatural. Hitchcock's special effects, which took years to produce, themselves have a deeply uncanny artificiality, a bizarre, mechanical affect that heightens rather than diminishes the terrifying effect (Paglia 1998: 14–15). Beyond the birds themselves, it is of course uncanny that the attacks begin with the arrival of Melanie. The film implies that Melanie's arrival and the attacks constitute some kind of synchronicity, a set of events related by some principle the nature of which is not (yet) clearly known (Jung 1960). At a certain point, a hysterical woman suspects Melanie has somehow caused the attacks. 'I think it's you, you're the cause of all this. I think you're evil!', she shrieks.

*Witch hunt.*

We will return to this accusation. But let's begin with what Freud might say about *The Birds*. In his 1919 essay Freud says that the feeling of the uncanny always derives from two sources: the return of repressed childhood traumas, and the recursion of the mind to primitive patterns of desire and belief (Freud 2003: 147). Freud in fact hypothesised that all uncanny experiences, in one way or another, ultimately betray the presence of psychic atavisms, and the threat of regression to that earlier moment in human history he called the 'primitive animist phase'. Freud describes this as an era of universal infantile narcissism, in which humanity believed the world was responsive to our desires in a way that the current scientific worldview no longer validates. In the unconscious, however, we still believe in our powers to communicate with the world on a deeper level, and this belief must be repressed in order to free ourselves from any sense of obligation to nature, let alone to angels, daemons, or ancestral spirits.

*infantile narcissism.*

> The analysis of cases of the uncanny has led us back to the old *animistic* view of the universe, a view characterised by the idea that the world was peopled with human spirits, by the narcissistic overrating of one's own mental processes, by the omnipotence of thoughts and the technique of magic that relied on it, by the attribution of carefully graded magical powers (*mana*) to alien persons and things, and by all the inventions with which the unbounded narcissism of that period of development sought to defend itself against the unmistakable sanctions of reality. It appears that we have all, in the course of our individual development been through a phase corresponding to the animistic phase in the development of primitive peoples, that this phase did not pass without leaving behind in us residual traces that can still make themselves felt, and that everything we now find 'uncanny' meets the criterion that it is linked with these remnants of animistic mental activity and prompts them to express themselves. (Freud 2003: 147)

Freud goes on to argue that, to the extent that we are unhappy or neurotic, and suffer from complexes in dealing with the trauma incumbent upon development, we are all more or less vulnerable to suggestions in our environment that seem to confirm the truth of an earlier era, a period not only of childhood fantasy, but of the primitive animist phase of human society, itself. Thus, according to Freud, those who have been traumatised and have not yet recovered are more susceptible than others to belief in telepathy, precognition, oracles, the messages of synchronicities, even to the possibility of mental control over matter (Freud 2003: 157).

In the case of *The Birds*, from a Freudian point of view, the attacks are symptomatic of impasses in the relationships between Mitch, Lydia and Melanie. That is to say, from a clinical perspective, because they signify the presence of regressions and fantasies, uncanny events are bound to occur at the site of unresolved conflicts. In *The Birds*, the attacks signify rivalries and antagonisms. For example, one can see the violence of the birds' attacks as expressive of the thwarted nature of Mitch's libido. Mitch has not fully detached from his mother. He still visits her every weekend, and Melanie is just the latest in a series of women who were unable to break through the spell of Lydia's hold over Mitch. In part the film dramatises the frustrations a male libido trapped in the maternal cul-de-sac represented by Bodega Bay. Here, a man is slowly drowning in the sterile waters of an ageing, bereaved woman, a mother without a man of her own. Perhaps more precisely, what the bird attacks symbolise is how Mitch's displaced libido becomes *displaced* onto Lydia, giving her the preternatural power to become a Queen of the Birds, able to call down vengeance on her son's unfaithfulness. At the same time, the attacks symbolise Melanie's frustrated attempt to seduce and dominate Mitch. Melanie's self-absorption and frigid demeanour betray a lack of depth to her affections.[5]

There is much truth to these observations, and psychoanalytical readings of Hitchcock generally have born much fruit.[6] But there is something missing in this line of interpretation, and what is missing is linked directly to Freud's conception of the uncanny. The paradox of Freud's account in his famous 1919 study, a paradox many readers have noticed, is that while Freud reduces the uncanny to a fantasy that cannot withstand the test of the reality principle, Freud himself cannot seem to shake the suspicion that the uncanny derives not from something known about fantasy (that it is a regression), but something as yet unknown about reality – namely, that the reality principle itself cannot establish the certainty of a disenchanted, silent universe of inert matter and indifferent force. Uncanny phenomena suggest the world is strangely animated, and that this animus is something to which we are connected and with which we communicate at occult levels.

Freud himself seems to fear that such a conclusion awaits his study of the uncanny. He confesses to having had a number of uncanny experiences, including the experience of 'randomly' wandering into the same red-light district three times in an Italian town he had never visited before, and where he did not know his way around (Freud 2003: 144). But because of his dedication to the scientific worldview, Freud must deny, even in his own case, that we can make claims for the reality of imperceptible conjunctions between psychic and non-psychic, human and animal, natural and cultural realms. Not wishing to give scientific credence to what he called the 'black mud' of occultism, Freud maintained a strict dualism between the meaningfulness of the uncanny, reducible to unconscious wish-fulfilment, and the meaningless nature of the non-psychic world (Jung 1989: 150).[7] That world, for Freud, operates in a way that is fundamentally separate from and indifferent to particular human desire and purpose. This dualistic, Cartesian and Newtonian worldview was the one to which Freud remained faithful.

## Beyond the Reality Principle

But Freud's worldview, and the reading of the uncanny it supports, is challenged by Hitchcock's film in a wry and highly ironic fashion. *The Birds* directs our attention not only to impasses in psychodynamics, but more profoundly to causes and consequences of our unhappy rapport with nature – as Cavell puts it, here 'the universe now sees to it that the consequences of our actions haunt us to a conclusion' (Cavell 1979: 65). Hitchcock himself was in fact inspired to make the films after a series of real-life incidents of bird attacks in California. In his interviews with Truffaut he described the real-life attacks as 'a form of rabies' (Truffaut 1967: 216), and said in another interview that 'all you can say about *The Birds* is that nature can be awful rough on you. If you play around with it. Look at what uranium has done. Men dug that out of the ground. *The Birds* expresses nature and what it can do, and the dangers of nature' (Gottlieb 1995: 294). As he puts it an another interview:

Basically, in *The Birds*, what you have is a kind of an overall sketchy theme of everyone taking nature for granted. Everyone took the birds for granted until the birds one day *turned* on them. The birds had been shot at, eaten, put in cages. They'd suffered *everything* from the humans, and it was time they turned on them. Don't mess about or tamper with nature . . . Who knows? It's feasible in the year 3000 or 4000 for *all* the animals to have taken over![8]

As ever, there is a supreme irony in Hitchcock's statements, since obviously the film is not about dangers of nature without being about the impasses of culture, and its deadlocks of desire. It is part of Hitchcock's genius that he is able to direct our gaze towards what is awry in our relations to the unknown in nature by simultaneously directing it to its connection to desire, at the site of what Deleuze and Guattari call those as yet unrealised capacities for 'unknown Nature – *affect*' (Deleuze and Guattari 1987: 240) that haunt and disturb the psyche. What Hitchcock shows so brilliantly in *The Birds*, in all of its terrifying and violent ambiguity, is the Deleuzo-Guattarian theorem that the ultimate stake of the antagonism surrounding unconscious impulses is *not simply* whether we have the clinical means to assuage neurotic (paranoid or hysterical) formations.

What is at stake is not merely our inability to love and be loved by human others, as those in *The Birds* are so obviously failing to do. What is at stake is also a massively disordered relation to nature, a properly 'cosmic' problem that determines the unconscious to seek relations (and perhaps, strictly speaking the unconscious *is* this seeking) outside the positions on the familial and political Oedipal t(ri)angle. Hitchcock's genius here may have been to realise the urgency of modernity's growing ecological crisis – seeing, as early as the 1950s, what would take the ecology movement (and decades of industrial waste) decades to clearly expose to public light. But it was not only that, but also to present the problem of human relations to nature with the sophistication to know that one cannot solve this problem directly, that we cannot in theory or in practice pass directly to the relation to nature, outside the mediations of culture. The relation to nature is mediated by and an effect of the deadlocks and impasses of culture.

For both Hitchcock and Deleuze, what a strictly Freudian view of the uncanny forecloses is the real – and truly uncanny – potency of intermediary zones, regions *between* psychic and non-psychic, cultural and natural, human and animal spheres. These are the zones, beyond the reality principle of an indifferent cosmos, to which an uncanny film like *The Birds* invites us to pay careful attention. If a strictly Freudian (and *mutatis mutandis* any reductively naturalistic) view of reality forecloses on the imperceptible interrelations and subtle interconnections uncanny phenomena seem to suggest are real, both Hitchcock and Deleuze invite us to *explore further* the latent connections between presumably isolated minds and materials, desires and objects of desires, human and non-human agencies. As Deleuze argues with Guattari (1987: 238–45), the feeling of the uncanny is due not to fantasy but to *fascination*, and uncanny phenomena of desire are manifestations of otherwise imperceptible resonances in converging and diverging series of forces, zones of attraction and areas of elective affinity between seemingly unrelated but genuinely connected events. To think of the human subject as isolated from the universe rather than as embedded in a network of material and semiotic forces, many of which are unconscious, is to miss much of what the unconscious itself may contribute to a more profound idea of learning.

In a way that Freud could not recognise, thought itself must be positively identified with unconscious fixations. We must learn the uncanny: the peculiar fascination exerted by uncanny phenomena, like the attacks in Hitchcock's film, do not signify the return of the repressed without also indexing novel experiences we do not yet have the wherewithal to undergo, let alone comprehend. A more comprehensive view of the uncanny as an invitation to learning would be one that seeks not to ward off the impending threat of regression to the animist phase, or to reject its suggestions as infantile, but to take the uncanny as an opportunity to learn to navigate a novel set of possibilities. Here the political, as well as pedagogical stakes begin to become clear: the self more open to its fascinations might navigate a set of potentials present in the multiplicities immanent to our imperceptible interconnections with a variety of others with whom we normally only unconsciously communicate – including the unknown in nature as much as in culture.

Hitchcock demonstrates just how difficult this is for the paranoid and hysterical modern mind. In a famous scene inside the Tides Restaurant, the citizens of Bodega Bay demonstrate all the typical reactions to an uncanny event: an elderly ornithologist attempts to explain it away, an hysterical mother overreacts in fear and flees, a drunk salesmen advocates annihilating the birds (domination of nature), and yet another drunk takes it as divine judgement: 'it's the end of the world', he quips. The film presents no clear way to understand the birds' attack, let alone escape them. And yet, to somehow follow or follow up on such an uncanny event without the havoc and destruction (or just plain insanity) normally involved would be, in the end, precisely an ethical imperative for which Deleuze and Guattari would argue.

## Becoming-Cosmic

What is at stake here is both political and cosmic. If the reductive view of nature complicit with capitalist administration is linked to a reductive view of human nature that gives no credence to the uncanny, then by becoming more open to uncanny phenomena we would simultaneously encounter a nature and a human nature beyond the requirements of a fully administered and totally instrumentalised world. Freud himself was ready to admit that uncanny phenomena are utterly common and everyday events. Might what is uncanny in many of our desires be simply signs of ordinary interactions that are foreclosed by an instrumental view of 'the environment' or 'resources' or 'human resources', an instrumentality that leaves too much of the self unrecognisable to itself? Contra Freud, human flourishing might be linked to the possibility not of reconciling ourselves, though analysis, to the fact that the universe is a hostile and indifferent place, but might indicate on the contrary that the hospitality and care we share with one another, and the passions and peculiarities of how we express our own natures, might be irreducibly bound up with perceptual and affective capacities that permeate any fixed border between subject and object, self and other, nature and culture. The experience of the uncanny might not be a regression but a genuinely communicative action, an irreducibly meaningful yet completely natural event.

In strident and exotic terms, Deleuze and Guattari call such modes of communication 'unnatural participation' (Deleuze and Guattari 1987: 240): unnatural because such participation cannot be coded as natural if by nature is meant within the fixed boundaries of species, organisms and cellular individuals. There is another nature, they argue, that remains to be thought, one that communicates and propagates not by hereditary and filiative means – through sexual reproduction – but by infection or contagion among irreducibly heterogeneous terms. As they put it:

> Unnatural participations are the true Nature spanning the kingdoms of nature. Propagation by epidemic, by contagion, has nothing to do with filiation by heredity, even if the two themes intermingle and require each other . . . These combinations are neither genetic nor structural, they are interkingdoms, unnatural participations. For us . . . there are as many sexes as there are terms in symbiosis, as many differences as elements contributing to a process of contagion. We know that many beings pass between a man and a woman; they come from different worlds, are borne on the wind, form rhizomes around roots; they cannot be understood in terms of production, only in terms of becoming . . . These multiplicities with

heterogeneous terms, cofunctioning by contagion, enter certain *assemblages*: it is here that human beings affect their becomings-animal. (Deleuze and Guattari 1987: 241–2)

One can see just such an assemblage at work in *The Birds*. The reductively Freudian reading obscures the fact that Melanie, in addition to being the object of Mitch's castrated desire, is also the *subject* of a peculiar fascination with birds. The ordeal of her unsuccessful tryst with Mitch produces a novel result, even if by way of catastrophe: Melanie enters into an intensified affective field where distinctions between the human and the animal break down. Melanie comes into visceral contact with the birds, entering a chaotic and epidemic space of infection or contagion where the distinction between her body and the birds is violated. As the plot unfolds, Melanie seems to detach more and more from her pursuit of Mitch, and to take a detour, what Deleuze and Guattari would call a 'line of flight' into another love affair, a sterile *hybrid* (Deleuze and Guattari 1987: 241) formed by alliance with the pack of birds. By the time of the climactic attack of the birds on the Brenner house, Melanie seems to be completely enraptured by this fascination, caught up in an uncanny mix of rapture and terror, as the birds swarm and swirl and peck in the family living room. There is truly something strange about her affect in these scenes, as if she were riding waves of strange attraction and aversion simultaneously. And to what can we attribute Melanie's survival, minutes later, when she ascends alone to the attic and finds an enormous hole through which the birds pour and attack her? And why does she go up there in the first place? Mitch finally breaks in to save her, but not until Melanie has been thoroughly infected with the pecks and claws of the pack, and emerging a changed woman.

What is the significance of Melanie's ordeal? Has Melanie, falling through the abyss of Mitch's castrated desire, fallen for the birds instead? This might be what a Freudian would have to say. But does Melanie's well-being (and/or Mitch's) really consist in a successful conjugal pairing? Does the consummation of desire consist simply in the tidying up of our Oedipal triangles? Might Melanie find something in conjunction with the birds that is not a substitute for, but a threshold of some other kind of desire, altogether?

In the end, what is really uncanny in this film is not the birds' attack but Melanie herself. The birds see that there is something truly strange, truly uncanny about Melanie. Camille Paglia, in her virtuosic study of the film, notes that Hitchcock constantly suggests that Melanie has a telepathic relation to the birds, as she seems to be able to sense and even hear their approach when it is invisible to others, a sign that she 'really is something like a vampire attuned to nature's occult messages' (Paglia 1998: 74).

It is especially significant in this connection that Melanie is portrayed as an unusual or inappropriate *woman*. Women, whether as witches or just as wombs, are suspected of enjoying preternatural connections to nature, to animals and to cosmic dynamics, generally. What is uncontrollable or uncanny in what women want is linked to the chaos of nature outside of masculine enculturating and dominating forces. Women more generally have always been marginalised and seen as problematic moral subjects – incapable of virtue or duty – precisely to the degree that they maintain deep and imperceptible modes of communication with nature.

Bizarre as this thought may seem,[9] what Melanie really wants cannot be understood apart from the distinct (if obscure) ways in which her desire links her with the birds, in what Deleuze and Guattari would call a becoming-bird of Melanie and a becoming-Melanie of the birds. A Freudian might argue that we must maintain the distinction between reality and fantasy, and that we must read the perversity of the birds attacks, and the dysfunction of the natural order with which it is bound up, as a simple fictional dramatisation of psychic disorder. But neither Hitchcock nor Deleuze would agree that things are so simple, and insist, *contra* Freud, that what is really uncanny is that the extent to which humans fail to resolve their own crises and complexes is also the extent to which they live, suffer and enjoy the universe, affect its dynamics, and are deeply affected in turn. Hitchcock himself ironically suggests that our tragic ignorance of the complicity between humanity and the animal world is the whole point of the film. In the 'lecture' he gives in the film's theatrical trailer, he pontificates, with hilarious irony, on all the ways birds have been useful to us and thus how kind we have been to them, all throughout our history. Given all this, the birds would never attack us . . . Unless . . . and just as Hitchcock sits down to eat a roast chicken, the strange and eerie sound of a bird attack begins.

## The Politics of Sorcery

*The Birds*, in short, can be read as a fable exemplifying the stakes of denying the level of reality laid out by Deleuze and Guattari in *A Thousand Plateaus*. They write:

> A multiplicity is not defined by its elements, nor by a center of unification or comprehension . . . Since its variations and dimensions are immanent

to it, it amounts to the same thing to say that each multiplicity is already composed of heterogeneous terms in symbiosis, and that a multiplicity is continually transforming itself ... If we imagined the position of a fascinated Self, it was because the multiplicity toward which it leans, stretching it to the breaking point, is the continuation of another multiplicity that works it and strains it from the inside. In fact, the Self is only a threshold, a door, a becoming between two multiplicities ... And at each threshold or door, a new pact? A fiber stretches from a human to an animal, from a human or an animal to molecules, from molecules to particles, and so on to the imperceptible. Every fiber is a Universe fiber. (Deleuze and Guattari 1987: 249)

Melanie was indeed stretched to the breaking point in *The Birds*. Although she thought she was in control, she clearly met her match, the 'continuation of another multiplicity' that 'works' and 'strains' her from the inside: the birds. Melanie finds herself matched not by the masculinity of Mitch (clearly impotent), nor by the maternal powers of Lydia, but in the multiplicity that binds her to a particular fibre, a universe fibre: an unknown Nature connecting her with the birds. What this 'something' is, is not a bird, but something the birds draw out of her: the multiplicity of powers and relations as yet unrealised.

It is here that we reach the cosmic dimension of desire, in all its uncanny ambiguity. Is this why Hitchcock advertised the film by saying, after *Vertigo* and *Psycho*, that *The Birds* 'could be the most terrifying picture I have ever made!'?[10] And yet, from a Deleuzo-Guattarian perspective, it is only at the sites of such impasses, such apocalyptic outbreaks – the sites of the emergence of schizoid potencies in all their terrifying ambiguity – that health, and for our purposes *learning*, truly begins. Hitchcock hints this might be possible, as the battered souls drive into the arising dawn, away from the deadlocks of Bodega Bay. But perhaps a contagion, a global catastrophe has now been unleashed. Hitchcock leaves it up to us to decide whether it will always have been too late for those who cannot truly love to learn to do so, and by learning to love stave off a destruction as much natural as it is cultural.[11]

As Mitch's attempt to discipline Melanie, and Lydia's attempt to control her, both fail, what we are left with is an elusive power (*dynamis*) that continues to fascinate Hitchcock, a power he calls up, in perhaps his most psychologically sophisticated film, as the threatening force of a neglected Nature. Is Hitchcock's fascination with the rogue woman, the powerful insouciance of a society girl who is beautiful, dirty and rich, also his fascination with an Outside of modern schemes of control and domination, whether psychic or industrial-military (Hitchcock famously hated and feared the police)? In some ways, *The Birds* is Hitchcock's *Lear*, the work in which he sends all his protagonists towards madness and death in a nature gone to the dogs, or rather to the birds. Here one might sympathise, after all, with where we began, in Plato's desire to offer the human mind a metaphysical buttress against the possibility of total destruction by insisting upon the organisation of potencies in hierarchical schemes, a vision of a cosmos disciplined in advance of its uncanny becomings.[12] But such moralising becomes impossible once we recognise that the disturbing interconnectivity and uncanny interdependence implied by the events of *The Birds* defies the idea that humans can define well-being in advance of encounters that will re-shape that being itself. What it would mean to re-define human well-being in broader terms, in terms of multiplicities, is a much larger, longer and more difficult project, but it is the one that Deleuze and Guattari suggest can only be undertaken through a rigorous exploration of the uncanny. Deleuze and Guattari go further, and suggest that we need not only an ethics but even an entire politics of the uncanny, a 'politics of sorcery' (Deleuze and Guattari 1987: 239–49), that would regard marginal or outlying or 'anomalous' personae (such as Melanie, but also such as sorcerers) as persons who are not different from everyone else, but who uncannily represent what life truly is, at micro-perceptual and subpersonal levels of connectivity and in relations of strange alliance and unnatural affiliations with other beings.

The gambit of a politics of sorcery would be that the strange or unusual connections entertained by sorcerers (and others like them, such as artists, children and mystics) with non-human life and non-ordinary states of consciousness are in some sense normative for human life. The perspective of such a politics can in some sense be summed up in the claim that uncanny connections, such as Melanie's connection with the birds, might only *appear* to be pathological or destructive relative to an artificially restrictive social formation in which desire (and perhaps especially desire gendered feminine) is subject to instrumentalised domination – and it may have been Hitchcock's genius in *The Birds* to leverage a scathing critique of the symmetry between psychic and ecological dysfunction in the zenith of just such a smug post-war industrialised world.

But learning the uncanny is not a prelude to an ethic or politics of heroism, or of stoic resolve. In the end, Deleuze and Guattari are not arguing that each of us *should* seek the kind of disastrous extremes in which Melanie (to say nothing of Artaud or Michaux) finds herself. Rather, the argument is that, given that we *do* find ourselves in an ongoing ecological and erotic nightmare of which *The Birds* is no more than a slight exaggeration, it is imperative to seek to cultivate societies capable of an approach to the 'interkingdoms' of the uncanny that is neither catastrophic nor only 'for the birds' (such as those 'birds' like Melanie – beautiful, powerful, libertine women with the leisure to exploit their elusive status). The politics of sorcery pursues nothing more (and nothing less) than the instauration of a 'people to come' (cf. Semetsky and Delpech-Ramey 2011), one capable of a deeper ecology of desire, an ethos where we might find ourselves at home in the *unheimlich*.

# Notes

1. For an elaboration of Deleuze on perception as creation, see Rölli 2009.
2. *'Unheimlich nennt man Alles, was im Geheimnis, im Verborgenen ... bleiben sollte und hervorgetreten ist'*. As quoted from Schelling's *Philosophy of Mythology* in Daniel Sanders' *Wörterbuch der Deutschen Sprache* of 1860. See Freud 2003: 132.
3. Paglia (1998: 10) notes that birds had already been a subtextual motif in many of Hitchcock's earlier films, and that the theme of birds and bird-like women form a kind of motif across both his work and life.
4. Be that as it may, Hitchcock was inspired to make the film after he learned of several bird attacks in California (Paglia 1998: 11). Although he had Daphne du Maurier's script under licence for some time, Hitchcock had originally planned to make *Marnie* next, but changed his mind at least in part because of the course of historical (and natural – preternatural? – events).
5. As Paglia confirms, the schoolteacher Annie Hayworth's deep sensuality and profound affections indict both Mitch's cluelessness as a man and Melanie's superficiality (Paglia 1998: 46).
6. The psychoanalytically oriented literature on Hitchcock is vast, but relevant here is particularly the work of Silverman (1988) and Žižek (2010).
7. For an uncanny confluence between Jung's psychology and Deleuze's philosophy in the specific context of education see Semetsky and Delpech-Ramey (2012).
8. *Inside Hitchcock* (1973), from *The Men Who Made the Movies*, series produced by the American Cinematheque, HPI Home Videos.
9. It is important not to misunderstand Deleuze and Guattari's practice of studying fictional and extreme cases of what occurs on the line of flight as if such studies revealed a set of straightforward normative claims, as if one should literally repeat the exploits of these fictional others, in a becoming-fiction. The extremities of intensification are dangerous, and normative claims about experimental living must be made locally (Deleuze and Guattari 1987: 251).
10. Could it be that, in *the Birds*, there is something more vertiginous and psychotic exposed than both the obsessive Scotty (in *Vertigo*) and the compulsive Norman (in *Psycho*)? Everyone in *The Birds* is, in a certain way, an hysteric – no one wants to commit to anyone else, everyone wants to play out his or her own fantasy or illusion, forcing the real to assert itself, to everyone's chagrin and potentially to the end of an apocalyptic destruction of culture itself.
11. Be that as it may, Deleuze and Guattari are nothing if not supremely *hopeful* about what the encounter with unknown nature portends (hopeful, since there

really is nothing else than an intensity of relation, becoming, communication, even love, that has not yet been fully realized). Here Hitchcock might maintain both his irony and his distance, where Deleuze and Guattari would join Blake in urging on us the prophetic significance of the depths of our impasse with nature:

> Will you suffer this Satan, this Body of Doubt that Seems but is Not,
> To occupy the very threshold of Eternal Life? If Bacon, Newton, Locke
> Deny a Conscience in Man and the Communion of Saints and Angels,
> Contemning the Divine Vision and Fruition, Worshipping the Deus
> Of the Heathen, the God of this World, and the Goddess Nature,
> Mystery, Babylon the Great, The Druid Dragon and hidden Harlot,
> Is it not that Signal of the Morning which was told us in the Beginning?
>
> (Jerusalem 93: 20–6)

Blake's warning (Blake 1997) here is also prophetic hope: the denial of the supernatural, upon reaching its nadir, may signal a new dawn of humanity. Meanwhile, Melanie could be read as an avatar of Blake's Babylon, a perverted cultural goddess who mirrors, and then meets her match in a deranged Goddess Nature, a Rotting Goddess (Rabinowitz 1998) whose caprice and power both mirror and absorb Melanie's capriciousness. The rivalry inherent in such mirroring is 'resolved' in the incestuous love-pecking attack in the attic (the 'ancient', the antique, the pagan), the place where Melanie is returned to a sacred feminine – Goddess Nature – whose unwitting cultural avatar she does not, or has not yet realised, she herself in some sense is.

12. If modernity has fully rebelled against any such psycho-politico Platonism, it has also changed what it means to learn, and to know, inviting us to play out (or act out) a desire for revelation (apocalypse) that risks total destruction for the sake of metamorphosis. Such are the dangers of complete 'deterritorialisation' onto cosmic forces against which Deleuze and Guattari warned us. These considerations point, in the end, to a problem of the necessity of 'relative hierarchy' or 'reterritorialisation' that has not been well considered by Deleuzian scholarship, which has been too long obsessed by the idea of difference as novelty and intensity as sheer break with normalised actuality. There is a way in which one can argue that for Deleuze and Guattari certain kinds of practices distinguish themselves as perennial and vital by comparison with others. Without claiming that these practices (such as those germane to sorcery and to the modernist avant-garde) have any kind of eternal prerogative, and with full recognition that such practices may change in relation to a changing cosmos, one is nevertheless constrained to admit that that a principle of intensifying participation, or increasing sensitivity to and sympathy with the resonance of the (divergent) whole connects various experimental practices in Deleuze's thought. Deleuze himself can be situated in a tradition of hermetic and esoteric thought that has always tried to 'attune' human reason and affective capacity to what it has interpreted as natural 'spirits' – whether these be construed as angelic, astral, daemonic, elemental, or, for that matter, aviary. Yet such powers cannot be identified in advance of the forms of relation into which they are ritually or liturgically invoked, and they have no actuality apart from their activation (or de-activation, through disenchantment) by human desire. Straddling the nature/culture and material/psychic divides, such spirits are truly uncanny. I have argued elsewhere (Ramey 2012) that there are political (and fundamentally anti-capitalist) reasons for highlighting the connection of Deleuze to esoteric spiritual traditions, since it is the 'abstract' power of capital that directly sunders us from responsive awareness to the details and decorum that contingently emerge in the broken interstices of ecological and social being.

From this perspective, learning from the uncanny would form one of the conditions without which an ethics and politics beyond the demise of capital would be impossible.

# References

Blake, W. (1997), 'Jerusalem' in *The Illuminated Works of William Blake, Vol. 1*, Princeton: Princeton University Press.

Cavell, S. (1979), *The World Viewed: Reflections on the Ontology of Film*, Cambridge, MA: Harvard University Press.

Deleuze, G. (1994), *Difference and Repetition*, trans. P. Patton, New York: Columbia University Press.

Deleuze, G. and F. Guattari (1987), *A Thousand Plateaus: Capitalism and Schizophrenia*, trans. B. Massumi, Minneapolis: University of Minnesota Press.

Freud, S. (2003), *The Uncanny*, trans. D. McLintock, New York: Penguin Books.

Gottlieb, S. (ed.) (1995), *Hitchcock on Hitchcock: Selected Writings and Interviews*, Berkeley: University of California Press.

Jung, C. (1960), *The Structure and Dynamics of the Psyche (Collected Works of Jung, Vol. 8)*, Princeton: Princeton University Press.

Jung. C. (1989), *Memories, Dreams, Reflections*, trans. R. and C. Winston, New York: Random House.

Paglia, C. (1998), *The Birds*, London: British Film Institute.

Plato (1997), *Complete Works*, ed. J. M. Cooper, Indianapolis: Hackett.

Rabinowitz, J. (1998), *The Rotting Goddess: The Origin of the Witch in Classical Antiquity*, Brooklyn: Autonomedia.

Ramey, J. (2012), *The Hermetic Deleuze: Philosophy and Spiritual Ordeal*, Durham, NC: Duke University Press.

Rölli, M. (2009), 'Intensity Differentials and the Being of the Sensible', *Deleuze Studies*, 3(1): 26–53.

Semetsky, I. and J. Delpech-Ramey (2011), 'Educating Gnosis/Making a Difference', *Policy Futures in Education*, 9(4): 518–27.

Semetsky, I. and J. Delpech-Ramey (2012), 'Jung's Psychology and Deleuze's Philosophy: The unconscious in learning', *Educational Philosophy and Theory*, 44(1).

Silverman, K. (1988), *The Acoustic Mirror: The Female Voice in Psychoanalysis and Cinema*, Indianapolis: Indiana University Press.

Truffaut, F. with H. G. Scott (1967), *Hitchcock*, New York: Simon Schuster.

Žižek, Slavoj (2010), *Everything You Wanted to Know About Jacques Lacan But Were Afraid to Ask Hitchcock*, London: Verso.

# Chapter 10

# Morphologies for a Pedagogical Life

*[handwritten: Camel to lion is "s.d / s.r / process"]*

*[handwritten: apollo.]*  *[handwritten: dionysi.]*  *[handwritten: child is dio with. apollo]*

## Jason Wallin

In *Pure Immanence* (2001), Deleuze argues that the three metamorphoses commencing *Thus Spoke Zarathustra* can be thought as composing a figural diagram for Nietzsche's life. Overburdened by the weight of pre-existing values and educational accretions, the camel travels into the desert where it transforms into a lion. Destroying the values, idols and burdens that weigh upon the beast of burden, the lion supplants the camel's duty to the other's command ('thou shalt!') by affirming a willing critique of establishment thought (I will!). Having instantiated the transformation of all accepted beliefs, the lion undergoes the final transformation of becoming-child which relaunches thought towards the creation of new values. Camel-becoming-lion-becoming-child, or rather, three imbricated metamorphoses for the creation of an original life. While designating modulations in Nietzsche's life and health, the opening story of *Thus Spoke Zarathustra* might concomitantly be thought in a manner unfettered from Nietzsche's conceptual persona. That is, while Deleuze operationalises the three metamorphoses as a diagram for Nietzsche's becomings, the opening of *Thus Spoke Zarathustra* concomitantly pertains to the pedagogical question of how a life *might* be composed. To relaunch such a question would constitute an important problematic for education in so far as the image of thought informed upon formal schooling already presumes how a life should be composed. Recommencing this educational problematic, the three metamorphoses might be taken as *Zarathustra*'s provocation on how the composition of life might create a maximum coefficient of freedom counterposed to the camel's dutiful encumbrances.

*[handwritten: is find troyuta free-spirit / nomadic way finder??]*

## Becoming-Camel

If Zarathustra's diagram can be thought as a pedagogical thought experiment for escaping an overdetermined life, it is one that constitutes an untimely interceder for contemporary educational thought. That is, institutional education inverts the becomings Zarathustra links to the liberation of life, organising its ideal image in the figure of the camel Zarathustra insists we overcome. The modern school overflows with beasts burdened by the accretions of their lessons, the conferrals of truth, and the dutiful abeyances of 'public professorship' (Deleuze and Guattari 1994). Far from being a maligned image of educational life however, the beast of burden constitutes a lionised image of educational success. Any good doctoral student knows that successful initiation into the life of the academy is correlative to the accrual of institutional capital as much as it is the ability to bear the weight of such accretions. The same might be said of the child who today faces a veritable onslaught of workflow to which they might learn to submit as a dutiful animal of labour. Ostensibly, the image of life implicit in orthodox educational thought is intimately wed to the production of subjects adaptable to immense burden. Such an adaptation cannot be thought in strictly pejorative terms, for as Zarathustra contends, the beast of burden is a 'courageous spirit' in its acceptance of 'pain and sickness, patience toward the chastiser, taste for truth even if given acorns to eat' (Deleuze 2006: 170). This posed, the educated ass could not be further from the figure of the lion necessary for the transmutation of values that over-encumber life. On this point, the implicit celebration of encumbrance in contemporary education is symptomatic of an inversion of Zarathustra's pedagogical diagram. The child's fabulations become overcoded by a rational appeal to what is. The lion is chained to an image of adolescent rebellion to be superseded by the duties of adult life. Child-becoming-lion-becoming-camel, or rather, three imbricated metamorphoses for the production of a moribund life.

Zarathustra's three metamorphoses become a way in which the orthodox image of life presupposed by contemporary education might be counter-actualised. That is, Zarathustra's pedagogy recommences the unthought question of life that orthodox schooling always already thinks on our behalf. This is to say that schooling is already informed by an abstract diagram that presupposes how pedagogical life should go. In education, this diagram might alternatively be dubbed the curriculum, or more adequately, the royal science otherwise known as the curriculum-as-plan, a term originally coined by Aoki (2005a).

Constituting a particular kind of abstract machine for educational thought, the curriculum-as-plan territorialises pedagogical life in an image of arboreality, covering over the question of how a life might go by transposing it upon a molar grid of objectives and outcomes that prescribe what teachers and students should do. It is in this way that the curriculum-as-plan functions in the spirit of reproducing the 'ideal circles' or constants to which royal science aspires (Deleuze and Guattari 1987: 367). Organised along the horizon to royal science, the curriculum-as-plan aims to fulminate itself as an axiomatic for 'pedagogical life'. Put differently, what we might call a pedagogical life becomes an epiphenomenon reflected in relation to the molar image in which it is conditioned.

As a power of stratification, the curriculum-as-plan might be thought as an abstract machine which functions to standardise educational thought and action by informing upon the concrete assemblage of the classroom. Therein, the plan functions as a machine of anti-production warding against singularity, thereby reducing what might be thought to an image in which everyone thinks just like us! The American Department of Education's Race to the Top Initiative constitutes a quintessential example of such institutional anti-production in so far as it stratifies the link between the curriculum-as-plan and the economic apparatus of the State. Put differently, the ideal actualisation of the abstract machine otherwise known as the curriculum-as-plan becomes bureaucratically linked to the fiscal rewards proffered to schools. Think like us or not at all. Regulated like zoo animals, teachers and students trace a deep rut at the threshold of their cages, habitually drawn back upon a course of life set out in advance. This is to say that the curriculum-as-plan constitutes a ready-made territory that always already marks a threshold for what should be thought or produced pedagogically. This is the bureaucrat's curriculum, and it might be known by the encumbering effect it has upon teachers and students who dutifully carry its mutilated image of life into their own. Citing the stressors of continual surveillance, impossible government targets, and the transference of workplace challenges into the personal lives of teachers, Britain's National Union of Teachers reported in 2008 that the suicide rate of teachers was 30–40 per cent higher than that of the national average (NUT Health and Safety Unit 2008).

While the sedimented image of life presupposed by the curriculum-as-plan composes a dominant architectonic stratum in contemporary educational thought, its diagram for living has roots in antiquity. As Pinar (1974) articulates in his analysis of pedagogical life, the etymology of the curriculum is derived from the Latin *currere*, meaning to run. In its most active sense, *currere* suggests a style of education (*educare*) that aspires to leading students from those habitual patterns and automatic responses that render thought docile (Colebrook 2008). Such a pedagogical style seems closer to what Deleuze has in mind when he suggests that 'our only teachers are those who . . . are able to emit signs to be developed in heterogeneity rather than propose gestures for us to reproduce' (Deleuze 2004: 26). Yet, it is this very reproductive tendency that inheres in *currere*'s reactive conceptualisation in the curriculum-as-plan, for while *currere* evokes an image of flight, it's origins concomitantly designate the Roman chariot-track as a highly coded territory of movement. Drawn from antiquity, *currere* designates a literal course run by slaves. Drawn upon the abstract machine of contemporary education, this reactive image of *currere* might otherwise be known via the symptoms it produces in the material life of the school. Akin to the chariot racers of ancient Rome, pedagogical life is made to orbit the interminable production of routine gestures, hence constraining movement to its most familiar circuits of action. It is this closed-circuit-machine that is carried into the formative models of such curriculum designers as Bobbitt (1928) and Tyler (1949), whose instrumental image of education functions to instil the normative conditions of State thought in every mind. The explicit pedagogical questions introduced by early curriculum design demonstrates a preoccupation with the organisation of educational experience and the conformity of student behaviours to pre-established norms (Tyler 1949). In other words, the content of *currere*'s course would be conceived in terms of its alignment to a predestined image of Being. Nietzsche (1969) would be echoed by the critical pedagogy movement of the 1970s when he argued that such conditions are optimal for the production of an easily manipulated, unthinking herd mentality.

The abstract-machine of bureaucratic educational thought produces its own illness. It is, as Guattari writes, a system 'of modeling in which we are entangled and which [is] in the process of completely polluting us, head and heart' (1996: 132). In part, this imbroglio points to a failure to ask how we got to where we are, or rather, to seek out singular models for the problems faced in education. Such a failure inheres in the damning critique of public schooling in the film *Waiting for Superman* (2010). In its documentation of the 'failure factories' that have ostensibly become America's public schools, the film is unsuccessful in rooting out the very image of life presupposed by contemporary education. In the absence of such an analysis, the film suggests that the decline of public schooling stems from a failure of correspondence between the abstract machine of curriculum-as-plan and the concrete assemblage of the educational organisation. This, however, constitutes a false problem in so far as it obfuscates difference by accepting the curriculum-as-plan as a transcendent axiom which the life of the classroom is presupposed to reflect. This situation is undoubtedly made worse by the fact that the film takes the axiom of the curriculum-as-plan for the real. This is to say that the impulse of *Waiting for Superman* acquiesces to the image of life as it is given, taking this reality as the only image of thought it is capable of sensing (Deleuze 2006). Like the dutiful camel who knows only the burden weighing upon it, this critique of public schools dare not say no to those machines of State thought from which its critique automatically follows.

＊＊＊

## Becoming-Lion

Were the curriculum-as-plan the only image of life informing on the material life of the school, the prospect of thinking education as an act of freeing life would be nigh impossible. That is, a style of education premised on leading out from established habit cannot simply be a matter of repeating in so far as must necessarily involve the active linkage of heterogeneic signs. To draw from Deleuze, it is inadequate for the student learning to swim to mimic the gestures of the instructor when finding themselves faced with conditions qualitatively distinct from those practised in the sand. The ideal stroke might very well prove itself insufficient in turbulent waters, where replication by rote would ensure trouble if not an outright drowning. 'Learning to swim . . . means composing the singular points of one's own body . . . with those of another shape or element, which tears us apart but also propels us into a hitherto unknown and unheard of world of problems' (2004: 241). To take this seriously suggests that no transcendent image of life 'set against itself to limit itself' will be sufficient to produce a liberatory pedagogy (Deleuze and Guattari 1987: 503). Rather, education must become sensitive to the singularity of 'pedagogical life'. In this task, the abstract machine of educational orthodoxy known as the curriculum-as-plan must be differentiated in kind from its immanent encounter with the *living* multiplicity of the classroom (Aoki 2005b). In other words, where the curriculum-as-plan functions as *the* abstract machine for educational thought, designating what education's concrete assemblages *can do*, what we might call the *lived-curriculum* begins to palpate the virtuality that education's royal science attempts to capture in the circuits of its molar machinery.

The curriculum-as-lived might otherwise be dubbed the nomad science of educational thought. If there is one lesson that new teachers learn quickly, it is precisely this – not for want of trying, no amount of planning makes one adequate to an encounter with multiplicity. In part, the staggering rates of teacher self-attrition in North America are symptomatic of this most difficult lesson. The royal science in which pre-service teachers are often trained is ill equipped to affirm the multiplicity of desiring-forces encountered in schools. Despite the myriad instructional strategies and methods of classroom engagement imparted to pre-service teachers, education's essential image of life has remained fundamentally tethered to the closed-circuit, ends-means orientation of the Roman chariot track. Recognising 'only reactive forms of life', education suffers a paucity of images for thinking how a life might be composed (Deleuze 2001: 71). In this vein, the curriculum is the ass's idea of education, obfuscating its unequal relationship to a virtuality of potential life courses – 'as many as there are teachers and students' (Aoki 2005c: 426). It is on this point that we might return to the notion that teaching is not a matter of reproducing gestures and habits of thought (Deleuze 2006). That is, the question remains as to how the abstract machine of educational thought might be heterogeneously negotiated in its connection to the multiplicity of conditions with which it is pedagogically contracted. In a manner that avoids falling back onto the historical aspiration to homogenise 'pedagogical life' as a condition for the uncomplicated transmission of the curriculum-as-plan, education's nomad science orients pedagogy towards its most singular or otherwise, 'indefinite' form of composition (Roy 2003).

The lived-curriculum mobilises the problematic of how a life might be composed at the immanent contact point between the curriculum-as-plan and the virtual. It is this problematic that is affirmed in myriad Hollywood films focusing on the liberation of pedagogical life from under the stultifying powers of standardisation. Ostensibly, where teaching goes right is when it least resembles the imperial model it is meant to reflect. Among other things, Richard Linklater's oft-celebrated film *School of Rock* (2003) affirms the attempt to compose a singular life subtracted from all forms of standardisation and orthodoxy. Despite a near obverse filmic treatment of pedagogical life, Ryan Fleck's *Half-Nelson* (2006) palpates a similar affirmation. Each begins to think the composition of a line of escape forged amidst an otherwise banal or routine existence in schools. Such an affirmative escape is oriented at releasing those molecular impulses running subjacent to the molar institution, wresting pedagogical life back from its internment under the overdetermined image of either the school-as-barracks or the school-as-factory. Put differently, these 'pedagogical' films palpate immanence at that very moment when vital life is most radically drained from the institutional milieu. In a way that begins to parallel the scene in Dickens' *Our Mutual Friend*, of the nearly expired Rogue Riderhood, education's moribundity sparks an impersonal life, opening upon an immanent multiplicity for thinking how a life might go. In other words, pedagogy becomes a life when it achieves a necessary dilation that escapes its *a priori* image, composing in this way the potential for the reterritorialisation of a singular life that does not yet have a name. Across a litany of 'pedagogical films', it is this event that constitutes the most revolutionary act of education, one that is fundamentally counterposed to the camel's reactive image of thought.

In so far as the lived-curriculum might be thought as the composition of a smooth space between the curriculum-as-plan and the virtuality of a life, it becomes a corollary to the experimental nomad science of improvisation. Returning to Deleuze's example in *Difference and Repetition*, the lived-curriculum might be thought as the motile line composed between the official gestures of the swimming instructor and the multiplicity of conditions that a swimmer might encounter. In this way, the lived-curriculum necessitates the deterritorialisation of education's molar image, or rather, those official gestures born from the representational impulse of the curriculum-as-plan. For example, having sensed the pull of a rip current, it becomes utterly inadequate for the swimmer to represent the gestures taught to him poolside. One must not simply represent, but become prepared to deterritorialise with infinite speed such that the official gestures of the teacher can be modulated in connection with new problems. It is in this vein that the composition of a lived-curriculum necessitates that pedagogy task itself with both encountering and creating original problems through which new modes of non-representational experimentation might be operationalised. Only once pedagogy has become a matter of unleashing thought and action from material repetition will it become capable of creating new styles and images of living. If this sketch can be taken as a rough diagram for what it means to compose a lived-curriculum, then it is one that concomitantly relies upon inventive processes of improvisation, or rather, the composition of a smooth space where what is can be brought into relation with problems unthought by the given. This is to affirm the non-foundational character of the given by promulgating a creative phylum that functions by decoding the official educational refrain elsewhere dubbed the curriculum-as-plan. In this way, the lived curriculum might be thought as an affirmation that no longer takes on the 'burden of what is, but to release, to set free what lives' (Deleuze 2006: 174).

A condition for education's universalisation is the obfuscation of a pedagogical life, or rather, the overdetermination of the creative pedagogical phylum upon which a life might be composed. To rethink pedagogy alongside the practice of improvisation hence marks a departure from the circuit of instrumental thinking that informs the curriculum-as-plan. Improvisation is hence inherently dangerous in so far as it reveals an immanent creative phylum no longer submitted to the illusion of transcendence that occludes the necessity of composition. As an inexact yet rigorous concept for pedagogical thinking, improvisation reveals the plane of immanence unthought by the bureaucrat's curriculum. Twisting Spinoza, we do not yet know how a life might go. This is to say that a pedagogical life (*currere*) must first be made. This practical approach to the composition of a pedagogical life once again shares fidelity with musical improvisation in so far as it plots an escape from under the burden of representational thought. That is, where representation relies on the adaptation of thought to prior images and the integration of desiring-production within pre-existing circuits of enunciation, improvisation unleashes thought to seek out new arrangements and formations.

'To seek harmony is to kill nature, to stop its pulsations, and to embrace the dead corpse that is left behind' (Suzuki cited in Aoki 2005b: 371). Constituting a noological ideal for thinking the course of a life, the image of integration, adaptive harmony and synthesis in education has its musicological equivalent in the classical orchestra (Holland 2004). That is, the organisation of the classical orchestra functions to capture difference by emphasising practices of tracing and representation, hence producing a coded block of antichaos that delimits experimental forces according to an organising score (Attali 1985). As Canetti (1962) argues, the conductor and score exert powers of life and death over the 'voices' of the symphony. While the hierarchical power of the score ensures the coordination of the orchestra, such unity comes at the cost of the orchestra's assent to a prior image of what a (musical) body might do. In this division of labour, the player becomes obedient to the score as a transcendent authority to which desiring-production becomes passively circuited. Indeed, the valuation of the orchestral player is predicated on their fidelitous tracing of a pre-established enunciative refrain. This, however, is yet to think in terms of the non-representational and non-repetitive force of improvisation.

While the compositions of such experimental musicians as John

Zorn, Don Van Vliet, or Mike Patton draw upon similar musicological resources, they productively fail to represent given musicological territories. This is to say that their art does not seek to reproduce, but rather functions to desediment and seek new formations of sound via a process of improvisational creation. In this vein, improvisation actively deviates from any notion of a prior course (score) or orthodox image of thought in its mapping of singular territories that do not yet bear a proper name (Deleuze 1995). Rather than being an iteration of a prior route then, improvised music might more adequately be dubbed itinerary (Holland 2004). Put differently, as it might be linked to the notion of dehabituation intimate to *educare*, improvised music does not trace, but travels, often deploying a multiplicity of musicological forces (tempos, keys and styles) simultaneously. Such compositions thus plot a line of escape from under the ideal of unification, breaking apart orthodox circuits of relation and exchange while eluding capture by representational or repetitive powers. In the absence of a formal leader for example, improvisational composition becomes immanent to the desiring-production of a collective no longer reducible to the individual. Further, unlike classical symphonic orchestration in which the drive of the player is circuited to the reproduction of the musical score, improvisational music becomes open to affirming disjunctive divergence from within. The 'fiction of sameness' that defines the curriculum-as-plan and organises orthodox desiring-production in schools might be similarly dilated by the nomad science of improvisation (Aoki 2005d: 161). That is, when the curriculum-as-plan is encountered in the mode of improvisation, the immanent flows of classroom life deform and assemble in singular ways. Such immanent morphologies are not those of an artificial life circuited to a transcendent ideal, but those of a life in the process of becoming.

Karateka Jesse Enkamp provokes the instructors at his dojo: 'become a master teacher, I dare you!' This provocation is far from an entreaty to be well planned, in fact, Enkamp derides planning as an impediment to a teacher's becoming. The risk of Enkamp's dare extends from his assertion that to be a master teacher necessitates becoming a skilled improviser. In part, this pedagogical appeal is an admission that no amount of planning will be sufficient to help the teacher anyway. That is, while planning might allow the instructor to navigate a plan without faltering, this is not yet to affirm a style of pedagogy oriented to the challenge of preparing a supple plane for immanent thought and action. In other words, the instructor's finely laid plans are ill suited to the affirmation of pedagogy as a matter of creation, or rather, of treating pedagogical life as a work of art capable of instantiating an original and non-representational style of thinking and acting (Surin 2011). Where the instructor aims to project an habitual plan upon the life of the classroom or within the student, Enkamp asserts, (s)he has failed. This understanding is fundamental to the karateka, since to engage one's opponent following a series of preformulated moves or patterns of thought is surely to court a grievous beating. In contradistinction to the tracing of a well-plotted course, the pedagogue must always be 'on the lookout' in a manner sensitive to the reception of signs (Deleuze and Parnet 2008). As they are for the artist, the immanent production of untimely connections, the introduction of new problems, or the failure of old models become the 'matter' of a pedagogical life. It is in this way that pedagogy might become adequate to the creation of original actions qualitatively distinct from the production of counter-algorithms or new universals. Affirming pedagogy as an art of improvisation is to affirm that the composition of a pedagogical life is a matter of both skilful and practical experimentation always growing immanently, in the middle of things.

The creation of an experimental plane not yet overdetermined in the image of the curriculum-as-plan enters into fidelity with the lion's affirmation ('I will'). No longer aspiring to reflect the *a priori* course of ends-means, instrumental, or transcendent production, such a plane functions to affirm that a pedagogical life must first be made and, further, that its making involve the overturning of those established images that presuppose how a life ought to go. By thinking pedagogy as the task of founding a compositional plane, pedagogical life is given back to becoming unanticipated by an antecedent being. As Daignault avers, 'the curriculum does not exist, it happens' (cited in Hwu 2004: 183). Despite the camel's insistence otherwise, the curriculum is not yet a thing that weighs upon it. The problem all along, Aoki (2005a) observes, is that we have become accustomed to thinking the curriculum as a noun and thereby ascribing it a reality from which life in schools is thought to arboreally extend. In contradistinction, Daignault (2008) palpates the curriculum-event, or rather, the notion that a pedagogical life is always actual-virtual, dilating through digressive connections or untimely occurrences to create new terrain for unanticipated thought and action. This is what the molar machines of institutional standardisation cannot think in so far as they continually confuse their particular abstract machine with the indeterminate plane of composition itself (Rajchman 2000).

'[Like a cat] I am on the watch', Daignault writes of life in the classroom, 'for a hint that, no matter how small it is, will allow me to open up a parenthetical remark and take a step outside' (2008: 56). To rethink *currere* as a process, however, is to appeal neither to a Heraclidian view of life nor to a postmodern celebration of continual semiotic digression. As Deleuze and Guattari (1984) contend, every vector of deterritorialisation reterritorialises somewhere else. While the search for new formations of *currere* (a course of a life) require the continual freeing of life from prior circuits of capture, this task must continually be connected to the composition of singular territories, lest 'education' fall prey to the image of perpetual training, interminable prolongation, and associated debt intimate to its recommencement under neo-liberalism. What remains pedagogically relevant in the otherwise cliché-laden *Karate Kid* (1984) is precisely this: the force of pedagogy is not merely to forge new ground or survey some new ethics of knowledge, but to sustain singular terrain such that a new style of living can become through it. As painting to a canvas, pedagogy might be thought as the act of composing curriculum (*currere*). Put differently, pedagogy might be thought as the act of sketching out *currere*'s course. It is this vague noology of pedagogical life that is ostensibly closer to the lion's affirmation that the transmutation of established values is necessary, that one might affirm difference and overcome the nihilistic admonition that life is simply what others have already made of it. Yet, as Deleuze and Guattari (1994) remark on the perennial problem of the painter, the canvas is always already populated by the hard to overcome clichés and the willing-encumbrance of the camel who clings to its 'personal' microfascisms.

## Becoming-Child

*" bring it all togetha ".*
*y peTse foram urtue for*

Historically, the role of the pedagogue was performed by a slave entrusted to safely accompany the student between home and school. While the conceptualisation of pedagogy as the act of leading the student from one ordinal (molar) point to another (be it a developmental benchmark, rank, class, or institution) insists within contemporary schooling, an 'art of pedagogy' might alternatively be understood as the composition of a life in conjunction with forces 'outside' of or alien to such molar points. That is, in its historical sense, the pedagogue had no formal position within the schoolhouse, occupying instead a position peripheral to the molar institution. While the pedagogue would have functioned *in loco parentis*, ensuring that the student arrive safely at her proscribed destination, the 'art of pedagogy' might have more radically entailed a creative encounter and negotiation with the subtle variations of city life. Put differently, the pedagogue of antiquity would have occupied a quasi-nomadic relationship to the molar institution by composing a zone of proximity with the impersonal forces of the city. Counterposed to the molarising power of the classroom then, the pedagogue might have shared a closer fidelity to the molecular forces of the street. Herein, the burden of tracing a habitual line between the ordinal points of home and school is eclipsed by the potential encounter with 'outside forces' largely unthought within contemporary education (Deleuze and Guattari 1987).

While the pedagogue of antiquity would have been invested in the care of her charge, her pedagogy would have been concomitantly connected to the impersonal modulations, flows and fleeing lines of the city. It is in this way that the ancient role of the pedagogue might be rehabilitated as a means of overcoming an enslavement to movement by ordinal or molar coordinates. Put differently, if pedagogy can be thought as an art of palpating the impersonal, it might become capable of liberating life from the grip of the transcendent, be it the illusion of universals, the ethics of knowledge, or the individual schema (Deleuze and Guattari 1987). For as much as pedagogy continues to be defined in terms a relationship between people, such a characterisation has become incapable of detecting the inhuman forces that draw life into composition with what it is not yet. It is in this manner that we might begin to think 'the art of pedagogy' as less connected to the education of individuals than an encounter with those non-personal haecceities that make pedagogy more than personal. Such a pedagogy might recommence 'a belief in the world and the potentials of a life' freed from their organisation in some prior image of life (Deleuze 2001: 18).

In *Cinema 2*, Deleuze writes that the ostensibly banal processes of mechanised reproduction utilised by Warhol are marked by small differences that subtract the artwork from standardisation. More adequately, Deleuze's treatment of Warhol's art palpates a mode of subtraction crucial to thinking beyond the circuit of representation where the notion of difference is always cathected to a *prior thing*. To take seriously Deleuze's provocation that creative repetition entails the return of difference itself is to impose a radical caveat against the illusion of standardisation. In *Thus Spoke Zarathustra*, the eternal return is not the 'same', but 'a thought of the absolutely different' (Deleuze 2006: 46). As Deleuze remarks, '*return is the being of that which becomes*' (2006: 24). Open to the multiplicity of the future, being is no longer simply itself, but a differentiating potential for *becoming*. In other words, the eternal return is for Deleuze the affirmative and constitutive power of the future. It is in this vein that the kind of complex repetition upon which the standardisation of education relies disguises variability. Amidst the bureaucrat's image of the classroom as a closed laboratory for the technical repetition of learner and behavioural objectives, shreds of difference continually return in so far as the act of composing *currere* opens upon an unknown future. Even the most seasoned teacher might admit to commencing a new semester of teaching with apprehension over the dice throw that is beginning of *currere*'s composition.

The 'art of pedagogy' is as much about the sensitive reception and creation of signs as it is an ethics of *amor fati*, or rather, of affirming and maximising the potential of that which returns. As Deleuze (2006) writes, it is the affirmation of the return of difference that marks the most difficult task for the teacher Zarathustra. Akin to the risk of thinking pedagogy in the mode of improvisation, we simply do not know how the dice will fall back. This is the affirmation of chance – the very chance that cannot be wagered under the governmental image of standardised education. The poverty connected to this obfuscation of difference is that *educare* become a matter of retarding movement, or tracing worn paths of thought. Apart from the presumption of conscious selection or the intentional composition of the course of 'pedagogical life' (*currere*), the eternal return palpates another kind of life irreducible to the life of the student, teacher, or even the historical life of educational content. This life constitutes the unthought within Hollywood's teacher melodrama, which continuously bear upon the narratological life of the student and teacher.

While the difference inhering in the return of the dice throw might become distorted by its forced adaptation to representational thought, impersonal differences return in affirmation of the change and becoming that are the hallmarks of a pedagogy that enhances the potential to think and act in original ways. Yet, even in the bleakest scenario where a pedagogue habitually traces an organisational pattern or associative circuit, such repetition already inheres in the act of selecting from a multiplicity of potential itinerant routes. In this way, repetition is at least minimally counterposed to the slave mentality demanded by education's royal science, since the pedagogue must continually select, even if such selections assume the character of reactive thinking that separate a life from what it can do. This however, is yet to affirm a kind of difference no longer cathected to a prior thing. Indeed, one of the highest aspirations of the pedagogue must be to adequately affirm how the dice return, or rather, how the return of difference continually requires new practices and images for thinking pedagogically. As Guattari (cited in

Guattari and Rolnik 2009) suggests, the images that we have of education have largely failed to liberate life from under the human-all-too-human molar machines of orthodox education. Indeed, the very notion of 'public education' is contemporarily travailed by problems Deleuze and Guattari (1994) ascribe to the public professor. That is, the standardising impulse of contemporary educational thought has aspired to produce a public unquestionably adapted to the desiring machines of the State, pathologising difference as a defect made manageable through the control mechanisms of continual monitoring and performance evaluation. Eroding the very mechanisms that once functioned to protect the singularity of pedagogical composition, the State war against tenure being mobilised across the United States is preparing a new form of social insecurity through which it will exert finer measures of biopolitical control upon the lives of both educator and educated.

To accept Deleuze's iteration of the eternal return is to reject the nihilism of the desert and the over-encumbrances of the camel. It is to think in place of the lion. That is, amidst the ostensible repetition and encumbrances of universal life, the lion commences the willing affirmation of difference. Herein, the lion's joyous pronouncement 'I will' has nothing to do with the exertion of power, but is, rather, the willing affirmation of difference for the 'transmutation of values' (Deleuze 2001: 60). Apart from the molar identities by which pedagogy is most typically known then, the lion commences two jets of becoming germane to pedagogical life. The first might be thought as a corollary of composition in so far as lion's emphatic 'No!' is levied against the transcendent powers of representational thought. As Deleuze writes, 'in the lion, negation becomes a power of affirming . . . to create, not to bear, put up with or accept' (2006: 173). Marking the 'negation of reactive forces themselves', the lion's 'No!' palpates the creative phylum necessary for the composition of an original life (*currere*) that 'no longer has a name, though . . . can be mistaken for no other' (Deleuze 2006: 65; 2001: 29). Where for the camel the desert is populated by mirages taken as reality, the lion's desert might be thought as an immanent plane upon which thought might be recommended. In place of a reactive nihilism that acquiesces to what is, the lion overturns the power of the transcendent by imparting the lesson that things might be made differently. Destroying idols and sedimentary accretions, the lion's deterritorialisation of accepted values concomitantly palpates immanence, commencing a desert plane of released nomadic flows.

In Zarathustra's three metamorphoses, the nomadic plane prepared by the lion's affirmation is subsequently populated by a people-yet-to-come figured in the final metamorphosis, becoming-child. As Deleuze enigmatically writes, however, the child is pre-individual, vaguely resembling all other children. While possessing 'barely any individuality', Deleuze writes, the child possesses singularities that are not yet 'subjective qualities' (2001: 30). 'A smile, a gesture, a funny face', or rather, virtualities not yet captured in an actual strata. The pedagogy of the lion's nihilism is hence dislocated from the recuperation of a new individuality. Summoning the plane of immanence, the lion prepares the way for a style of living composed of singularities rather than representational identities. That is, in so far as pedagogy is typically characterised by a duty to the molar child, Zarathustra's metamorphoses create a circuit-breaking force, suggesting that pedagogy pertains less to 'actual' children than to the non-personal singularities that make up a life. As Deleuze suggests, becoming-child has nothing to do with becoming recognisable according to the generalised traits of creativity, naivety, or fascination attributed to children, but instead, with commencing an indeterminate plane of composition upon which singularities might mix and coalesce into new formations unfettered from their association to a molar identity.

Becoming-child recommences pedagogy's 'ancient' task of composing *currere*. Yet more radically, it marks a dilation of the actual upon a singular life, or rather, a life composed of subindividual forces that fail to reterritorialise upon an orthodox image of molar identity. It is in this vein that pedagogy might eclipse the gravitational pull of representational thought in so far as Zarathustra's becoming-child ushers the nomadic forces unleashed by the lion's 'negation of negation' into new, less burdensome formations. Ultimately, becoming-child is both an affirmation of the new and a pedagogical challenge to experiment with the creation of new arrangements of life. Such a challenge minimally inheres in the pedagogy of Célestin Freinet, whose experimental connection of unconscious desiring-production with the printing press fabulated a new, freer form of enunciation and collective production within institutional space. This is to say that the kind of life promulgated by becoming-child is sensitive to those molecular forces that pass through and escape the clutches of representation, constituting original forms of life and powers of enunciation. Here, becoming-child might enter into a productive relation with alien forces, or rather, singularities that escape the capture of representation such that being might be given back to becoming. It is in this way that becoming-child suggests a pedagogical style oriented to the affirmation of untimely singularities through which thought might be recommenced. Daignault affirms such a singularity when he insists that the curriculum does not exist, 'it happens' (cited in

Hwu 2004: 183). 'It' happens is the eternal return, happening again and again, year after year, class after class. Yet, 'it' happens concomitantly marks the untimely and pre-personal interceder that introduces new problems for the composition of pedagogical life. What, in this manner, constitutes a pedagogical life but the eternal return and the willing affirmation or *amor fati* of composing *currere* from the difference with which it repeats? The camel becoming lion becoming child, or rather, sedimented life becoming affirmed difference for the composition of the singular – three metamorphoses for the composition of a pedagogical life. Herein, education (*educare*) is no longer a matter of individualising life, but of constituting an indeterminate plane of composition for the recommencement of ontology, or rather, a style of living that attends to education's obfuscated question of how a life might go. Rather, it is to dilate pedagogy upon the virtual as a tactic for recommencing a style of *currere* unlinked from prior circuits of tracing, be it the linearity of instrumental thought or an image of circular return that fails to affirm disjunctive lines of flight. What teacher does this better than one who approaches pedagogy as both physician and artist, affirming the lived curriculum in the year omega of representational thought (Surin 2011)? This is not only to follow Bloom's (1997) provocation to begin as if one did not yet know, but more importantly, to approach pedagogy as the task of creating a life. Such a task is increasingly important in an age wherein the image of life assumed by orthodox education is increasingly overdetermined.

As Foucault (1994) argues in *The Order of Things*, the idea of life is relatively recent. Nonexistent prior the eighteenth century, the idea of life comes to constitute a transcendent plane upon which 'political man' emerges as an epiphenomenon. A homogenising vitalism is instantiated in lieu of life composed from a diversity of social relations. One life emerges in place of an 'unlimited finity' (Deleuze 1988: 131). Reterritorialised in the image of transcendent life, 'man' is reordered according to *a priori* exigencies that retroactively constitute a means for regulating and managing the subject according to the image of life they presuppose. In this scenario, 'man' becomes educated because it is a requirement of life. Yet, it is this very presupposition that constitutes a perennial crisis in education manifest in the often heard student reproach that school fails to recognise the lives of those that undergo it. This posed, educational thought must go further still in its attempt to detect a kind of life not yet captured in the molar image of the individual or otherwise, the image of personal desire that has driven the rise of 'boutique education' under neo-liberalism. To think in terms of the inhuman life of pedagogy, or rather, the pre-individual plane of immanence that constitutes the unthought within contemporary education, is to rethink education as first a project of creation. To what should education aspire but the detection of a creative phylum capable of differentiating education from education in general? As Deleuze (2004) suggests, it is only when the student learning to swim is able to differentiate between her lessons in general and their necessary counter-actualisation in relation to new problems that she might truly become capable of swimming. This is already to think pedagogy as a matter of detecting the plane of immanence whereupon new relations and heterogeneic connections might be machined. And where pedagogy becomes oriented to the composition of singularities already suggests thinking a life without a transcendent image – a life containing only events (Deleuze 2001). Counterposed to the actualisation of how pedagogical life should go, a pedagogical life might be rethought as an experimental approach to the difference with which the same continually returns. Swimming is never the same twice and to learn this necessitates the affirmation of the eternal return. This is to say that for as much as the figure of the camel has come to constitute a lauded image of 'educated man', another style of pedagogy is necessary to recommence a kind of education (*educare*) that aspires to voyage out from habitual tracts of thought and action. For that, pedagogy must prepare a plane for thinking what resists in standardisation. This is to commence pedagogical life in a style closer to that of Nietzsche's Zarathustra. To become-lion to unfetter thought from what is – to become-child to apprehend the potential that life might be composed differently.

# References

Aoki, T. (2005a), 'Legitimating Lived Curriculum: Toward a Curricular Landscape of Multiplicity' in W. Pinar and R. Irwin (eds), *Curriculum in a New Key: The Collected Works of Ted T. Aoki*, Mahwah, NJ: Lawrence Erlbaum Associates, pp. 199–218. (Originally published in 1993.)

Aoki, T. (2005b), 'Sonare and Videre: A Story, Three Echoes and a Lingering Note' in W. Pinar and R. Irwin (eds), *Curriculum in a New Key: The Collected Works of Ted T. Aoki*, Mahwah, NJ: Lawrence Erlbaum Associates, pp. 367–76. (Originally published in 1991.)

Aoki, T. (2005c), 'Locating Lived Pedagogy in Teacher "Research": Five metonymic moments' in W. Pinar and R. Irwin (eds), *Curriculum in a New Key: The Collected Works of Ted T. Aoki*, Mahwah, NJ: Lawrence Erlbaum Associates, pp. 426–32. (Originally published in 2003.)

Aoki, T. (2005d), 'Teaching as Indwelling Between Two Curriculum Worlds' in W. Pinar and R. Irwin (eds), *Curriculum in a New Key: The Collected Works of Ted T. Aoki*, Mahwah, NJ: Lawrence Erlbaum Associates, pp. 159–65. (Originally published in 1986.)

Attali, J. (1985), *Noise: The Political Economy of Music*, trans. B. Massumi, Minneapolis: University of Minnesota Press.

Bloom, H. (1997), *The Anxiety of Influence*, Oxford: Oxford University Press.

Bobbitt, F. (1928), *How to Make a Curriculum*, Boston: Houghton Mifflin.

Canetti, E. (1962), *Crowds and Power*, New York: Viking.

Colebrook, C. (2008), 'Leading Out, Leading On: The Soul of Education' in I. Semetsky (ed.), *Nomadic Education: Variations on a Theme*, Rotterdam: Sense, pp. 35–42.

Daignault, J. (2008), 'Pedagogy and Deleuze's Concept of the Virtual' in I. Semetsky (ed.), *Nomadic Education: Variations on a Theme*, Rotterdam: Sense, pp. 42–60.

Deleuze, G. (1988), *Foucault*, trans. S. Hand, London: Athlone.

Deleuze, G. (1995), *Negotiations 1972–1990*, trans. M. Joughin, New York: Columbia University Press.

Deleuze, G. (2000), *Proust and Signs*, trans. R. Howard, Minneapolis: University of Minnesota Press.

Deleuze, G. (2001), *Pure Immanence: Essays on a Life*, trans. A. Boyman, New York: Zone Books.

Deleuze, G. (2003), *Cinema 2: The Time-Image*, trans. H. Tomlinson and B. Habberjam, Minneapolis: University of Minnesota Press.

Deleuze, G. (2004), *Difference and Repetition*, trans. P. Patton, New York: Continuum.

Deleuze, G. (2006), *Nietzsche and Philosophy*, trans. H. Tomlinson, New York: Continuum.

Deleuze, G. and F. Guattari (1984), *Anti-Oedipus: Capitalism and Schizophrenia*, trans. R. Hurley, M. Seem and H. R. Lane, Minneapolis: University of Minnesota Press.

Deleuze, G. and F. Guattari (1987), *A Thousand Plateaus: Capitalism and Schizophrenia*, trans. B. Massumi, Minneapolis: University of Minnesota Press.

Deleuze, G. and F. Guattari (1994), *What is Philosophy?* trans. H. Tomlinson and G. Burchell, New York: Columbia University Press.

Deleuze, G. and C. Parnet (2008), Overview of *L'Abecedaire de Gilles Deleuze, avec Claire Parnet*, dir. Pierre Andre Boutang (1996), by C. Stivale <http://www.langlab.wayne.edu/cstivale/d-g/ABC3.html> (accessed 19 September 2012).

Foucault, M. (1994), *The Order of Things*, New York: Routledge.

Guattari, F. (1996), *The Guattari Reader*, ed. G. Genosko, Oxford: Blackwell.

Guattari, F. and S. Rolnik (2008), *Molecular Revolution in Brazil*, Los Angeles: Semiotext(e).

Holland, E. (2004), 'Studies in Applied Nomadology: Jazz Improvisation and Post-capitalist Markets' in I. Buchanan and M. Swiboda (eds), *Deleuze and Music*, Edinburgh: Edinburgh University Press, pp. 20–35.

Hwu, W. (2004), 'Gilles Deleuze and Jacques Daignault: Understanding Curriculum as Difference and Sense' in W. M. Reynolds and J. A. Webber (eds), *Expanding Curriculum Theory: Dis/positions and Lines of Flight*, Mahwah, NJ: Lawrence Erlbaum Associates, pp. 181–202.

Nietzsche, F. (1969), *Thus Spoke Zarathustra*, trans. D. Smith, Oxford: Oxford University Press.

NUT Health and Safety (2008), 'Teacher Stress in Context' <www.teachers.org.uk/files/TEACHER-STRESS_0.doc> (accessed 14 June 2011).

Pinar, W. F. (1974), 'Currere: Toward Reconceptualization' in J. Jelinek (ed.), *Basic Problems in Modern Education*, Temple: Arizona State University, College of Education, pp. 147–71.

Rajchman, J. (2000), *The Deleuze Connections*, Cambridge, MA: MIT Press.

Rajchman, J. (2001), 'Introduction' to G. Deleuze, *Pure Immanence: Essays on a Life*, New York: Zone Books, pp. 7–23.

Roy, K. (2003), *Teachers in Nomadic Spaces: Deleuze and Curriculum*, New York: Peter Lang.

Surin, K. (2011), 'Existing Not as a Subject But as a Work of Art': The Task of Ethics or Aesthetics' in N. Jun and D. W. Smith (eds), *Deleuze and Ethics*, Edinburgh: Edinburgh University Press, pp. 142–53.

Tyler, R. (1949), *Basic Principles of Curriculum and Instruction*, Chicago: University of Chicago Press.

# Chapter 11

# Deleuze, *Edusemiotics*, and the Logic of Affects

*Inna Semetsky*

The term *edusemiotics* in the title of this chapter translates as educational semiotics and designates a cutting-edge direction in educational theory (Semetsky 2010a). It addresses the value of experiential knowledge, partaking of the practical art of interpreting signs and is irreducible to a preconceived theoretical judgement. In the context of education, an *informal* learning site permeated with signs represents a *milieu* for the transformational pragmatics of experience. For the founder of modern semiotics, Charles Sanders Peirce, the whole universe is 'perfused with signs, if . . . not composed exclusively of signs' (Peirce CP 5: 448).

Deleuzo-Guattarian semiotics, as noticed by Genosko (1998), is a conceptual mix of Peirce's relational logic and Hjelmslev's linguistics, both frameworks opposing Saussurean semiology. In contrast to substance metaphysics and the law of identity based on the logic of the excluded middle pertaining to the analytic tradition, Deleuze's philosophy – not unlike the pragmatism of Peirce, John Dewey and Alfred North Whitehead (cf. Semetsky 2006, 2009a, 2010a) – deploys process-ontology and the 'logic of multiplicities' functioning on the basis of 'a theory and practice of relations, of the AND' (Deleuze and Parnet 1987: viii, 15), the conjunction *and* functioning as the included middle. Such logic is a distinctive feature of semiotics characterised by the 'unit' of analysis represented by qualitative multiplicities, that is, signs as relational (and not substantial) entities.

Peirce defined his three-relative universal categories as follows: 'Feeling is First, Sense of reaction Second, General conception Third, or mediation . . . Chance is First, Law is Second, the tendency to take habits is Third. Mind is First, Matter is Second, Evolution is Third' (Peirce CP 6: 7). A static logical copula gives way to the relational dynamics which is not 'subordinate to the verb to be' (Deleuze and Parnet 1987: 57). The primacy of relations defies static *being*; the logic of lived experience is triadic and formed by 'the semiotic machine, the referred object and the enunciative subject' (Guattari, original French, in Bosteels 1998: 167) embedded in the dynamics of *becoming*. The cardinality of Peirce's categories ensures that 'there are two in the second, to the point where there is a firstness in the secondness, and there are three in the third' (Deleuze 1989: 30).

Each *and* forms a sign, 'a being-multiple' (Deleuze and Parnet 1987: viii) enabled by a conjunction that marks 'a new threshold, a new direction of the zigzagging line, a new course for the border' (Deleuze 1995: 45) expressed in the newly created concept. For Deleuze, concepts are fragmentary wholes created in experience 'as a function of problems which are thought to be badly understood or badly posed (pedagogy of the concept)' (Deleuze and Guattari 1994: 16). Learning is 'infinite [and] of a different nature to knowledge' (Deleuze 1994: 192), and pertains to informal pedagogy as a practical invention of concepts.

## Pedagogy of the Concept

Novel concepts are to be invented or created in order to make sense out of singular experiences embedded in concrete events such as 'a day, a time of day, a stream, a place, a battle, an illness' (Deleuze 1995: 141). An experiential event is as yet subject-less because we as human subjects are constituted within the multiplicity of events by experience from which we can learn. Experience is what produces thinking, and a *learning experience* is one during which, instead of repetitively 'displaying phenomena or statements', we form 'a transversal or mobile diagonal line' (Deleuze 1988a: 22) that intervenes as a conjunction: the *and* in its mediative, indirect function.

If a dyad amounts to the identity between two terms, a triad representing a genuine sign is based on *difference* that intervenes as the included middle. It is the included 'third which . . . disturbs the binarity of the two, not so much inserting itself in their opposition as in their complementarity' (Deleuze and Parnet 1987: 131). Deleuze considered difference to be not only an existential but an ontological category, 'the noumenon closest to phenomenon' (Deleuze 1994: 222); still one that is never beyond experience because every phenomenon is conditioned by difference.

We are made up of relations, says Deleuze (2000), and events will make sense to us not if we understand them theoretically but when we experience in practice the very difference that makes each singular event significant. All thinking proceeds in signs, and the continuous process of *semiosis* provides a stream of events for the practical 'experimentation on ourselves'. *This experimentation is the core of edusemiotics.* Multiple becomings involve 'the harshest exercise in depersonalization' (Deleuze 1995: 6), and experimentation 'is our only identity, our single chance for all the combinations which inhabit us' (Deleuze and Parnet 1987: 11). For Deleuze, genuine education proceeds through deregulation of the senses and a shock that compels thought against its will to transcend its ordinary operations. He called for education of the senses by means of exploring the faculties of perception above and beyond empirical sense-data. It is the very presence, that is, the included middle of the transversal link that characterises Deleuze's *transcendental empiricism*, which does not rely on absolutes but aims to creatively 'bring into being that which does not yet exist' (Deleuze 1994: 147).

Deleuze's philosophical method is empirical by virtue of the object of inquiry regarded as real, even if sub-representative, experience. Yet, it is radically transcendental because the very foundations for the empirical principles are left outside the common faculties of perception. Transcendental empiricism purports to discover conditions above and beyond actual commonsensical experience. An object of experience is given only in its tendency to exist, or rather to subsist, in a virtual, non-representative, format. The actualisation of the virtual exceeds a physical effect following its cause in a mechanistic manner. Deleuze's *quasi-cause*, importantly, is 'nothing outside of its effect . . . it maintains with the effect an immanent relation which turns the product, the moment that it is produced, into something productive' (Deleuze 1990: 95). A sign as a multiplicity would not subscribe to the law of non-contradiction: the included middle is a repetitive conjunction 'and . . . and . . . and' (Deleuze 1995: 45) that, by virtue of interfering in between what analytic philosophy traditionally presents as dualistic opposites, forms a smooth space as 'a field . . . wedded to nonmetric, acentered, rhizomatic multiplicities' (Deleuze and Guattari 1987: 381).

## The New Image of (Affective) Thought

Deleuze's biological metaphor of a rhizome refers to the new image of thought contrary to the old dogmatic image, one that manifests in 'new connections, new pathways, new synapses [produced] not through any external determinism but through a becoming that carries the problems themselves along with it' (Deleuze 1995: 149). Rhizome describes the mode of experimental thinking whose central concept, in contrast to the ontology of static being, is a process-ontology of dynamic becoming:

A line of becoming is not defined by points that it connects, or by points that compose it; on the contrary, it passes *between* points, it comes up through the middle . . . A line of becoming has only a middle. The middle is not an average; it is fast motion, it is the absolute speed of movement. A becoming is neither one nor two . . . it is the in-between, the border or line of flight. (Deleuze and Guattari 1987: 293)

Becoming manifests as 'an extreme contiguity within a coupling of two sensations without resemblance or, on the contrary, in the distance of a light that captures both of them in a single reflection . . . It is a zone of indetermination, of indiscernibility . . . This is what is called an *affect*' (Deleuze and Guattari 1994: 173). The 'logic of affects' (Guattari 1995: 9) demands the presence of the transversal because it is the transversal link that establishes 'coupling' as a semiotic bridge, the included middle along the line of flight, and where the dualistic opposites coalesce so that they 'show the imperceptible' (Deleuze 1995: 45) amidst the apparently illogical (but only within the narrow boundaries of classical logic) 'possibility of the impossible' (Deleuze and Guattari 1994: 60).

Positioning the 'origins' of philosophical thinking at the level of practice, of life, Deleuze brings *thought* into intimate relation with *non-thought*, or the as yet unthought, unknown, and unpredictable. Something in the experiential 'world forces us to think. This something is an object not of recognition but a fundamental "encounter" . . . It may be grasped in a range of affective tones: wonder, love, hatred, suffering. In whichever tone, its primary characteristic is that it can only be sensed. In this sense it is opposed to recognition' (Deleuze 1994: 139). Thinking without recognition operates as a thought without image and is semiotic to its core: it interprets, or evaluates, experience, and 'beneath the generalities of habit . . . we rediscover singular processes of learning' (Deleuze 1994: 25).

Experience permeated with signs presents a plurality of problems rather than a single solution, and the coexistence of moments that defy representation because a rhizomatic process enables any single line to be potentially connected with any other line. As a symbol for unlimited growth through the multitude of its own transformations, the rhizome is contrasted with a tree, the latter symbolising direct and linear, arborescent, reasoning. The tree metaphor reminds us of the tree of Porphyry, which is an example of a classificatory system or a hierarchical structure based on precise definitions that serve as the foundation for rationally demonstrable knowledge. The tree metaphor incorporates the logic of the *excluded* middle pertaining to Aristotelian syllogisms. However experimental learning is 'more like a grass than a tree' (Deleuze 1995: 149); a rhizome organically 'grows from the middle' (Deleuze and Parnet 1987: viii) in accord with the affective logic of the *included* middle.

This logic cannot be reduced to 'the logic of a language. It is a description of the structures that appear when being is understood as the encounter of events and series' (Williams 2008: 23). Amidst the affects permeating experience, 'once one ventures outside what's familiar and reassuring, once one has to invent new concepts for unknown lands, then methods and moral systems break down and thinking becomes . . . a "perilous act," a violence, whose first victim is oneself' (Deleuze 1995: 103). Such a perilous act of thinking is embodied in the maximum intensity of experience as '*a power to affect itself, an affect of self on self*' (Deleuze 1988a: 101, original emphasis) that leads to our learning from experience and becoming-other.

The underground sprout of a rhizomatic plant, rather than having a traditional root, has a stem, the oldest part of which dies off while simultaneously rejuvenating itself at the top. This metaphor is poignant: it is precisely when the old is dying off that the new, as becoming-other, may be created. It is the rhizomatic process-structure, which is capable of producing something new 'when it [thought] acceded to the infinite movement that frees it from truth as supposed paradigm and reconquers an immanent power of creation' (Deleuze and Guattari 1994: 140). At this critical point a rhizomatic line – betraying 'the principle of linear progressive "building up knowledge"' (Deleuze 1995: 139) – would zigzag into new directions potentially filled with new sense (Deleuze 1990). Deleuze's *Logique du sens* refers to both meaning and direction pertaining to practical life. It necessarily includes Peirce's category of Firstness in the form of an affective dimension described as the 'quality of a possible sensation [which] is felt, rather than conceived' (Deleuze 1986: 98).

## Affects, Percepts, Concepts

Deleuze stresses the triad of affects, percepts and concepts comprising a genuine sign. The irreducible triad represents a major Peircean inflection in Deleuze's philosophy, according to which a concept 'should express an event rather than an essence' (Deleuze 1995: 25) and – itself a genuine sign of transformational pragmatics – exists in a triadic relationship with percept and affect: 'you need all three to *get things moving*' (Deleuze 1995: 165, original emphasis). A concept necessarily has two other dimensions, percepts and affects. Percepts [are] packets of sensations and relations that live on independently of whoever experiences them. Affects . . . are becomings that spill over beyond whoever lives through them (thereby becoming someone else) . . . Affects, percepts, and concepts are three inseparable forces, running from art to philosophy and from philosophy into art. (Deleuze 1995: 127)

Deleuze's new image of thought is aesthetic because 'art thinks no less than philosophy, but it thinks through affects and percepts' (Deleuze and Guattari 1994: 66). Accordingly, life informed by the pedagogy of concepts is 'ethical and aesthetic, as opposed to morality' (Deleuze 1995: 114), with the latter's dualistic moral algebra.

A much-talked-about educational aim is therefore intrinsically ethical (May and Semetsky 2008), oriented to evaluating experience in practice, in life, in terms of the polyvocality of multiple directions taken by rhizomatic lines: 'which of the lines are dead-ended or blocked, which cross voids . . . and most importantly the line of steepest gradient, how it draws in the rest, towards what destination' (Deleuze and Parnet 1987: 120). Because every newly created concept must embody a singularity of experience, it 'speaks the event, not the essence' (Deleuze and Guattari 1994: 21).

The event is a prerogative for becoming, and the process of becoming embedded in Peirce's semiosis is unlimited: 'becomings evolve' (Deleuze 1995: 45). Signs permeating experience demand the 'corresponding apprenticeship' (Deleuze 2000: 92) when mediated by other signs creating meanings for the series of events. Thinking as a learning process is grounded in the affective logic of the included middle and can traverse existing boundaries, not unlike the witch's flight. The flight, bordering on immaterial vanishing through an imaginary event horizon, creates its own terms of actualisation, thereby leading to an 'intensification of life' (Deleuze and Guattari 1994: 74) by virtue of the transformational pragmatics whenever signs, with which according to Peirce the world is always already perfused, become lived through, experienced and apprehended.

Deleuze (2000) discusses Proust's *À la recherche du temps perdu* as the story of the narrator's apprenticeship in signs (cf. Bogue 2004; Bogue and Semetsky 2010; Semetsky 2007), tracing the events through which the young Marcel learns that signs are to be apprehended in terms of immanent problematic instances embedded in experience. Without the relation between signs and the corresponding apprenticeship, signs would forever remain sense-less: 'Sense is essentially produced' (Deleuze 1990: 95). It is along the transversal link that a meaningful concept, filled with sense, is produced: novelty and creativity are concepts intrinsic to edusemiotics. Signs can be subtle and barely perceptible, 'speaking' but in silent discourse (cf. Semetsky 2010b); still, Deleuze purports to show that which is as yet imperceptible by means of laying down a visible map of an invisible, yet intelligible, territory. Experience is fundamental: 'Only empiricism knows how to transcend the experiential dimension of the visible without falling into Ideas, and how to track down, invoke, and perhaps produce a phantom' (Deleuze 1990: 20) as the potential expression of sense.

The proverbial relationship between a map and a territory avoids the trap of representation; the dynamics of semiosis ensures that 'the map ... merges with its object, when the object itself is movement [and] the trajectory merges not only with the subjectivity of those who travel through a milieu, but also with the subjectivity of milieu itself, in so far as it is reflected in those who travel through it' (Deleuze 1997: 61). Everything has 'its geography, its cartography, its diagram. What's interesting, even in a person, are the lines that make them up, or they make up, or take, or create'; 'a "map", or ... a "diagram" is a set of various interacting lines' (Deleuze 1995: 33), among which it is a line of becoming or a line of flight that does not represent but engenders a new territory.

## The Thirdness of a Diagram

Diagram is a Peircean concept that, as a mediatory 'third' (Deleuze and Parnet 1987: 131), disturbs the binary opposition between signifiers and signifieds, between words and objects. A diagrammatic mode serves as a connective link along which new knowledge is produced: in its 'piloting' role (Deleuze and Guattari 1987: 142), a diagram forms 'a bridge, a transversality' (Guattari 1995: 23) crossing over an a-signifying gap by virtue of its own 'extreme contiguity' (Deleuze and Guattari 1994: 173). Deleuze understands semiotics as a-signifying, that is, as defying a presupposed signifier-signified identity. His emphasis is on the dynamical and triadic nature of signs, that is, their having an 'increasingly intimate' (Deleuze 2000: 88) relation with their enfolded meanings which are never given but depend on signs entering into 'surface organization which ensures the resonance of two series' (Deleuze 1990: 104) thereby converging on a paradoxical differentiator, which becomes 'both word and object at once' (Deleuze 1990: 51).

A diagram is a necessary third in the dynamic process-structure of a genuine sign. A diagram acts as a connection between the planes, and its purpose is to 'pursue the different series, to travel along the different levels, and cross all thresholds; instead of simply displaying phenomena or statements in their vertical or horizontal dimensions, one must form a transversal or mobile diagonal line' (Deleuze 1988a: 22). A diagram

> has only 'traits' of content and expression, between which it establishes a connection . . . The diagram retains the most deterritorialized content and the most deterritorialized expression, in order to conjugate them. . . . The diagrammatic or abstract machine does not function to represent, even something real, but rather constructs a real that is yet to come, a new type of reality . . . The diagram knows only traits and cutting edges that are still elements of content in so far as they are material and of expression in so far as they are functional, but which draw one another along, form relays, and meld in a shared deterritorialisation. (Deleuze and Guattari 1987: 141–2)

'Traits' are like traces of involuntary memories, always below the level of consciousness, therefore capable of manifesting as affects, and not yet concepts, which are to be invented or created. Traits have no *explicit* content. Deleuze posits the grammar of disequilibrium – the existence of the a-signifying gap – as a precondition for the production of sense. Experiential meanings are conferred not by reference to some external object but by virtue of their enfoldment in the rhizomatic network of signs. As embedded in the perplexity of experience, the rhizome goes in diverse directions instead of a single path, thus establishing the multiplicity of links in the open-ended smooth space of its growth. The unpredictable connections presuppose not the transmission of 'the same old' but the creation of the different and new: a process that has important implications for education as an *experimental practice of the invention of new concepts.*

Deleuze (1990) points out that uncertainties encountered in experience cannot be reduced to subjective doubt but are derived from the objective structure of the event, in so far as it moves in two directions at once, and in so far as it fragments the subject following this double direction. Reading Proust from the perspective of triadic semiotics, Deleuze asks: 'What is a young girl or a group of young girls? . . . They have in common the imperceptible . . . Proust describes them as moving relationships of slowness and speed, and individuations by haecceity which are not subjective' (Deleuze and Parnet 1987: 93) but always relational, of the nature of signs that defy subject-object dualism. The exteriority of relations presents 'a vital protest against principles' (Deleuze and Parnet 1987: 55) that present the universal reference point, the view from nowhere.

## 'Learning to Swim'

It is the difference encountered in the here-and-now of each experiential event that presents a shock to thought, thereby transcending the faculties of perception above and beyond 'given' sense-data. The rhizomatic distributions break down 'the sedentary structures of representation' (Deleuze 1994: 37) whenever a thought encounters a crisis as in the case of a novice athlete who is thrown into water. In *Difference and Repetition*, Deleuze (1994) presents a story of an athlete who learns to swim by means of becoming. The novice athlete struggles against the waves because she is facing the unknown and *unthought*. Not-yet-knowing-how-to-swim, the athlete's movements do not resemble the movements of the wave. Nor do they imitate the instructor's movements given while not in the water but on the shore. For this athlete who finds herself in a novel situation, there is literally no solid foundation under her feet, and the world that she has to face loses its reassuring power of familiar representations.

The dynamics of semiosis as a *virtual* 'foundation' for knowledge cannot be based on an *a priori* recognition, and Deleuze would have agreed with John Dewey that 'there is an impact that precedes all definite recognition of what it is about' (Dewey 1934/1980: 145), an affective, shocking, impact! The bulk of theoretical knowledge is transformed into practical apprenticeship: the swimmer is learning 'by grasping . . . signs' (Deleuze 1994: 23) in practice, within the experiential *milieu*. The athlete has to *invent a novel concept* of what it means to swim in the midst of the very encounter with an unknown problematic 'structure [which] is part of objects themselves, allowing them to be grasped as signs, just as the questioning or problematising instance is a part of knowledge allowing its objectivity and its specificity to be grasped in the act of *learning*' (Deleuze 1994: 64, original emphasis). As Deleuze says:

Learning to swim or learning a foreign language means composing the singular points of one's own body or one's own language with those of another shape or element, which tears us apart but also propels us into a hitherto unknown and unheard-of world of problems. To what are we dedicated if not to those problems which demand the very transformation of our body and our language? In short, representation and knowledge are modelled entirely upon propositions of consciousness, which designate cases of solution, but those propositions by themselves give a completely inaccurate notion of the instance which engenders them as cases, and which they resolve or conclude. By contrast, the Idea and 'learning' express that extra-propositional or subrepresentative problematic instance: the presentation of the unconscious, not the representation of consciousness. (Deleuze 1994: 192)

Deleuze considered the unconscious – unthought-of at the cognitive level – to be just as profound as the unknown of the body, at the level of affects permeating experiential encounters. As an unconscious *desire* in contrast to one's conscious *will*, an erotic element of affect is fundamental for Deleuze's philosophy. The unconscious, or unthought, dimension is a-conceptual, 'located' amidst affects. Even as a concept inhabits our experience as a *living* concept in its as yet unconscious or *virtual* form, a practical task remains 'to set up . . . to extract' (Deleuze and Guattari 1994: 160) the very sense of this empirical event as the newly created concept in our *actual* experience.

## Constructing the Plane of Immanence

The creation of concepts is impossible without 'the laying out of a plane' (Deleuze and Guattari 1994: 36). To think means to construct a plane: to *show* that it is there so as to pragmatically 'find one's bearings in thought' (Deleuze and Guattari 1994: 37). The plane of immanent consistency is laid down via the infinite becoming of the virtual qua virtual; this process is described in a sort of Neoplatonic language: 'From virtuals we descend to actual states of affairs, and from states of affairs we ascend to virtuals, without being able to isolate one from the other' (Deleuze and Guattari 1994: 160). While not all of the virtualities may become actualised in the present, they are nevertheless real. Because virtual ideas exist as implicit tendencies they define the immanence of the transcendental field: 'immanence is the unconscious itself' (Deleuze 1988b: 29), and the creation of concepts always takes place 'in and through the unconscious, thereby establishing the bond of a profound complicity between nature and mind' (Deleuze 1994: 165); such conjunction of matter and mind determines what Alfred North Whitehead called a semiotic threshold. The plane of immanence is pre-rational and a-conceptual, ultimately enabling 'the conquest of the unconscious' (Deleuze 1988b: 29) due to the very logic of affects. The actualisation of the virtual, ontologically, is then akin, in terms of practical unorthodox 'epistemology' – or, rather, apprenticeship to signs – to the unconscious-becoming-conscious, thereby traversing what ordinarily appears to be a 'fundamental distinction between subrepresentative, unconscious and aconceptual ideas/intensities and the conscious conceptual representation of common sense' (Bogue 1989: 59). The plane of immanence is to be constructed: 'immanence is constructivism, any given multiplicity is like one area on the plane' (Deleuze 1995: 48). That's how Deleuze and Guattari defined the plane of immanence which, for them, was not in any way reduced to reasoning with pre-existent concepts:

> Precisely because the plane of immanence is prephilosophical and does not immediately take effects with concepts, it implies a sort of groping experimentation and its layout resorts to measures that are not very respectable, rational, or reasonable. There measures belong to the order of dreams, of pathological processes, esoteric experiences, drunkenness, and excess. We head for the horizon, on the plane of immanence, and we return with bloodshot eyes, yet they are the eyes of the mind. (Deleuze and Guattari 1994: 41)

The eyes of the mind imply the awakening of the inner eye (cf. Noddings and Shore 1984) as opposed to the cold, dispassionate and unblinking gaze of the epistemological subject, a spectator. The eye of the mind 'sees' with the uncanny, extra, sixth, sense; and Deleuze's method of transcendental empiricism indeed 'seems to be patterned after Bergson's intuition' (Boundas 1996: 87). Intuition enables the reading of signs, symbols and symptoms that lay down the dynamical structure of experience. Intuition works, 'it presupposes an impulse, a compulsion to think which passes through all sorts of bifurcations, spreading from the nerves and being communicated to the soul in order to arrive at thought' (Deleuze 1994: 147), thereby producing *sense* in a series of signs being translated into other 'more fully developed' (Peirce CP 5: 594) signs.

Thinking-in-signs highlights 'the genesis of intuition in intelligence' (Deleuze 1991: 111) and constitutes 'the supreme act of philosophy: not so much to think THE plane of immanence as to show that it is there, unthought in every plane, and to think it in this way as the outside and inside of thought . . . that which cannot be thought and yet must be thought' (Deleuze and Guattari 1994: 59–60). The virtual, which cannot be thought, *must* be thought when actualised in the process of 'differentiations of an initially undifferentiated field' (Deleuze 1993: 10), which subsists in its virtual mode of existence. Deleuze describes the transcendental field as a pure stream of a-subjective, impersonal and immediate consciousness without object or self. The traces of the self in this field are as yet non-conscious, enfolded in the multiplicities, in signs. Contrary to the linguistic turn of analytic philosophy, Deleuze's philosophy manifests a semiotic turn which is effectuated by the presentations of the unconscious that may be linked transversally – that is, via Thirdness which, by definition, always already contains an affective Firstness in itself – with the representations of consciousness.

The unconscious affects are implicated at the level of microperceptions that are part and parcel of the cartographic microanalysis in the mode of 'an unconscious psychic mechanism that engenders the perceived in consciousness' (Deleuze 1993: 95). It is not the Cartesian *Cogito* but indeed 'an economical balance of the unconscious and the conscious' (Dewey 1991: 215–16) that determines the success of education as a holistic practice embodied in experience, in life. Because becomings are 'the most imperceptible, they are acts which can be only contained in a life' (Deleuze and Parnet 1987: 3), in embodied practice. The unconscious qua affect is not opposed to intentionality qua conceptual content but is being enfolded into 'its very heart' making the 'unthought therefore not external to thought' (Deleuze 1988a: 97) as it would be in conformity with the classical logic of the excluded middle. That is how a body lives and what describes a body's mode of existence: 'it is by speed and slowness that one connects with something else. One never commences; one never has a *tabula rasa*; one slips in, enters in the middle' (Deleuze 1988b: 123).

Ontologically, the 'intentionality of being is surpassed by the fold of Being, Being as fold' (Deleuze 1988a: 110). The fold is a powerful symbol that overcomes the habitual binary opposites of analytic thinking due to 'a different logic of social practice, an intensive and affective logic of the included middle' (Bosteels 1998: 151). The experiential world is folded – perfused with signs! It unfolds in an unpredictable manner, and it is impossible to know ahead of time what the body (at once physical and mental, corporeal and incorporeal) can do; life becomes an experimental and experiential affair demanding learning as an apprenticeship in signs by means of immanent evaluations of the modes of existence: *learning from experience*. No need for *formal* instruction! In fact, it is counterproductive. As Dewey said nearly a century ago:

> To 'learn from experience' is to make a backward and forward connection between what we do to things and what we enjoy and suffer from things in consequence. Under such conditions, doing becomes a trying; an experiment with the world . . . the undergoing becomes instruction – discovery of the connection of things. (Dewey 1916/1924: 164)

Dewey described such learning staying at the existential level of actual experiences. Deleuze takes it to the level of the virtual which is no less real than any actual existence. Experience cannot be limited to what is immediately perceived by senses: the Deleuzian line of flight or becoming is real even if 'we don't see it, because it's the least perceptible of things' (Deleuze 1995: 45). We are affected by experience, and think-ing enriched with affect is always experimental, like a process of trying, testing and creating a real-life experiment with what is new, or coming into being, therefore becoming via 'an intrinsic genesis, not an extrinsic conditioning' (Deleuze 1994: 154). Deleuze insists that

> we learn nothing from those who say: 'Do as I do'. Our only teachers are those who tell us to 'do with me', and are able to emit signs to be developed in heterogeneity rather than propose gestures for us to reproduce . . . When a body combines some of its own distinctive points with those of a wave, it espouses the principle of a repetition which is no longer that of the Same, but involves the Other – involves difference, from one wave and one gesture to another, and carries that difference through the repetitive space thereby constituted. To learn is indeed to constitute this space of an encounter with signs, in which the distinctive points renew themselves in each other, and repetition takes shape while disguising itself. (Deleuze 1994: 23)

Those who keep on telling us, do as I do, will be reproducing the same and simply reinforcing the dogmatic image of thought. But signs permeating our experience defy Cartesian substance dualism with its apparent opposites of body and mind, of corporeal and mental. These are not binaries but multiplicities reinforced 'by their mutual solidarity, and neither of them can be identified otherwise' (Deleuze and Guattari 1987: 45). Thinking as infinite learning replaces the Cartesian point of departure. Thinking is not a natural exercise but always a second power of thought, born under constraints of experience as a material force; still capable of transcending this experience, that is, freeing it from these con-straints, hence paradoxically, yet necessarily, complementing Deleuze's empirical philosophy with its transcendental dimension. Affecting itself, the concept at the 'untimely' moment of its very creation posits itself and its object simultaneously, thus defying the dualistic split between subject and object, matter and mind, immanence and transcendence, science and art; these binary opposites embedded into one 'inseparable process' (Williams 2010) of semiosis.

## Nomadic Education

In order to find one's way, one's bearings or whereabouts in life as 'a theatre of problems and always open questions' (Deleuze and Guattari 1994: 241), one must feel and experience as much as see or listen. Those expanded faculties of perception capable of apprehending signs pertain to 'nomadic education' (Semetsky 2008) grounded in the logic of the included middle. The nomad is always in-between, always in the process of becoming: in accord with the logic of affects, 'the life of the nomad is the intermezzo' (Deleuze and Guattari 1987: 380). The affective logic of nomads' lived experience precludes experiential signs from meeting 'the visual condition of being observable from a point in space external to them' (Deleuze and Guattari 1987: 371) – in accord with Dewey's rejecting a spectator theory of knowledge in favour of logic as a theory of inquiry (Dewey 1938).

Deleuze referred to ideas as '"differentials" of thought, or the "Unconscious" of pure thought . . . related not to a Cogito . . . but to the fractured I of a dissolved Cogito' (Deleuze 1994: 194). To genuinely learn means to piece the fractured pieces together, to actualise the virtual in practice, to literally construct the plane of immanent consistency in the process of an informal and immanent pedagogy of concepts irreducible to formal instruction. Rational consciousness as the sole constituent of thought is insufficient because what is yet unthought-of is equally capable of producing practical effects at the level of experience in accord with Peirce's pragmatic maxim: 'Consider what effects, that might conceivably have practical bearings, we conceive the object of our conception to have. Then our conception of these effects is the whole of our conception of the object' (Peirce CP 5: 402).

It is practical experience that breathes life into philosophy; immanence as 'a life' (Deleuze 2001) accords with Dewey's vitalist definition of education:

> What [a person] gets and gives as a human being, a being with desires, emotions and ideas, is . . . a widening and deepening of conscious life – a more intense, disciplined, and expanding realization of meanings . . . And education is not a mere means to such a life. Education is such a life. (Dewey 1916/1924: 417)

Deleuze's experiential pedagogy of the concept is devoted precisely to the realisation of meanings, to making sense out of the problematic situations and events abundant in life. Concepts do not simply link propositions; as embodied in experience, in life, they partake of corporeality. A sign filled with sense is produced under the *proviso* of transversal communication between the series of events operating along different planes or levels so that these planes become related: they form a multiplicity, a Janus-faced genuine sign functioning as a semiotic bridge between different planes even without actually passing from one to another (cf. DeLanda 2002: 103).

Only transversally can communication literally make the same sense for both 'participants' that, while 'belonging' to different series, are nonetheless embedded in 'a transcoded passage' (Deleuze and Guattari 1987: 313). *Transcoding* is a Deleuzian neologism that marks an element of creativity, of invention. Nomadic education defies a habitual transmission of given facts from a teacher to a student; instead education becomes 'a transcoded passage from one milieu to another . . . whenever there is transcoding . . . there is . . . a constitution of a new plane, as of a surplus value. A melodic or rhythmic plane, surplus value of passage or bridging . . . The components as melodies in counterpoint, each of which serves as a motif for another' (Deleuze and Guattari 1987: 313–14). The oft-cited example is potent:

> The line or block of becoming that unites the wasp and the orchid produces a shared deterritorialisation: of the wasp, in that it becomes a liberated piece of the orchid's reproductive system, but also of the orchid, in that it becomes the object of an orgasm in the wasp, also liberated from its own reproduction. (Deleuze and Guattari 1987: 293)

Thus, education informed by Deleuze's pedagogy of concepts and the logic of affects becomes possible providing a teacher and a student together become a motif for each other, both embedded in a transcoded passage and ultimately going through a 'shared deterritorialization' (Deleuze and Guattari 1987: 293) by virtue of their convergence on the line of flight whence each-becomes-other. Thinking through affects is liberating; it brings an element of non-thought into a thought; such a forceful, as if physical, intensity of an encounter with an affect marks the passage between the experiential states of the body. Accordingly, a body's power and its capacity for action subscribe to the transformational pragmatics of experience. We are never separated from the world: rhizomatic lines connect 'the interior [as] a selected exterior [and] the exterior, a projected interior' (Deleuze 1988b: 125) that form experiential folds (Semetsky 2010c).

The network of connective lines constituting the rhizome serves as a diverse means to express the reciprocal ways in which signs can affect and be affected. At the level of perception by regular senses such connections would remain imperceptible. But learning via signs-becoming-other-signs enables one's perception to vitally increase in power, thereby becoming able to perceive something previously imperceptible. Connecting the dots in the multileveled rhizomatic network enables one to make sense out of experience, that is, to de-stratify one's old way of thinking by means of newly created concepts. Nomadic education that employs the multiplicity of unthought-of-affects is equivalent to 'experiencing, experimenting . . . and what we experience, experiment with, is . . . what's coming into being, what's new, what's taking shape' (Deleuze 1995: 104).

## The Learning Paradox

Learning from experience and creating novel concepts in practice – whenever affects 'spill over beyond whoever lives through them' (Deleuze 1995: 127) – inevitably problematises the so-called learning paradox articulated in the famous Socratic dialogue with Meno (Semetsky 2004, 2006, 2009b). Sure enough, it is the logic of affects foregrounding edusemiotics that allows us to accept the apparent equivocation of paradoxes as the necessary – albeit dark, pushing to the very limits of knowledge, power and subject – precursors for 'the creation of the New' (Deleuze 1989: 146) despite – or, rather, due to – their apparent 'logical invalidity' (Williams 2008: 24). A resolution to the learning paradox involves two modes, thought and un-thought, one with 'conscious cogitation and [one] with the unconscious' (Williams 2008: 73).

The learning process, understood as an experiential inquiry, always takes place through the unconscious, leading to the conjugation which determines the threshold of consciousness: unconscious-becoming-conscious because of the folded – semiotic – relationship between the two, inconsistent with 'the operation of the principle of non-contradiction *as a response to paradoxes*' (Williams 2008: 71, original emphasis). Itself paradoxical, the logic of the included middle would never allow 'the submission of the line to the point' (Deleuze and Guattari 1987: 293); a point being the metaphor for identity, for the exclusion of Thirdness as a semiotic interpretant or a diagram that enables evolution, growth and multiple becomings, which inevitably betray 'common sense as the assignation of fixed identities' (Deleuze 1990: 3).

It is the affective logic, the uncanny logic of differences pertaining to a diverse regime of signs irreducible to verbal propositions but encompassing involuntary memories, images and non-discursive formations. The line of becoming itself is the included middle by means of which the complex and forever incorporeal concept, or pure event, expresses itself in the corporeality of experience, of life, hence making sense via its very embodiment. The affective logic bridges the dualistic opposition between sense and nonsense, between subject and object, between inside and outside, between consciousness and the unconscious.

The unconscious forms a 'floating signifier' that can nonetheless donate meaning to the series of events. The difference encountered in experience functions as 'a "donation of sense" ... it generates a paradox' (Williams 2008: 72) qua *nonsense* because this experience qua affect is simply felt and not recognised, hence does not yet make sense. Nonsense (non-sense) is neither true nor false but has its own intrinsic value indeed because of its ability to make sense. Nonsense is necessary for sense because a sign is Janus-faced; it functions as a paradoxical 'entity [that] circulates in both series ... and [is] equally present in the signifying and signified series [as] at once word and thing, name and object ... It guarantees ... the convergence of the two series which it traverses, but precisely on the condition that it makes them diverge' (Deleuze 1990: 40). This convergence/divergence is a feature of a genuine, triadic, sign in which the a-signifying rupture is bridged by the conjunction *and* by virtue of the affective logic of the included middle as a distinguished feature of semiotics.

## Conclusion

Education informed by semiotics will necessarily 'bring something to life, [will] free life from where it's trapped, [will] trace lines of flight' (Deleuze 1995: 141), therefore embracing the pedagogy of novelty and creativity rather than a given curriculum. We never have a *tabula rasa*, said Deleuze; nor are we born with a reservoir of actual concepts. They subsist at the level of the virtual, and it is the affective conditions of experience that produce a shock to thought, making it 'wide awake' (Dewey 1991: 57) and capable of actualising the virtual in practice, in life. Signs embedded in experience are 'the symptoms of life gushing forth or draining away ... There's a profound link between signs, events, life and vitalism' (Deleuze 1995: 143). Rhizomatics traces the lines that connect diverse experiences as a means for making sense out of them via 'an infinite succession of linkages and changes in direction' (Deleuze and Guattari 1987: 494).

Learning implies an increase in knowledge qua a newly created concept via the diagonal, transversal link leading to the thought's increase in power. An increase in power is almost literal: if there was an exponential growth inscribed in the learning process, then the transversal communication would have carried an exponent towards its limit, crossing the otherwise asymptotic line. It cannot be otherwise because it is events that present us with uncanny experiences, which elude recognition; hence we simply must 'invent new concepts for unknown lands' (Deleuze 1995: 103). The edusemiotic process is based on experimentation that 'forces us to frame a new question' (Deleuze 1995: 114) which engenders an uncharted and unbounded territory of new concepts and new modes of existence.

Edusemiotics is indeed 'not just a theoretical matter. It [is] to do with life itself' (Deleuze 1995: 105). Genuine teachers as *edusemioticians* would be capable of reading, interpreting and creating signs that 'imply ways of living [and] possibilities of existence' (Deleuze 1995: 143). These possibilities are implicit in experience permeated with signs that logically exceed any given system of significations but bring into being novelty, creativity and the emergence of *sense* as 'an increase in valence, a veritable becoming' (Deleuze and Guattari 1987: 10). Teachers-as-edusemioticians would agree with Deleuze that everything which genuinely 'teaches us something emits signs; every act of learning is an interpretation of signs' (Deleuze 2000: 4). These educators partake of what Deleuze designates as people to come (cf. Semetsky and Delpech-Ramey 2011), whose function is to be clinicians of culture and inventors of new immanent modes of existence. These people themselves are produced by virtue of experimentation; they belong to 'an oppressed, bastard, lower, anarchical, nomadic, irremediably minor race. They have resistance in common – their resistance to death, to servitude, to the intolerable, to shame, and to the present' (Deleuze and Guattari 1994: 109–10). The people to come in education are nomads capable of overcoming the limits of *being* and tapping into multiple *becomings*.

# References

Bogue, R. (1989), *Deleuze and Guattari*, London and New York: Routledge.

Bogue, R. (2004), 'Search, Swim and See: Deleuze's apprenticeship in signs and pedagogy of images', *Educational Philosophy and Theory*, 36(3): 327–42.

Bogue, R. and I. Semetsky (2010), 'Reading Signs/Learning From Experience: Deleuze's pedagogy as becoming-other' in I. Semetsky (ed.), *Semiotics Education Experience*, Rotterdam: Sense, pp. 115–30.

Bosteels, B. (1998), 'From Text to Territory: Felix Guattari's Cartographies of the Unconscious' in E. Kaufman and K. J. Heller (eds), *Deleuze and Guattari: New Mappings in Politics, Philosophy, and Culture*, Minneapolis: University of Minnesota Press, pp. 145–74.

Boundas, C. (1996), 'Deleuze-Bergson: An Ontology of the Virtual' in P. Patton (ed.), *Deleuze: A Critical Reader*, Oxford: Blackwell, pp. 86–106.

DeLanda, M. (2002), *Intensive Science and Virtual Philosophy*, London and New York: Continuum.

Deleuze, G. (1986), *Cinema 1: The Movement-Image*, trans. H. Tomlinson and B. Habberjam, Minneapolis: University of Minnesota Press.

Deleuze, G. and C. Parnet (1987), *Dialogues*, trans. H. Tomlinson and B. Habberjam, New York: Columbia University Press.

Deleuze, G. (1988a), *Foucault*, trans. S. Hand, London: Athlone.

Deleuze, G. (1988b), *Spinoza: Practical Philosophy*, trans. R. Hurley, San Francisco: City Lights.

Deleuze, G. (1989), *Cinema 2: The Time-Image*, trans. H. Tomlinson and R. Galeta. Minneapolis: University of Minnesota Press.

Deleuze, G. (1990), *The Logic of Sense*, trans. M. Lester with C. Stivale, New York: Columbia University Press.

Deleuze, G. (1991), *Bergsonism*, trans. H. Tomlinson, New York: Zone Books.

Deleuze, G. (1993), *The Fold: Leibniz and the Baroque*, trans. T. Conley, Minneapolis: University of Minnesota Press.

Deleuze, G. (1994), *Difference and Repetition*, trans. P. Patton, New York: Columbia University Press.

Deleuze, G. (1995), *Negotiations 1972–1990*, trans. Martin Joughin, New York: Columbia University Press.

Deleuze, G. (1997), *Essays Critical and Clinical*, trans. D. W. Smith and M. A. Greco, Minneapolis: University of Minnesota Press.

Deleuze, G. (2000), *Proust and Signs: The Complete Text*, trans. R. Howard. Minneapolis: University of Minnesota Press.

Deleuze, G. (2001), *Pure Immanence: Essays on A Life*, trans. A. Boyman, New York: Zone Books.

Deleuze, G. and F. Guattari (1987), *A Thousand Plateaus: Capitalism and Schizophrenia*, trans. B. Massumi, Minneapolis: University of Minnesota Press.

Deleuze, G. and F. Guattari (1994), *What is Philosophy?*, trans. H. Tomlinson and G. Burchell, New York: Columbia University Press.

Dewey, J. (1916/1924), *Democracy and Education*, New York: Macmillan Company.

Dewey, J. (1934/1980), *Art as Experience*, New York: Perigee Books.

Dewey, J. (1938), *Logic: The Theory of Inquiry*, New York: Henry Holt and Company.

Dewey, J. (1991), *How We Think*, New York: Prometheus Books.

Genosko, G. (1998), 'Guattari's Schizoanalytic Semiotics: Mixing Hjelmslev and Peirce' in E. Kaufman and K. J. Heller (eds), *Deleuze and Guattari: New Mappings in Politics, Philosophy, and Culture*, Minneapolis: University of Minnesota Press, pp. 175–90.

Guattari, F. (1995), *Chaosmosis: An Ethico-Aesthetic Paradigm*, trans. P. Bains and J. Pefanis, Bloomington: Indiana University Press.

May, T. and I. Semetsky (2008), 'Deleuze, Ethical Education and the Unconscious' in I. Semetsky (ed.), *Nomadic Education: Variations on a Theme by Deleuze and Guattari*, Rotterdam: Sense, pp. 143–58.

Noddings, N. and P. J. Shore (1984), *Awakening the Inner Eye: Intuition in Education*, New York and London: Teachers College, Columbia University.

Peirce, C. S. (1860–1911), *Collected Papers of Charles Sanders Peirce*, Vols 1–6, eds. C. Hartshorne and P. Weiss, Cambridge, MA: Harvard University Press.

Semetsky I. (2004), 'The Role of Intuition in Thinking and Learning: Deleuze and the pragmatic legacy', *Educational Philosophy and Theory*, 36(4): 433–54.

Semetsky, I. (2005), 'Semiotics' in A. Parr (ed.), *The Deleuze Dictionary*, Edinburgh: Edinburgh University Press, pp. 242–4.

Semetsky, I. (2006), *Deleuze, Education and Becoming*, Rotterdam: Sense.

Semetsky, I. (2007), 'Towards a Semiotic Theory of Learning: Deleuze's philosophy and educational experience', *SEMIOTICA*, 164(1/4): 197–214.

Semetsky, I. (ed.) (2008), *Nomadic Education: Variations on a Theme by Deleuze and Guattari*, Rotterdam: Sense.

Semetsky, I. (2009a), 'The Magician in the World: Becoming, creativity, and transversal communication', *ZYGON: Journal of Religion and Science*, 4(2): 323–46.

Semetsky, I. (2009b), 'Deleuze as a Philosopher of Education: Affective knowledge/effective learning', *The European Legacy: Toward New Paradigms*, 14(4): 443–56.

Semetsky, I. (ed.) (2010a), *Semiotics Education Experience*, Rotterdam: Sense.

Semetsky, I. (2010b), 'Silent Discourse: The language of signs and "becoming-woman"', *SubStance #121*, 39(1): 87–102.

Semetsky, I. (2010c), 'The Folds of Experience, or: Constructing the pedagogy of values', *Educational Philosophy and Theory* (special issue *Local Pedagogies/ Global Ethics*), 42(4): 476–88.

Semetsky, I. and J. Delpech-Ramey (2011), 'Educating Gnosis/Making a Difference', *Policy Future in Education* (special issue *Deleuze, Pedagogy and Bildung*), 9(4): 518–27

Williams, J. (2008), *Gilles Deleuze's* Logic of Sense: *A Critical Introduction and Guide*, Edinburgh: Edinburgh University Press.

Williams, J. (2010), 'Immanence and Transcendence as Inseparable Process: On the relevance of arguments from Whitehead to Deleuze interpretation', *Deleuze Studies*, 4(1): 94–106.

# Chapter 12

# Time and Education in the Philosophy of Gilles Deleuze

## James Williams

> The activity of the narrator no longer consists in explication, to deploy a content, but to select, to choose a non-communicating part, a non-communicating vessel, with the self enclosed in it. (Deleuze 1970: 154)

## A Gift in Time

When he was a child in the 1920s my grandfather suffered from severe ear infections. These were treated by crude surgery on both his inner ears. He was left deaf. At the back of his school classes, he could not follow the lessons, yet could already read and write. One of his teachers, noticing a pupil eager to learn, gave him the works of Shakespeare to read and report on during lessons. Though he did not continue school beyond sixteen, this thoughtful act helped my grandfather, in one of many different jobs, to become a proof reader for the press. Much more than that, though, it gave him an inner record of language, wisdom and human experience adapted to almost any challenge life could conjure up. This benefited me and everyone else who met this balanced and kind family man, since not only were our minor disasters and frustrations met with good humour and stoical yet streetwise advice, they were also accompanied by a more mysterious, sometimes apparently inapposite, yet invariably enticing and eventually enabling Shakespearean verb and lore.

What time-frame was that caring educator teaching for? Was it the time of a peaceful classroom? Or was it the later useful employment of a man? Perhaps it was for the fullness of a whole life, lived in tune with the best of humane art? Or was it to benefit a community, cohering through the harmony of its different members in the edifying effect of their common cultures? Perhaps, in continuing the deep influence of

Shakespeare's works, it was a gesture towards the past, as much as to the present or future; a stewardship of the past.

Or maybe it went well beyond all these virtues by combining them, since in contributing to a good life, that teacher also contributed to all the lives it touched and will continue to enrich, including mine and now those of my children and their cousins in counties, countries and cultures far from the murky and treacherous waters of the Thames in London, where my grandfather swam and one of his brothers drowned as a child, a few wharfs from the site of Shakespeare's Globe theatre. In writing these lines, I also launch a small part of that example of good teaching a little further on in time through any reader, even one who might come to disagree with everything I will go on to claim.

## Selection in a Multiplicity of Times

> . . . it is because time, ultimate interpreter and ultimate to interpret, has the strange power to affirm simultaneously pieces that do not make a whole in space, no more than they form one by succession in time. Time is exactly the transversal of all possible spaces, including spaces of time. (Deleuze 1970: 157)

One of my arguments, drawn from the philosophy of Gilles Deleuze, will be that there is more to reality than actual events gauged either according to individual lives and the linear clock time it takes them to fill, or according to some account of time and space taken from classical physics. The essence of good teaching according to this philosophy is to adapt to singular circumstances and individuals by drawing from an ideal virtual reserve, beyond actual occurrences and reference points. This reserve demands a different and complicated account of time, where time is viewed as a nexus of interacting dimensions of times. Much of Deleuze's philosophy is concerned with the implications of this multiplicity of active and passive syntheses of times and, therefore, of processes for teaching and apprenticeship to life, for instance in his readings of Plato, Bergson, Sacher-Masoch, Proust, Kant and Nietzsche.

Here is this nexus of times rendered as a grid:

|  | First synthesis of time (synthesis in the present) | Second synthesis of time (synthesis of the past) | Third synthesis of time (synthesis for the future) |
|---|---|---|---|
| Present | As prior selection | As made to pass as the most contracted state of the pure past | As incapable of returning and as caesura, assembly and seriation |

| Past | As dimension contracted into the present through a singular selection | As synthesis of the pure past | As selected to return as pure difference and as symbolic process |
| Future | As dimension contracted into the present as a range of possibilities assigned given probabilities | As freedom and destiny | As eternal return of difference |

The processes described in each box are not independent of one another, but rather determine each other such that individual boxes are always incomplete. Any event is a conjunction of all nine processes and a 'transversal' product of their mutual determinations.[1] Time is a multiplicity of processes of reciprocal determination. These determinations are defined according to the concepts of dimension and priority. On the left to right diagonal each time is defined as a prior process, one that takes the others as dimensions by determining them but not by being determined by them in return. All processes not on that diagonal are dimensions of ones on it. This means that Deleuze's definition of multiple times is asymmetrical. Time flows for Deleuze and has an irreversible quality. Unlike traditional concepts of the irreversible flow of time from past to future, Deleuze's time has multiple dimensions that cannot be reversed, including from future to past, present to future and present to past.

For Deleuze, the present is defined as a prior selection. It is a determination of time by a selection in the present highlighting a path in the past, by increasing its significance, and altering possibilities in the future, by reassigning their probabilities. This explains the importance of selection in his account of the apprenticeship to signs in his work on Proust in the above quoted passages.[2] The apprentice to signs must learn to select and to select well, in relation to all of the past and all of the future, but where time is never a perfect whole but rather a series of parts or non-communicating vases.

The present is therefore a reassignment of the past in degrees of significance and a recombination of the future through a change in probabilities. Deleuze calls this a concentration of the past and of the future. When a teacher makes an example of a pupil, for instance in choosing one for a special role or favour, the past is selected in a particular way and the future is altered in its possibilities. *I always regret having been the one chosen for banishment.* This active selection is, however, passive when taken as a dimension of the past, that is, as it passes away into the past and changes in its significance. In addition to selection, every present is a passive fading away into the past. *Even as I resisted its mark, banishment was to be my destiny and stain.* The present is not only passive to a calling into the past. It is also passive in relation to the future. This is because new presents will replay the past present by transforming its original passing away and selections. *I did not know banishment would become such a mark of infamy.* It is also because the condition of an open future erases all marks of identity as either necessary or settled since all can be reassembled and set into new series. *I had nothing to resist the freedom and power of the future.*

Due to the role of selection in a complex and irreducible nexus of dimensions, against the ground of past, present and future passivity and action, Deleuze's philosophy is a practical philosophy. Practice is not about prescription, nor is it regulated by it. This is because the asymmetries and multiplicity of times mean that determination is not uniform and universal, as it would be in simple versions of causal determination according to a now out-dated account of natural laws, for instance. Neither is practice about ethical obligation, since the determination allows for no overarching transcendent moral laws. There is neither 'is' nor 'ought' in this philosophy of time, only a more speculative set of guidelines in relation to an essentially problematic and event-led frame.

Deleuze's philosophy of time, or at least my version of it, translates into practical guides. Here is the nexus of time translated into a set of paradoxical maxims, questions and challenges for apprenticeship. The guides are for apprentice teachers and apprentice learners, for no one is simply one or the other:

|  | First synthesis of time (synthesis in the present) | Second synthesis of time (synthesis of the past) | Third synthesis of time (synthesis for the future) |
|---|---|---|---|
| Present | Your selections in the present concentrate all of the past and all of the future. *How will you select past degrees and future probabilities against the whole of time?* | Your present passes away not into an unchanging record but into a shifting set of values. *How will your selection be affirmative and resilient to its passing away into pure differences of value?* | The present will never return. It is a cut that reassembles the whole of time and sets it into a new series. *All your actual existence will pass away, never to return. How will your selections reassemble time and determine new series?* |
| Past | The past is revised by your selections. *Seek to revise the past well and to avoid resenting it.* | All values of the past are at play in the passing of any present. There are no pure acts and no pure good or evil. *All acts are a matter of degree, but degrees always matter.* | The past only returns as pure difference in a symbolic replaying. *What symbols need to be reworked to express the pure difference you want to connect to?* |

| Future | The present alters probabilities for all future possibilities. *Which possible lines does your selection make more likely, which less so?* | The future is free from the past as actual contraction but determined by it as destiny to replay values. *How are you free? Try to divine your destiny.* | The future is the eternal return of difference. *How to live with the challenge that only difference returns and never the same?* |
|---|---|---|---|

The teacher and the apprentice in time have therefore to select on the transversal line: selection in the present, with the transformation of degrees of pure values in the past and their return in the future, free of any former identities and representations. *Who? Where? How to select? Which values to intensify? Which to call to return?*

This transversal line is described in detail in Deleuze's work on Proust and apprenticeship. It can be read as leading into, then following, Deleuze's work on time in *Difference and Repetition*. The book is bridged by the two editions of Deleuze's Proust work; they share and expand upon the crucial idea of dimensions of time. Given the different dimensions of time, actors and narrators, apprentice-teachers, must replay fragmented parts in time. They must seek to select well in each dimension as different and irreducible to all the others. Yet this act will still unify them, but only as dimensions of one another, rather than as a single total unity of time in which subjects and objects are well-placed in unique space-time:

> Since, if a work of art communicates with a public or, better, calls forth a public, if the work communicates with others by the artist, and calls for new ones, it is always in this dimension of transversality, where unity and totality are established for themselves, without unifying or totalising objects or subjects. The work is the supplementary dimension added to those occupied by the characters, events and parts of *In Search of Lost Time* – that dimension in time with no common measure with the dimensions they occupy in space. (Deleuze 1970: 202–3)

Any selection is therefore a balancing act with different relations to time. Teachers and apprentices will never have a secure and certain solution to the problem of how to teach and learn in a given situation. Instead, each act is experimental and only open to guidelines. If we accept Deleuze's fragmentation of time into dimensions, then teaching will always remain an experimental and singular practice: a transversal practice.

This insistence on the individual and singular within a patchwork of connections and disconnections informs Deleuze's appreciation of teachers. When he turns to the difficult task of writing elegies for friends, Deleuze frequently isolates the feature making them a special teacher, unlike others yet in the service of an innovative connection to pupils and comrades. For François Châtelet, for instance, he draws attention to the capacity to create novel groups of their famously talented and quarrelsome set of friends, some of whom became their colleagues at Vincennes. Châtelet is a 'group star', an educator who makes collectives creative. This is his singularity:

> But what is remarkable, is not simply [François'] pedagogical care and taste. It is certain that he was a great teacher, but what was important is that the direction of collective work allowed him to trace new paths. He was not doing history. It was really new tracks. (Deleuze 2003: 249)

Deleuze values teachers. According to his philosophy, great teachers create by aligning their singular powers with those of others in order to usher in the new. Theirs is a collective apprenticeship to differences and to novelty in an act of creation. It can never simply be passing on of knowledge, or learning, or skills, but must constitute a novel event out of historical fragments: the lesson as event and encounter. This is why Deleuze's philosophy of time forms the context for his sketches of teaching and apprenticeship. It is also why the nurturing environment for his thinking about teaching and apprenticeship can be found not in pedagogical theory, but in the works and practice of artists and philosophers.

## Practice Under the Demands of Purity and Abstraction

> Similarly, in Masoch even order-words and descriptions are surpassed towards a higher language. But this time, everything is persuasion, and education. (Deleuze 1967: 20)

> In the pedagogical undertaking of Masoch's heroes, in the submission to the woman, in the torments they suffer, in the death they come to, there are as many moments of ascension to the Ideal. (Deleuze 1967: 21)

In Deleuze's philosophy, the complex multiplicity of times and the roles of the pure past and of the future as eternal return of difference mean that any singular selection in the present is made against the background of a virtual reserve of the pure past, return of difference and passing of sameness and identity. According to this account of virtual reserve implied by each of these dimensions, because of their asymmetrical reciprocal determinations, teaching is a dedication to pass on pure and abstract values – the virtual reserve of difference – so lives have a greater potential to be lived well. Any act is a redistribution of degrees of intensity of pure values. Paradoxically, these values have no meaning at all, if we understand meaning to be an association of a fixed signification with a given referent, act, or picture. They are instead transformations in the intensity of relations between abstract processes (to trust, to love, to bind, to free, to kill, to torture, to caress, to betray, to support, to mock, to nurture . . .).

These relations can be grouped under 'Ideas', which themselves must not be confused with meaning but rather with complex problems. For example, we might speak of the 'idea' of the internal combustion engine, but from Deleuze's philosophical structure this conceptual representation is but a fraction of the actual expression of, say, the Idea of the Age of Oil and its problematic legacy around the abstract processes of 'to hope', 'to destroy', 'to use', 'to build', 'to exhaust', 'to heat', 'to grow', 'to divide', 'to accelerate', 'to pollute', 'to make', 'to discover' and many more besides. Crucially, just like the mutual reciprocal determinations of the dimensions of times, an Idea is incomplete without its expression in actual things and meanings and these actualities require Ideas not only for their explanation but their genesis. Virtual and actual are in circles of mutual genesis, determination and expression.[3]

The association of the Idea with teaching and apprenticeship therefore takes a quasi-Platonic form, that is, a reversal of Platonism where Ideas become pure values in process, rather than eternal pure identities or oneness.[4] That's why the future as eternal return of *difference* is so important to Deleuze's philosophy of time. The passages from Deleuze's book on Sacher-Masoch quoted above demonstrate the importance of this move to the Ideal in Deleuze's work. It would be a mistake, therefore, to connect Deleuze's account of apprenticeship strictly to the actual practices of masochism. Instead, it is the dialectical rise to an ideal that most concerns him:

> From the body to the work of art, from the work of art to Ideas, there is all of an ascension that must be made through lashes of a whip. A dialectical spirit animates Masoch. Everything begins in *Venus in Furs* with a dream that occurs with an interrupted reading of Hegel. But it is mainly about Plato; if there is Spinozism in Sade, and a demonstrative reason, there is Platonism in Masoch, and a dialectical imagination. (Deleuze 1967: 21)

The important lesson here is that any teaching and learning taken from within Deleuze's philosophy of time must be more than an aim towards actual aims and objectives, however worthy they might seem. The practice must have an ideal horizon in a change in the realm of values.

Abstract processes, such as 'to divide' or 'to love' and their intense relations are the highest values due to the demand, in any given situation, to seek to intensify their connections and to include as many of them as we can. *How can I reveal, transform and intensify the abstract processes sitting as a potential in this given situation?* A child cut off from the class through the ablation of one of his senses is reconnected to the abstract values in the most intense way through the loan of books. But is this gift not the most concrete of acts, rather than anything virtual, abstract and pure? The book, the loss of hearing and the classroom are all concrete and actual. However, their potential to connect past and future events, against an unpromising situation, is not an actual entity, neither is their degree of significance, for instance as hurt or hope. This significance, this intensity of relations of values, relies on actualisation for determination, but far exceeds any given actualisation in range of possibilities and potentialities to be revealed in others. Any act is in touch with *all* others through its struggle with value. *You have betrayed humanity.*

Might it have been better to do nothing, or do more, or offer a different gift? What would have happened then? What is the connection between different possible lines and different intense investments and experiences? Potential and possibility exceed concrete actualities in something intangible but very important. This is the condition for the explanation not only of the difference between alternate actual actions but also for the difference in value between them. The condition is a virtual differentiator of value and destiny. A teacher does not have to be conscious of this to depend upon it. In sensing that something must be done and in seeking the best thing to do, we divine into the future through our feel for the past and our attunement to signs of actual stress and opportunity. Perhaps this also explains the delayed gratitude for those teachers who sought to nurture our own singularity, and the loathing for those that failed it. *The change made, in that angry and long-smarting slap, to the intensities of 'to love' and 'to forgive' in their relations to 'to hate'.*

The pure values affirm the transformation of all meaning and set orders. To express their abstract quality, and the changing intensity of their connections, we must seek to go beyond and transform any given situation. The transformation of pure values requires actual becoming, rather than stasis. The situation treated as self-sufficient is incomplete and insufficient in relation to intensity, connection of relations and abstractness, understood as freedom from specific referents, acts and pictures. How could such transformation and therefore denial and destruction of what we hold dear and live by at any given time be considered the highest and most pure values? They are pure exactly because they are free of specific meaning and identity, of all identifying marks limiting them and trapping them at a particular time and place. They are the highest of all values since they call into question all others and remind us of their exclusions, faults and redundancies. Most importantly they stress the failure of set values to be adequate to novelty and to difference. *How to escape entrenched yet worn rules without depending on others?*

So when an educator decides, against the grain, to divide or to assemble a class in order to release a different potential and respond to demands from the past, present and future, this act challenges and destroys a given order, but it also experiments with a different one. According to Deleuze's philosophy and its pure values, set concepts of division and assembly are not values in themselves. No set concept is a value in itself. Instead, different situations, events and individuals call for different responses seeking to release new potential. Value and intensity are explained through the potential. Sometimes connection and intensification could be by assembly; sometimes they could be by division. It is the effect in the virtual realm of pure values that counts in assessing and explaining the act. *Has there been an increase in the intensity of connections of pure values?*

In answering these questions there is no direct way into those effects and potentialities. They are not actualities we can touch or see. Instead, we must seek signs of the increase in intensity and connection in actual signs, such as a child developing because she has been set apart from others and been given special treatment, or such as children being given confidence and a sense of belonging when they are assembled with all others and not treated as different or inferior. We must also seek to express these novel connections of pure values and intensities through the creation of novel ideas.

These ideas cannot be mere slogans with their simple meaning and dependence on familiar value sets and preconceptions. They must instead be new concepts and acts that express a problematic coming together of different stresses and pulls within a field of possible answers. A new Idea, with its novel concepts, does not solve a problem. It expresses it as a challenge to find solutions, but also with the critical power to call any answer back into question. The problem and the Idea are therefore invitations to act but also to criticise any act and to put it into suspense. No answer is final. No answer is universally valid. It all depends on the relation between the situation, the events, the individuals and the effects. This is why Deleuze's philosophy of learning and teaching is one of singular events and local practice against a shifting cosmos (a chaosmos). This philosophy is never about universal concepts and laws. It is a speculative philosophy of experimentation and apprentice-ship to changing practice, rather than a philosophy of knowledge and regular application.[5]

## Against Utopia

> Classical humour and irony, as used by Plato, as they dominated thought of the laws, are found to be reversed. The double margin, represented by the foundation of the law on the Good and by the approval of the sage in function of the Better, is reduced to nothing. There is only the indetermina-tion of the law on the one hand, and the precision of the punishment on the other. (Deleuze 1967: 75)

Is it not absurd to include 'to torture' or 'to kill' in a list of abstract processes to be connected to and to intensify as values? No. The task is to intensify their relation to other abstract values to connect them and thereby to deny their independence, not only as processes that can be enacted without connection to others, as if a killing could ever be free of a terrible connection to the murder of a loved one, but also as potential relations in other processes, as if love could ever be free of dark connections to pain and injury. There is a dark realism, a quality of chia-roscuro, to Deleuze's philosophy. It eschews the blithe utopianism of a world future-directed towards a pure identity in the Good or Absolute, but it also resists the deepest pessimism of a world vision drawn around brutal power and the struggle for survival as sole rule. So the highest value lies in revealing the connections of violence and apparently merely good processes. It also, though, lies in diffusing violence and cruelty through their connection to shared nurture, growth and dependence.

Paradoxically, the purity of values, the abstract nature of the Idea and the recurrence of the problem underwrite their potential to bend to novelty and singularity. Good teaching and apprenticeship are hence relentlessly critical of given values, including their own. They are also the creation of new Ideas, of new connections to and intense links between abstract processes, for novel situations and different individuals and groups. In Deleuze's philosophy every individual is a group and every such group is all worlds under a certain perspective or determination. In this education, actual lives are enriched, but the condition for this gift is the reserve of pure, virtual, yet real values. These are the values released with the critical and creative novelty of works of art, science and philosophy, such as those expressed in the works of Shakespeare for my forefather, in the intensity, self-destructive fragility, and polyphonic tones of Shakespearean love in its embrace with violence and mistrust.

This is why Deleuze admires teachers and apprentices (Sade, Masoch and Kafka) whose acts show the emptiness of the law, its lack of determination. There is no eternal law – including our current law of naturalist subservience to scientific method and liberal economics. One of the roles of humour in teaching is to draw this out. Another role is to undermine the teacher or sage as guardian of what is better. Irony and humour are essential to teaching. They must be self-destructive as much as anything else. Without this self-undermining, a false law takes root with sages as its custodians: 'There has only ever been one way of thinking law, a comedy of thought, made of irony and humour . . . Sade and Masoch represent the two great efforts of contestation, of a radical reversal of the law' (Deleuze 1967: 75).

Values defined in opposition to laws are always repeated and expressed as new gifts, though to varying degrees, each time we recite lines or simply draw on cultural memory. In its actual acts and legacy, teaching revivifies this virtual reserve in its necessary exchange with actual lives and cultures. Together, actual lives – past, present and future – benefit from and contribute to those virtual values. When we say Shakespeare is eternal, maybe we have an intuition of this counterpoint of re-enactment and virtual reserve; embodied first in the work itself and then in the hinterland of ever-changing pure values it expresses. This counterpoint and Deleuze's insistence on the singularities of teachers and apprentices form a powerful opposition to the current obsession with centralised curricula and methodology. Together, these enforcements of uniformity seek to deny the dappled quality of a world evolving at different speeds in multiple times.

Good teaching is also therefore destructive and self-destructive.[6] It has a duty to run counter to establishment and to smash icons. This is no license to annihilation, though. Destruction only has value where it serves the past, present and future of the individuals and events it depends on for its ongoing exercise and for its nurturing of new forms of value. There is no intensification of values where the individuals capable of carrying them are eliminated or hopelessly stunted. Deleuze's philosophy inherits the deep philosophical problem of dosage. This is the experimental practice of weighing out what an individual body can do and take as it evolves with novel events, in relation to all the other bodies its life connects it to under a certain perspective. Dosage balances between two disasters.

There is the disaster of conservatism, where order chokes on its own faded certainties. Then there is the disaster of the bloodthirsty rush to wipe out all of the past. The two are twins. Conservatism is nostalgia for earlier destructive ages, with their violence conveniently overlooked. The bloodthirsty rush carries remnants of earlier ages elevated to eternal truth. Dosage in relation to teaching is therefore a question of continuity and discontinuity. Which past lines must carry forward in order to allow the creative destruction of others? Which future lines must be sacrificed in this selection from the past in the present? A teacher is on the cusp of history and in a singular situation, having to divine what the future might hold while nurturing the present thanks to the past. This explains why all teaching is political. It is a struggle with different claims from the past and different calls from the future within a care for multiple demands in the present.

The time we teach for is then impossible to circumscribe in general plans and objectives, though many today wish to do just that by reducing teaching to training for specific time-limited tasks and abilities, or, in the realm of morals, to fixed forms of comportment or supposedly universal and timeless laws. The utilitarian outcomes will necessarily become redundant over periods defined by technical innovation, economic cycles, political fashions, social change, the sheer multiplicity of directions and comportments open to desires, and the ubiquity of wear and burgeoning among living beings. Imagined benefits will mostly fall stillborn, given the bureaucratic lag between the political and corporate specification of needs and their inscription into syllabus.

Populists and technocratic managers are rarely good at divination. They are even worse at eternal pure values, since they choose the false pretence of controlling the forces buffeting them and those they seek to dupe with aged and simplified solutions or one-dimensional techniques presented as economic necessities. Feeling the way into the future is a call better performed by philosophers, scientists and artists. Tentative experimentation by thinkers attempting to open up to the new will outlive the more confident yet also more fragile fixities of rulers and administrators, because time is not governed by eternal rules but rather by eternal change and becoming.

## Signs and Learning in the Philosophy of Time

Apprenticeship is not in the relation of representation to action (as reproduction of the Same), but in the relation of sign to response (as encounter with the Other). The sign involves heterogeneity in at least three ways: first, in the object carrying or emitting it, necessarily presenting two orders of size or two disparate realities between which the sign flashes; second, in itself, because the sign envelopes another 'object' within the limits of the carrying object, incarnating a power of nature or spirit (Idea); finally, in the response it draws out, where the response movement does not 'resemble' that of the sign. (Deleuze 1968: 35)

Learning for Deleuze is apprenticeship, not a learning 'that' tending towards a 'knowing that', but an apprenticeship to 'acting thus in response to this'. Unlike the knowledge and behaviours following from learning 'that', which are settled and acquired once and for all, 'thus' is always in a process of evolution because it responds to a different 'this', to ever-changing material and situations, to 'an encounter with the other'. This process is forward and backward facing, that is, past apprenticeship is reviewed in the present as an attitude towards the future, between the emission of a sign and 'the response it draws out'.

Let's be clear, none of this implies that education should not involve knowledge. It is rather that knowledge alone is insufficient. Knowledge also requires an apprenticeship to evolving practice. This practice is not a matter of knowledge. It is a matter of experimental doing and acting, when knowledge is not enough, when knowledge fails. *A gardener on new soil in a changing climate. A cyclist going beyond her limits on a hill taken too fast. A teacher in front of a class each new day. A musician with a new instrument or a new score. A writer essaying the next sentence. A child balancing without Mummy's hand. The first day without a loved one . . . and the hundredth. A scientist with new results. Parents skirmishing with an anguished teen.*

There is a fundamental trap here around the concepts of the new and of the insufficiency of knowledge. It is not that apprenticeship has its proper place solely where there is novelty and where established knowledge reaches a limit. Learning always involves knowledge and apprenticeship, but to differing degrees. More importantly these degrees cannot be known at the time of learning, rather, they are discovered at a later time when the learning is put into practice again, tested anew, set in a different situation. This later time is itself under review by further apprenticeship such that instead of fixed aims or goals, or fixed review or judgement points, we instead have an infinite speculative cycle, where each new present is a speculative re-take on all of the past and all of the future. Selections must be made in this cycle and the infinity is not an excuse for inaction. Instead, the speculative nature of apprenticeship implies an awareness of necessary error, review and replay.

The lapse and mismatch between emission and response, both in relation to an encounter with something other and in relation to each other as 'other', as novel, leads Deleuze to redefine the sign. A sign is not a symbol, associating an image with a fixed meaning. It is not the arbitrary unity of a signifier and a signified. Nor is the sign a formal trigger or token. Nor is the sign a sense that can be put into circulation and reliably substituted and exchanged. Instead, the sign is a change of intensity registered sensually between two heterogeneous orders where both are forced to change but not according to a same logic or function: 'presenting two orders of size or two disparate realities between which the sign flashes'. An object carries the sign. It could be a stick, a word, a body-part, a movement. But the sign is a multiple effect of that object, not the object itself.

The book is given to the pupil, but the real sign is the flash between physical joy and intellectual growth, two orders altering in different ways through the work of the sign. The wider object is then the ideal horizon of these effects, the changing intensities in values embodied in the local gesture of the gift of the book and in the wider and wider effects on bodies and values: 'because the sign envelopes another "object" within the limits of the carrying object, incarnating a power of nature or spirit (Idea)'. In turn, the response to the sign, the way it is carried forward, does not resemble the sign because it is responding to other encounters and forming its own signs. The gift of the book is not carried forth simply through a further gift of the same book (it is never the same gift). Instead, the flash between orders and the ideal and physical effects are echoed in a new sign which therefore responds to the earlier without resembling it, 'in the response it draws out, where the response movement does not "resemble" that of the sign'.

So knowledge is always misrepresented in relation to learning when it is given as self-sufficient, because all learning is also a matter of apprenticeship, whether we are aware of it or not. Again, all is degree and unconscious relations over time. An encounter with the new and the strange could well turn out to be at a low degree apprenticeship when viewed from a later experience or test. *You travelled the world but never learned how to dwell.* The acquisition of set knowledge with little apparent novelty and discovery can turn out to be the most intense period of apprenticeship, for instance where learning by rote or through repetitive knowledge turns into a deep preparation for later encounters. *Her deep knowledge of sail patterns revealed the battle to her long before it began.*

Apprenticeship is about time because it is only revealed over time and because it develops over stretches of time with no inherent boundaries. We must therefore understand apprenticeship within Deleuze's multiple nexus of dimensions of time. Apprenticeship is selection in the present, a passing away into the pure past, a divination of the future, an experimental and risky struggle with destiny, a necessary oblivion and a necessary return as pure difference through pure values. As soon as apprenticeship is understood as a time-bound task or as a way to fulfil a pre-known and fixed objective it is fundamentally misunderstood as active and passive comportment in times.

In *Difference and Repetition*, Deleuze is therefore critical of mistaken or backhanded gestures towards time in learning. 'To learn that' (*apprendre*) is never 'to be an apprentice to signs' (*l'apprenti*): 'And even if one insists on the specificity of learning, and on the *time* implied by apprenticeship, it is to appease the scruples of a psychological conscience that certainly does not allow itself to dispute the innate right of knowledge to represent all of the transcendental' (Deleuze 1968: 215). So long as learning is set within an account of knowledge whereby everything can be, by right, learned as knowledge, then learning is limited to an interval between two points in time: 'To learn is but the intermediary between not-knowing and knowing, the living passage from one to the other' (Deleuze 1968: 215). To escape from these limits, Deleuze invokes the extreme case of learning as bounded by knowing: absolute knowledge in Hegel. Once again, Plato shows the way out of this trap: 'Because, with [Plato] to learn is really the transcendental movement of the soul, irreducible to knowledge as much as to lack of knowledge' (Deleuze 1968: 215–16).

By transcendental movement in apprenticeship, Deleuze means a movement beyond known boundaries set by internal rights, recognition of limits and representation of internal spaces. A transcendental movement is a radical experimentation free of known goals and recognised limits and represented methods and actors. It is a leap into the unknown, but not one free of any determination, for it owes its structure to the structure of time: 'Thus a time is introduced into thought, not as the empirical time of the thinker submitted to factual conditions, for whom thinking takes time, but rather as a time of pure thought (time takes thought)' (Deleuze 1968: 216).

## Notes

1. For my full interpretation of Deleuze's philosophy of time, see Williams 2011a. I have used this interpretation and accompanying grid of time in other essays on time and objective-setting and on time and objects (see Williams 2011b, 2011c).
2. For a detailed analysis of Deleuze's apprenticeship to signs see Sauvagnargues 2009, esp. pp. 123–48. Sauvagnargues insists on four facets to apprenticeship: the encounter with the sign, the art of apprenticeship, its local specificity and apprenticeship as practice: 'A sensibility to signs. Every apprentice is an

Egyptologist . . . it is the recourse to art as artisanal making and regulated prac-tice' (2009: 145). Levi Bryant has a shorter set of references to apprenticeship 'in' signs in his *Difference and Givenness* (2008). Partly this is because Bryant stresses the encounter aspect rather than the subsequent apprenticeship, as if the apprenticeship is in how to encounter rather than a broader learning as set out by Sauvagnargues and here: 'such thought requires an apprenticeship or training in signs to engender an openness to the encounter, prevent it from covering over the difference which manifests itself with the subjects and objects resulting from the syntheses of habitus' (Bryant 2008: 77).

3. There is a deep discussion, with rich examples and explanation, of this inter-dependence of the virtual, the unconscious and the actual in Todd May and Inna Semetsky's 'Deleuze, Ethical Education, and the Unconscious' (in Semetsky 2008: 143–58). Their insistence on the importance of freedom in education follows from the roles of the virtual and the unconscious: 'A free thought is capable of realizing its creative potential, of actualizing the virtual' (Semetsky 2008: 154). David Cole's book on Deleuze and education also has as a detailed and subtle analysis of the role of the virtual in education in relation to practice. Similar to the argument set out here, the importance of multiplicity and singularity is emphasised: 'The primary and yet malleable connection between the construction of the virtual and learning that we may derive from the philosophy of Deleuze, lies in the conception and deployment of multiplicities' (see Cole 2012: Chapter 5).

4. Claire Colebrook shows this reversal within Platonism through the anti-Platonic side of Socratic Elenchus: 'Deleuze's overturning of Platonism deconstructs the opposition between truth and sophistry: there is a truth of appearances, an ability to think the truth of what appears, not as some hidden content, but as the life or difference of appearances. In Socratic pedagogy, for example, Socrates's interlocutor is often not led towards some content, but is exposed to the move-ment of dialogue and to a sense of the limited nature of already constituted terms' (Colebrook 2008: 40).

5. That this account of practice in relation to signs offers many fruitful connections to the pragmatism of Dewey and Peirce is explained in detail in Semetsky 2006, esp. Chapter 2, 'Becoming-sign'.

6. Ronald Bogue shows this critical dimension to teaching and to apprenticeship in his very beautiful essay 'Search, Swim and See: Deleuze's Apprenticeship to Signs and Pedagogy of Images': 'Hence, the pedagogy of signs entails first a critique of codes and conventions, an undoing of orthodox connections, and then a recon-nection of elements such that the gaps between them generate problems, fields of differential relations and singular points' (Bogue 2008: 15).

# References

Bogue, R. (2008), 'Search, Swim and See: Deleuze's Apprenticeship to Signs and Pedagogy of Images' in I. Semetsky (ed.), *Nomadic Education: Variations on a Theme by Deleuze and Guattari*, Rotterdam: Sense, pp. 1–16.

Bryant, L. (2008), *Difference and Givenness*, Evanston, IL: Northwestern University Press.

Cole, D. (2012), *Educational Life-Forms: Deleuzian Teaching and Learning Practice*, Rotterdam: Sense.

Colebrook, C. (2008), 'Leading Out, Leading On: The Soul of Education' in I. Semetsky (ed.), *Nomadic Education: Variations on a Theme by Deleuze and Guattari*, Rotterdam: Sense, pp. 35–42.

Deleuze, G. (1967), *Présentation de Sacher-Masoch*, Paris: Minuit.

Deleuze, G. (1968), *Différence et repetition*, Paris: PUF.

Deleuze, G. (1970), *Proust et les signes*, 2nd edn, Paris: PUF.

Deleuze, G. (2003), 'Il était une étoile de groupe' in *Deux régimes de fous et autres textes (1975–1995)*, ed. D. Lapoujade, Paris: Minuit.

Sauvagnargues, A. (2009), *Deleuze: l'empirisme transcendental*, Paris: PUF.

Semetsky, I. (2006), *Deleuze, Education and Becoming*, Rotterdam: Sense.

Semetsky, I. (ed.) (2008), *Nomadic Education: Variations on a Theme by Deleuze and Guattari*, Rotterdam: Sense.

Williams, J. (2011a), *Gilles Deleuze's Philosophy of Time: A Critical Introduction and Guide*, Edinburgh: Edinburgh University Press.

Williams, J. (2011b), 'Objects in Manifold Times: Deleuze and the speculative philosophy of objects as process', *Cosmos and History, the Journal of Natural and Social Philosophy*, 7(1): 61–74.

Williams J. (2011c), 'Identity and Time in Gilles Deleuze's Process Philosophy' in M. Schultz, S. Maguire, A. Langley and H. Tsoukas (eds), *Constructing Identity in and Around Organizations*, Oxford: Oxford University Press, pp. 180–200.

# Notes on Contributors

**Julie Allan** is Professor of Education at the Stirling Institute of Education, University of Stirling, Scotland and Deputy Head of Department. She is also visiting professor at the University of Borås, Sweden. Her research interests encompass inclusion, children's rights, the arts (especially disability arts) and social capital and she has published widely in these areas. Among her most recent books is *Rethinking Inclusive Education: The Philosophers of Difference in Practice* (Springer), which considers the work of Deleuze, Foucault and Derrida. She has also published *Doing Inclusive Education Research* (with Roger Slee, published by Sense) and *Social Capital, Professionalism and Diversity* (edited with Jenny Ozga and Geri Smyth, published by Sense).

**Ronald Bogue** is Distinguished Research Professor of Comparative Literature at the University of Georgia. He is the author of *Deleuze and Guattari* (Routledge, 1989), *Deleuze on Literature* (Routledge, 2003), *Deleuze on Cinema* (Routledge, 2003), *Deleuze on Music, Painting, and the Arts* (Routledge, 2003), *Deleuze's Wake: Tributes and Tributaries* (SUNY, 2004), *Deleuze's Way: Essays in Transverse Ethics and Aesthetics* (Ashgate, 2007), and *Deleuzian Fabulation and the Scars of History* (Edinburgh University Press, 2010). He has also published numerous essays on Deleuze in various collective volumes and in the journals *SubStance, Man and World, Concentric, Interventions, Symposium, CiNéMAS, Revue internationale de philosophie, Educational Philosophy and Theory* and *Deleuze Studies*.

**Mark Bonta** earned his BA in geography from Penn State, MA in geography from the University of Texas-Austin, and PhD in geography from Louisiana State University. He is currently Visiting Associate

Professor of Geography and Sustainable Development at Delta State University, and resides with his family in Philadelphia, Pennsylvania. He has worked extensively on the relationships of Deleuze and Guattari to geography, and co-authored *Deleuze and Geophilosophy: A Guide and Glossary* with John Protevi (Edinburgh University Press, 2003).

**David R. Cole** is Associate Professor in English and Pedagogy at the University of Western Sydney. David has edited three books: *Multiple Literacies Theory: A Deleuzian Perspective* with Diana Masny (Sense, 2009), *Multiliteracies and Technology Enhanced Education: Social Practice and the Global Classroom* with Darren Pullen (IGI, 2009), and *Multiliteracies in Motion: Current Theory and Practice* with Darren Pullen (Routledge, 2009). He published a novel in 2007 called *A Mushroom of Glass*, and his latest monograph is *Educational Life-Forms: Deleuzian Teaching and Learning Practice* (Sense, 2012). David uses his knowledge of Deleuze and multiple and affective literacies to investigate areas of educative interest.

**Christopher M. Drohan** is currently an Assistant Professor at Sheridan College, Ontario, teaching in Sheridan's School of Community and Liberal Studies. He graduated from the European Graduate School of Media and Communications in 2007, and has worked as an Assistant Director for the School's Canadian division ever since. He is the author of *Deleuze and the Sign* (Atropos Press, 2009) and an executive member of the Toronto Semiotic Circle at Victoria College.

**Rocco Gangle** is Associate Professor of Philosophy in Endicott College, MA, and the co-director of the Center for Diagrammatic and Computational Philosophy. He is the translator of François Laruelle's *Philosophies of Difference* (Continuum, 2010) and the author of numerous articles on Spinoza, Peirce, contemporary French philosophy and diagrammatic logic.

**David Holdsworth** is Associate Professor, Trent University, Canada, and Director of the Centre for Theory, Culture and Politics. His research focuses on environmental theory, valuation and interpretation of mathematics, as well as political discourses and cultural organisation of scientific community. Among his recent articles are 'Economics and the Limits of Optimization: Steps towards extending Bernard Hodgson's *Moral Science*'; 'The Cosmopolitan Foucault: Global practice within a micro-politics of thought', and 'Becoming Interdisciplinary: Making sense of DeLanda's reading of Deleuze'.

**Diana Masny** is Emerita Professor at the University of Ottawa, Canada. She teaches in language and literacies education, and minority language education. She has developed MLT: Multiple Literacies Theory, from a Deleuze-Guattari perspective. She is a founding member of the Multiple Literacies Research Unit Ottawa and Adjunct Professor at Queensland University of Technology, Australia. Her recent publications include a co-edited volume of *Multiple Literacies Theory: A Deleuzian Perspective* with D. R. Cole (Sense, 2009), *Lire le monde: les littératies multiples et l'éducation dans les communautés francophones* (University of Ottawa Press, 2009) and *Cartographies of Becoming in Education: A Deleuze-Guattari perspective* (2013). She has co-authored *Mapping Multiple Literacies: An Introduction to Deleuzian Literacy Studies* with D. R. Cole (Continuum, 2012).

**Joshua Ramey** is a Visiting Assistant Professor at Haverford College. He is the author of *The Hermetic Deleuze: Philosophy and Spiritual Ordeal* (Duke University Press, 2012). Ramey is the editor of 'Spiritual Politics After Deleuze', a special issue of *SubStance*, and the author of numerous articles on contemporary philosophy, aesthetics and cultural theory. His essays have appeared in *Angelaki*, *Political Theology*, *Discourse*, and the *Journal for Religious and Cultural Theory*.

**Inna Semetsky** is Adjunct Professor, University of Waikato, New Zealand. Her research strength is semiotics encompassing continental and pragmatic traditions represented by Charles S. Peirce, John Dewey and Gilles Deleuze. She has published *Deleuze, Education and Becoming* (2006); *Nomadic Education: Variations on a Theme by Deleuze and Guattari* (2008), *Semiotics Education Experience* (2010), *Re-Symbolization of the Self: Human Development and Tarot Hermeneutic* (2011) and *Jung and Educational Theory* (2012). She has entries on 'Semiotics' and 'Experience' in *The Deleuze Dictionary* (2005). Her forthcoming publications include *The Edusemiotics of Images: Essays on the Art~Science of Tarot*.

**Jason J. Wallin** is Assistant Professor of Media and Youth Culture in Curriculum in the Faculty of Education at the University of Alberta, Canada, where he teaches courses in visual art, media studies and cultural curriculum theory. He is the author of *A Deleuzian Approach* *to Curriculum: Essays on a Pedagogical Life* (Palgrave Macmillan), co-author of the forthcoming *Arts-Based Research: A Critique and Proposal*, with Jan Jagodzinski (Sense), and co-editor of the forthcoming collection *Deleuze, Guattari, Politics and Education*, with Matt Carlin (Continuum). Jason is assistant editor for the *Journal of Curriculum and Pedagogy* and reviews editor for *Deleuze Studies*.

**James Williams** is Professor of Philosophy at the University of Dundee. As a writer and lecturer, Williams has a specific interest in twentieth-century French Philosophy, Postmodernism, Poststructuralism, Aesthetics and Political Philosophy. His many books include *Deleuze's Philosophy of Time: A Critical Introduction and Guide* (Edinburgh University Press, 2011); *Gilles Deleuze's* Logic of Sense: *A Critical Introduction and Guide* (Edinburgh University Press, 2008) and *The Transversal Thought of Gilles Deleuze* (Clinamen, 2005). Professor Williams is a member of the Arts and Humanities Research Council peer review panel. Together with Ian Buchanan, he has recently launched a new theory series *Critical Connections* with Edinburgh University Press.

# Index